My Dear Martin,

Merry Christmas

Hope San

Much

Margaret
x

HOWARD

HOWARD

The Life and Times of Sir Howard Morrison

with

JOHN COSTELLO

ISBN 1-86947-113-X

© Moa Beckett Publishers Ltd

Published in 1992 by
Moa Beckett Publishers
P.O. Box 31-042, Milford, Auckland 10, New Zealand.

Typeset by
Typocrafters Ltd, Auckland.

Printed through
Colorcraft, Hong Kong.

To
Kuia
our children
our grandchildren
and
Mum

Acknowledgements

I have truly been the most fortunate of men.

I have a family I love and by whom I am loved. I have good friends with whom I have shared many ups and downs. I've been able to earn a comfortable living, travel many parts of the world and gain an ego-warming measure of acclaim just doing what I love: singing and entertaining.

My overwhelming feeling, as I look back at my very full and very rewarding life, is immense gratitude.

Grateful aroha to my mother and my late, still sorely missed father, who gave me a wise and loving upbringing.

Grateful love to my wife Kuia, and to my children Donna, Howard Jnr and Richard, whose love and support have always been there for me despite the long absences involved with my chosen career.

Grateful memories of my late brother Laurie, who I would have loved to have had with me all through the show biz years, loving thanks to my sisters and to my extended family.

A warm thank you to all the friends who have enriched my life. My gratitude to all the artists who ever performed with me (especially to Gerry, Wi and Noel of the Howard Morrison Quartet); to all the musicians who have backed me and the entrepreneurs and agents who have helped me; to Bruce Woodham and Paul Barnes of the Bic connection.

Thank you to that skilful man of words John Costello, who collaborated with me on this book and helped to draw all the strands of my life into a coherent whole. And thanks to the photographers who have captured on film the images of my life and times.

Finally, my heartfelt thanks to all you good people, who have followed and supported my career over the past 30 years and more.

God bless, and thanks for everything so far.

CONTENTS

INTRODUCTION

FOR THE VISITORS it was a fantastic scene, a mystical setting. The meeting house beside the lake, named for and embodying the person of Tamatekapua, captain of the Te Arawa canoe; St Faith's church to one side and St Michael's on the other; on either hand the clouds of steam from subterranean sources, veiling the old Ohinemutu village from the younger city behind it.

To the locals it was as familiar as concrete and glass canyons to a city dweller, as white Tasman spray on endless black beaches to Northland people, as the brooding presence of the sacred mountain to Taranaki people, as the mist-shrouded ridges and ravines of the Urewera country to the Tuhoe.

But perhaps even to the locals that Rotorua day in October 1990 had an extra burnished brightness.

For this was the day that Howard Morrison, whom they'd seen growing up as freezing worker, chainman and bush hunter, as a gifted local rugby player and dance hall troubadour, as a family man, a 'local boy made good', a hometown hero; this was the day he would officially become Sir Howard Morrison.

October 12, 1990 — the day of my investiture as Knight Bachelor. You may have seen it on the television news that night: Sir Howard Morrison, with tears streaming down his face. Or on the front page of the next morning's *Herald*: Sir Howard Morrison — in tears again.

Yet earlier that day I remember thinking, a bit smugly perhaps, that I was very together, very loose. Howard Morrison, Mr Cool even; comfortable in both worlds, accustomed to taking the stage before a sea of faces.

In the morning I had shed some private tears. That was when I looked out over Lake Rotorua from the home where Kuia and I now live to the family home across the bay and thought of my father and of my older brother, Laurie.

I knew they would have been so proud to have been there on this day. It would have meant so much to them; it would have meant so much to me. So I had my moment of silent tears. I thought it was better to get them over with before I faced the public.

By the time the press descended on me, later in the morning, I had it all together. To the reporters, who wanted to know how I felt, how my family felt, I said that I was, obviously, deeply honoured. To the Maori newsgatherers, I was able to explain that this gift, the knight-hood, wasn't just for me, to be enjoyed selfishly and personally, but an honour to my tribe, to the people.

We had some photographs taken while final preparations were being made at the marae. I was very relaxed, very comfortable about the whole thing. There was no nervous tension, no butterflies, because I'd been part of so many sacred occasions on our marae; all of them important, and me just as a participant, supporter, onlooker . . . feeling that sense of pride when different people had been honoured from the tribe or different important guests had been brought on.

I can remember Field Marshal Montgomery coming here after the Second World War and how we were proud that Rotorua greeted Monty not at the town hall but at this marae. I have to add that this marae, of Ohinemutu, is where the captain of our canoe, Te Arawa canoe, Tamatekapua, where his person, in the form of a meeting house, stands. So I'm right in the heart, the bosom, the poho as they say.

All the people were giving me kisses and hugs in anticipation of the arrival of the vice-regal party. We took our stations and the place was suddenly filling up with people that I'd known from all walks of life. They'd come from the South Island, they'd come from the north, they'd come from the east, the west, the four winds, Maori and pakeha.

As I say, I'm comfortable in both worlds. But suddenly the air is getting that thickness, that hum, that you get just before the curtain goes up on a big, sellout concert. And suddenly I'm not so comfortable, not quite so relaxed.

At the duly appointed time the Governor-General arrived and my daughter and two sons brought the vice-regal party and all the other distinguished guests on to the marae — the formal protocol.

About this time I was starting to get a little fuzzy in the head. Hang on a minute, this is all happening. I'm the star here — this is all for me! I remember my uncle was in a wheelchair beside me; he was recovering from a stroke. And I was hanging on to his hand, as the tangible bond with where I came from. Even though my uncle couldn't talk to me, he was there. And the spirit of my father, and my other uncles who had passed on . . . it was all there.

With the strength I was getting from that physical contact with my uncle, I was starting to loosen up again and enjoy things. I mean, I'm sitting there looking around . . . politicians, people from all walks of

'Arise, Sir Howard . . .' the moving moment when Sir Paul Reeves tapped each shoulder with the sword — and didn't take a shortcut in between. NZ Herald

life, the Governor-General — and they're all there for me. Now that's a buzz! It's the wrong word, I know, but I guess it says it.

Protocol having to be observed, we went on to the formal speeches. Our kawa, our rules, say that one speaks for this side, another speaks for their side. And the visitors might sometimes have more speakers than you, so it's up to you to find more — drag them out of bed if necessary! But we had the whole armoury there; we had all the sub-tribes, we had it more than covered.

The Governor-General, Sir Paul Reeves, was the last speaker. I understand that when he took up his vice-regal duties, his Maori was almost non-existent. But he'd certainly learned very quickly; he didn't try to be smart-aleck but he knew the basics, what to say and to say it correctly. Then he translated it into English, which was a nice touch.

'This will probably be my last investiture,' he said, 'and perhaps the most unique. Because as you think of knights, in the old days, you think of knights on horses. And Howard at the moment is on his horse around New Zealand . . .' (I was on the Ride for Life at that time; I'd finished the South Island part and flown back from Blenheim for the investiture.)

He was able to bring in that nice, humorous, common touch.

'As to my duties,' he said, 'I will, with my sword, touch him on the left shoulder and, without taking any short cuts, touch him on the right shoulder . . .'

And, of course, the crowd roared. He was quite brilliant. The dignity of his office was still there yet he was able to bring in that human touch and that bond, as a distant relative in Maori terms.

Then Sir Charles Bennett closed things off for our side. He said it was a great day for New Zealand, a great day, an important day, for both cultures. And he thanked me for getting famous enough to be knighted — to allow them this opportunity to celebrate the best of both cultures in such a dignified way.

Now the Governor-General asked me to come forward. We'd tried the stool out earlier and it was a bit shaky. I've got a bad right knee, anyway, so what with the ginky stool and my ginky knee, I was feeling a bit shaky as I knelt. The citation had been read before this, so without any further ado he took out his sword and touched me on the left shoulder, touched me on the right — without taking any short cuts, as he'd promised — and said: 'Rise, Sir Howard.'

I was still holding on to my emotions then. But now the whole of the tribe burst out into our challenge of mana, of ihi, of all the things you chant through pride of your people. When they did, that was when the emotions rushed in and I wished so much that my father could have been there to share the moment. I just couldn't hold back the tears!

I was very conscious of crying; I was conscious of the cameras looking at me. I was trying to control myself but I just . . . I didn't feel like a dork, but I didn't feel pretty, either! I lifted my head now and again while they were singing — they followed the chant with *Whakaaria Mai (How Great Thou Art)* — and as far as I could see, Maori and pakeha, there wasn't a dry eye on the marae! Everybody was just full of emotion.

I got my strength back giving comfort to the others. My wife Kuia and my mum are very strong. They kept their crying inside and were strong for me.

But the men! I was hugging a mate and he was crying his eyes out on my shoulder and a pakeha guy, from a well-known Rotorua family, said: 'Good on you, Howard. You give us a lot of love.'

Many, many things were said to me that day but that one thing, said on the spur of the moment, will stay with me for a long time.

So, there was the hugging and the crying, and the release of enormous emotion, and then we walked around the bay to the dining room. And that's when the tribe further honoured me by having the waka, our waka that had been at the Waitangi celebrations, come into the lagoon. That was an epic sight. Picturesque Ohinemutu was magnificent, with the lake and the meeting house, and St Faith's on one side and St Michael's on the other, and the waka coming in with the paddles flashing in the sun.

They had a military guard of honour as we came round and as the paddlers got out of the canoe they also formed a guard of honour, with paddles raised, and gave the haka.

That was what Sir Charles Bennett was talking about, the blending of two cultures — and it happened so naturally! It just showed again, for me, how beautiful our culture is when it can be shared.

I've always felt the media, especially television, has not just a responsibility but a bounden duty to help alleviate that huge chasm between understanding what a culture is and how to appreciate it. It's not so much us, but the next generation; the ones who haven't been stained by our bigotry. You can't change old dogs, who are set in their ways, but our kids deserve better.

That was the sort of thing that was going through my mind as we walked through the guards of honour; one in the European military tradition, one of Maori warriors in our ancient tradition. Why can't it be like this more often? It's happening so naturally, there's no one being intimidated by it.

There were friends of mine from the South Island who had never been on a marae for a formal occasion. But it was natural for them to respect the custom without feeling uncomfortable or intimidated.

It was a wonderful day, a magic day . . .

A marquee had been set up by the dining room, where the whanau had prepared beautiful food. And the elders had relaxed the rules for the occasion to allow some wine. Normally there is no alcohol on the marae but this occasion called for flexibility.

The Governor-General enjoyed himself. I mean, no one can act that well. A great guy, he looks you in the eye when he's talking to you, he shakes your hand firmly, hasn't got that patronising air you sometimes associate with 'representatives of the Crown, old boy' — he enjoys himself, he really does!

The Right Reverend Manu Bennett actually instigated holding the investiture at the Papaiouru Marae. From the time of the announcement of my knighthood he had insisted that everything should be done to make it a tribal occasion. I have a sneaking suspicion that he was also one of those who championed my cause.

Uncle Manu and I have always been close, not only in blood but in our work together in matters pertaining to family, tribe and country. I value his counsel and it was fitting that he took a forward role at my investiture.

My backing band was there, providing background music, and after kai we started ad libbing. I broke the ice by singing first and then others started coming up to the microphone. I got Koro Wetere up and he sang a song, beautifully. Some of the local wags got on the microphone — it was a great day.

It was on the news that night, showing Howard Morrison in full flight — crying my eyes out and looking about 108! Nothing like emotion to destroy your image. And on the front page of the *Herald* the next morning, crying again.

But seriously, it was a momentous occasion and it was reported as such. And I'll tell you what: it beats funerals. As some of us more cynical people in Maoridom say, who wants to wait till you're dead to be called a rangatira and have a big fuss made about you? I've been honoured while I'm still alive and kicking. Mind you, I've had a heart bypass and a gall bladder operation since!

Anyway, I certainly lived that day to the full. And I suppose it was natural that when it was all over, when Kuia and I were back home and the last guests and family had gone, that I began to drowsily think about where it all began, and all the turning points, and chance meetings, the carefully considered decisions and the spur-of-the-moment impulses that led me to this great day in my life.

1

BEGINNINGS

I WAS BORN to Gertrude Harete Morrison (nee Davidson) and Temuera Leslie Morrison on the 18th day of August 1935 at Rotorua Hospital.

The family name was established in New Zealand by a Scottish settler named James Thomas Morrison — my great-grandfather. Among our family memorabilia is a reproduction of an old magazine story which describes how my great-grandfather operated the Victoria Hotel in Harington St, Tauranga, from 1867 until early 1874, when the renewal of his licence was refused. This caused Great-Granddad considerable anguish at the time, but resulted in his moving to Rotorua and taking up the licence of the Rotorua Hotel at Ohinemutu later that year.

If this had not happened, of course, his son Jimmy (my grandfather, James Montgomery Morrison) would never have met my grandmother — and Howard Morrison would never have been born!

Granddad was born in 1871, so he was only three when the family moved to Rotorua. When he was 20 he married a local woman of high rank by the name of Ngapuia-Teriana Te Tupara Toko-Aitua. Their son, my dad Temuera, was the second youngest of six boys and one girl.

An article on Jimmy Morrison published in the *Rotorua Daily Post* in 1954 described him (at 82 years of age) as the town's oldest inhabitant.

Cavalry-moustached Jimmy can recall Maori War scares, the Tarawera eruption of '86 and has even shaken the hand of the famous Maori rebel, Te Kooti.

Jimmy was 15 when Tarawera erupted. 'It was a lovely sight,' he recalled. The people in the town panicked, according to Jimmy, and most left town on foot, horse or buggy. Jimmy, his mother and sister travelled to Awahou and stopped there for a couple of days.

He remembered Te Kooti well. 'I can still see him in my memory,' he said. 'I shook hands with the old devil — he was certainly a great old warrior.'

A former blacksmith, Mr Morrison attributes his alertness and toughness to 'plenty of hard work and plenty of beer'. He still likes to slip along to the pub and drink the odd pot.

This recipe saw Granddad out for another three years. He died in 1957, aged 85. Sadly, my dad did not inherit Granddad's longevity. He actually predeceased his father by three years, dying on December 31, 1954, when only 45.

Dad married my mother, Gertrude Harete 'Kahu' Morrison, in 1931. Mum has been known as 'Kahu', rather than by her given names, for as long as I can remember and longer. Mum tells me it was her grandmother's name. She and a childhood friend used to call each other by their grandmother's names and, in her case, it stuck.

The dominant Maori bloodline is descended from Te Arawa, which, around 1350, laid claim to the land area from Maketu (near Te Puke) to Tongariro. On my mother's side I have inherited Tainui blood — as well as a dash of Irish. That combination of bloodlines led Bob Parker on *This Is Your Life* to say that I was never going to lead an ordinary life. True!

My older brother Laurie (Laurance Whareporera Morrison) was born on December 6, 1931. His death in a car crash in 1974 was another tragic blow for the family. I was second in our family, following Laurie. Then there was another son, Charles Douglas, who died when he was only a toddler aged 17 months.

And then came four girls, Judith Merania, Rene Kahu, Adelaide Carol and Linda Moewaka.

My early childhood was post-Depression and Second World War years. Mum tells me that they were tough times but they made ends meet by sharing the extended family's food from land and lake.

Vegetables (mainly potato and kumara) were cropped seasonally and, with Dad having five brothers who were all expert hunters and fishermen, there was always plenty of kai.

It's hard, sometimes, to separate what you can remember physically from what you've been told. But I have visual memories from when I can't have been more than four or five.

Dad's grandfather, James Thomas Morrison (1839–79). Morrison family collection

Dad's grandmother, Henrietta (Fisher) Morrison (1844–1921). Morrison family collection

Dad's father, James Montgomery Morrison. Morrison family collection

Dad's mother, Ngapuia Teriana Te Tupara Tokaitua. Morrison family collection

Mum's father, Charles Davidson.
Morrison family collection

Mum's mother, Elizabeth (Bessie) Davidson. Morrison family collection

The family house had not long been built then. It was very modern for those days, with the latest wood and coal-burning stove. We had an outside cold-water tap and toilet; we used to fetch hot water from the nearby hot pool. By today's standards our house would be much admired, being positioned as it is on the shores of Lake Rotorua and 100 yards from the mouth of the Utuhina River. In those days, all of our outdoor social, cultural, recreational and spiritual activities were centred around our beautiful inlet and the Ruapeka (hot and cold in different places) Lagoon.

The river mouth and bay abounded with fresh-water crayfish (koura), trout and fresh-water mussels (kakahi; not that tasty, actually). The reeds off the bay were home to an abundance of multi-coloured carp.

The Maori name for carp is Morehana, which is the 'make up' Maori name for Morrison. It seems that the Morrison clan claim that one of them released the first carp into the bay.

In the winter when the carp were fat, it was a Sunday morning ritual (at daybreak, before the church bells) for men from the village to go out 'harvesting' carp. Of course, the lake was icy cold in the winter. But for half an hour before first light they would crowd into a hot pool — up to 20 men in a bath perhaps 10 feet by 15 — and get their blood really warmed up to go into the lake.

The men would go out to the reeds and form a picket line to drive the carp out and towards the shore, splashing and yelling, doing the haka . . . whatever. Then they would sit in the shallower water with their legs spread out, their feet touching, and catch the carp as they turned from the shore to escape back to the reeds.

The men would tie the fish on flax lines and then move to the deep of the lagoon where they dived for the fish which had nest holes in the muddy bottom. Some divers were so good they could stay down long enough to catch three or four carp in one dive.

Alas, this food source died out in the late 'fifties, another victim of foreign nutrients finding their way into the lake.

But it wasn't just food gathering in those days. It was a ritual, a spectacle, entertainment. Everyone in the village used to go out and watch, quite entranced; the men splashing and yelling, the flash of the carp breaking the water as they tried to escape, the yells of triumph as someone caught a fish — it was a real spectacle.

Funnily enough, not many of our lot participated — we were onlookers. Even though the village was small, there was a division on what we used to call 'the pa lot' and 'our lot'. We were the 'suburban marae Maori'. We would watch 'the pa mob' making their semi-circle, splashing, splashing, splashing, as they drove the fish into the bay.

Of course, everyone was mindful of what time and what day it was. They were out of the lagoon and back into the hot pool to warm up, then dressed by the time the church bells rang for Communion at

St Faith's, Mass at St Michael's.

These were war years and, though I remember them mainly as trouble-free times — indeed very happy times — the war did cast its shadow. It was a morning ritual for us kids to join Dad, his brother and others in the communal outdoor mineral pool (no roof, but with walls) and the discussion was usually about the progress of the Allies in the Middle East, especially news of the Maori Battalion.

We were all very proud of the exploits of 'the 28th'. I've read since that Rommel said in his memoirs: 'If I had one division of Maori on my side, we would not have lost the war in the desert.' I've also read that the Maori Battalion suffered more casualties per capita than the forces of any Allied country except Russia.

And my childhood memories include the times when the war news was of casualties — killed, wounded or missing in action — from B Company, who were the extended family either directly or through marriage. I remember well how the women would cry loudly while lovingly holding pictures of those killed.

I also learned, later rather than realising it at the time, that Dad was very hurt and angry because a perforated eardrum prevented him serving his country, as he put it. Mum wasn't angry, though, and I've no doubt us kids would have been as quietly relieved as she was that Dad was turned down for military service if we'd been able to comprehend the real risks of never seeing your loved ones again.

New Zealand had its own invasion, of course. The US forces used New Zealand as an assembly place for the Pacific War and I can remember convoys of trucks and tanks and artillery pieces by the hundreds trundling through our town. It was thrilling stuff.

The Americans had set up training camps at the back of Tarawera Mountain and Rerewhakaiti and during the Pacific campaign GIs from Auckland would travel down by train for rest and recreation in Rotorua. The socials arranged for them included tours, concerts (Maori culture) and dances.

I'm told that the Americans were very polite and many GIs charmed the knickers off our local lasses. According to Mum, there were a few two-legged parcels left behind after the war!

Growing up at this time wasn't hard for us kids and we never wanted for anything. It was the time of ration cards and, with only three children, we probably weren't as well off in that regard as larger families. But, by growing vegetables, with uncles who were expert hunters, and with fishing from the lake, there was never any shortage of food that I can remember.

Though we didn't take part in the 'pa lot' ritual of harvesting the carp, our family had its own fishing routine. Saturday mornings were clean-up time, in the yard and the garden. But this was usually preceded by early-morning fishing, and our quarry was not the carp, but

My family, my immediate family, is Church of England but others in the family are Roman Catholic. On a Sunday morning you can see one lot going to St Faith's, on one side of the marae, and another lot going to St Michael's. This goes right across our whanau, and thereby hangs a tale.

It seems that when the Catholic Church was trying to get established here, there was some conflict between families. So one of our chiefs, Pukuatua, gathered all our tribe here in the meeting house, Tamatekapua. Now Tamatekapua is our parliament, a mourning house, a church and all things tribal. After listening to all the tos and fros, the pros and cons, Pukuatua — this Solomon of Te Arawa — stood up and said: 'All those on the left hand side of the meeting house are now Catholic; all those on the right hand side are now Mihirangi, Church of England.' It didn't matter if brothers and sisters were on opposite sides of the meeting house. That was that.

Originally my dad was on the Catholic side, he and an older brother. The others, three brothers and a sister, were Church of England.

But there came a time when his oldest brother wanted to marry a Maori damsel who happened to be of the Catholic persuasion, which, certainly in those days, was much more inflexible about 'mixed marriages'. My uncle was quite prepared to change to Catholic, but he had to balance the books! He said to my father, would you be willing to change to Church of England so I can change to Catholic? And my father, only too readily, said yes — the Catholic Church was too strict for his nature. He was very happy to look across the bay and know he could go to St Faith's if he wanted to — not because he had to.

trout — out on the lake in our boat, trolling with spoons. No motor, it was oar power — my brother Laurie on one oar, me on the other. It was the years when I was eight and nine, my brother three and a half years older. It could be exhausting work, but it made us fit and built up our upper-body strength.

My dad was a very good psychologist in making everything, whether it was work or sport, a challenge rather than a chore. 'You're getting so much better at rowing now that I'll let you take us further out in the lake.' Or, 'If you keep improving the way you are on one oar, maybe, just maybe, I'll let you have a turn with both oars.'

Each harder step was an achievement, an honour.

I reckon we'd row about three miles in a morning, but it was something we always looked forward to. And we'd average three or four trout over the two hours. To Dad it was necessity, keeping food on the family table. But he made it a thrilling expedition for us kids. It was a bit like show biz: 'Preparation. anticipation . . . exhilaration.'

He knew the lake, where the holes were, where the trout were most likely to be. In the deep parts we might be barely moving; in the shallower water he'd give us an increased stroke rate so the spoons would rise. There were long quiet periods, Dad sitting at the back with a rod out each side and one between his legs, us kids pulling on the oars; and then the thrill as a fish would strike.

Those early mornings on the lake come back to me so clearly. In my mind's eye the lake is always placid and hazy, then brightening as the sun gets up. And there are always fish wriggling on the floorboards of the dinghy; if we ever came back empty-handed, my mind doesn't recall those trips.

There was another harvest from the lake. In certain parts there were cork floats which marked what we called a tau — native ferns interwoven with flax, maybe 25 feet long, and allowed to sink to the bottom of the lake. It would attract the koura, the freshwater crayfish, who would make their home in it. And after a certain period of time, maybe a few days or a week, it would be pulled up and harvested.

After the early Saturday fishing expeditions, it was round-the-house chores. And then the big treat; about 1pm every Saturday my brother and I had a shilling each for the pictures. Sixpence admission and sixpence to spend on fish and chips and a coffee bun. Our routine was to walk Dad to the pub and then go on to 'the flicks'. Favourite serials were *The Lone Ranger* and *Flash Gordon.*

Adventure rated high with me and my imagination was pretty vivid. The movies apart, my dad was a great story-teller and I can clearly remember a 'serial story' he used to tell me about an aboriginal hero called 'Sammy the Black Tracker'. My insatiable appetite for hearing the continuing saga led to me being nicknamed 'Sammy' and some of my older relatives still call me that.

Sir Sammy . . . how's that sound? No, I don't think so.

Halcyon days, they seemed to me.

But now came the first upheaval in my young life. My father was posted to Ruatahuna, in the Urewera country. I was 10. A new chapter in my life was about to unfold.

2

DAD, MUM AND RUATAHUNA

REMEMBER the trip to Ruatahuna; me, aged 10, with Dad and the driver in a truck loaded with everything including the kitchen sink. And in another truck were two Jersey cows; Betty and Daisy, who was in calf.

Taking those cows was an example of Dad's initiative. He had made a couple of advance trips and discovered that milk wasn't available in the district. He reckoned that growing kids needed fresh milk. Butter, too, was still rationed so the cows would be a handy source of home-made butter.

Well, one house cow would have been sufficient for our needs. But Dad could see that there would be a wider demand. And that led to me going into business at the tender age of 10, supplying milk to the postmaster, storekeeper, ranger, Sister Annie (a Presbyterian missionary who was famous in the Urewera country) and the school principal.

So why were we leaving the comparatively bright lights of Rotorua, over narrow, dusty, twisty metalled roads, for the remote bush settlement of Ruatahuna?

My father worked for the Maori Affairs Department. He started off taking contracts for scrub cutting, living in a tent with Mum when they were bringing up my brother Laurie; Mum washing the clothes beside a cold creek. He moved up with Maori Affairs during the war and he was a field officer when the war ended and the department started rehabilitation programmes for Maori farm units, trying to bring them back to the land.

They decided to send Dad to Ruatahuna where they were in a bit of cactus fungi; the land had gone back and a lot of farmers were in debt. I guess they thought Dad couldn't do any worse than what had been happening. The bottom line is, he got them debt-free in five years.

And I guess this is a good time to tell you something about my father.

Dad was a very good athlete and a very good rugby player. He made the Maori All Blacks and he was also selected for a team that was to tour Australia. But the way I remember hearing it, the tour was called off because of a strike on the *Wanganella*.

Dad in action in his rugby days. Not a classical tackle — but I reckon he makes it with the ankle tap!   Morrison family collection

He was the second youngest of five brothers and told me that he was originally the slowest. But he worked at improving his speed — his eldest brother was a good trainer — and Dad eventually became a very fast runner.

Part of our family lore is that Dad and his youngest brother competed against some English professional runners who came out before the war. There was prize money of two hundred pounds, a lot of money, and my eldest uncle had worked out a way to beat the Poms with a bit of team running. Dad was to be the rabbit and set a hot pace for the English runners, while his youngest brother would swoop on them in the last 50 yards. But it didn't work that way; they couldn't catch my old man!

Dad took a pretty technical approach to his rugby, too; to his training, to improving his ball skills, learning how to step off both feet. He was a very good five-eighth; he played through all the district rep teams and when he made the New Zealand Maori team his five-eighths partner was John Rowles' father, Eddie Hohapeta Rowles, who was also a very good player. And, as Mum says, they were both a pair of blow bags!

Dad was a bit of a Sheik Ben Hassan, according to Mum. She couldn't stand him at first, because he was a bit of a teaser and a show-off. I wondered where I inherited that from!

Anyway, I said to Mum — how come you got married?

Just one of those things, she said. A love-hate relationship, and the love got stronger than the hate.

Mum has been very frank. Dad was told by the elder brothers that he had to do the decent thing and marry Mum, and they just made it, to quote Mum. They got married and one month later my elder brother was born!

But those were the days when chivalry was alive and well. Those were the days of innocence, when sex education was non-existent. It had an advantage where the purity of the person was concerned; it had a disadvantage, in that innocence being exploited. But then, if a pregnancy was the result of taking advantage of a girl's innocence, then the young chap usually 'acted the man' and accepted his responsibilities.

So there was Dad, a great athlete but a bit of a go-getter in other ways, too. He created a lot of initiatives, made use of his natural talents and skills. OK, he was inclined to blow a bit . . . all the Morrisons are known as blow bags. But when the blowing was over, Dad had put his money where his mouth was. He was an achiever as well as a talker.

Of the five brothers, all of them as physically talented as Dad and some more, he was the one who made the New Zealand Maori team. And he was a success in his work as well, as his achievements in Ruatahuna showed.

I guess you can feel the threads of my admiration for my father showing through and why there has been a huge gap for me in my adult life . . . in what I've achieved, I've missed his acceptance, the pride I think he would have taken. It drew me closer to my uncles, two in particular. But there have been so many times in my life, like at the investiture, where I wished so much that Dad could have shared those moments.

Anyway, that was all a long way in the future as that little Maori boy and his dad arrived on the truck at Ruatahuna — to a culture shock!

For me, it was to discover that I wasn't a Maori — well, as far as the Ruatahuna kids were concerned I wasn't. You see, they all spoke Maori as their mother tongue; remember at that time the culture and language were alive and well, and the rural to urban drift had not yet occurred. I was the new breed of Maori, with English as the first language. I couldn't speak Maori at all.

So here was this new kid arriving at Huiarau Native School at Ruatahuna with his cap and tie and socks and shoes, as if he was still going to Rotorua Primary (Mum took pride, of course, in sending us off to school neat and tidy and 'dressed right'). The kids, of course, thought I looked a cissy. And they couldn't figure out how I could say I was a Maori when I could only speak pakeha — and looked like one!

I soon fixed the first part. There was a big rata tree on the way to school, with a hole in it. I'd stop off, take off my cap and tie, shoes and socks, stuff them in the hole and get a bit of dirt under my fingernails.

But the second part was tougher. I'd try to get the other kids to teach me Maori, in the playground. I was desperately trying to learn the language, just to a conversation level. I didn't realise how important it was, in a cultural sense; I just didn't want to stay on the outer.

But those were the days when you weren't allowed to speak Maori in the school grounds — the teachers would come down on you. It was all right for the other kids; they knew the language from their mother's knee. But I was trying to learn the language, and I guarantee I got the strap more than anyone for speaking Maori in the school grounds. I

Okay, we didn't have Leicas or Canons back in the 1940s. But the Box Brownie shows me, with sister Din on my shoulders, and brother Laurie at the back of the woolshed at Ruatahuna. Morrison family collection

don't know how many times I had to write on the blackboard: 'I will not speak Maori in the grounds again.'

One evening Dad found me having a bit of a cry behind the wood-shed, because I couldn't resolve the dilemma. The kids were giving me a hard time because I couldn't speak Maori; the teachers were giving me a hard time because I was trying to learn.

So Dad marched up to the school the next day and bailed them all up, teachers and pupils. He said to the kids, 'I realise there are going to be misunderstandings and a few fists flying but I don't want to hear of you kids giving my son a hard time for trying to learn what you have got by privilege, by your right, and he hasn't got it. If he's a showoff or whatever, you can give him a hiding if you like. But not for that.'

And he said to the teachers that they had to make an exception for me. And he got his way, too!

By the time I left primary school, I wouldn't say I spoke Maori because the chances to use it were too few. We didn't speak it at home; it was restricted at school. But I got the tone, the feel, the flavour. Forty years later I'm still weak on vocab. But it doesn't take long to come back when I'm among Maori people. Especially when I'm back there, at Ruatahuna.

Ruatahuna . . . Mum hated it. She'd had her fill of loneliness and isolation as a child. She'd become a 'city girl'. There was only generator power, which you could use only at certain times. It would be lights out, then you'd use candles. It could be hard there in the winters; it was a hostile environment. All the household tasks, with none of today's conveniences, would have made it hard for Mum.

But for me, once my assimilation problems were over, Ruatahuna was a boy's paradise . . . the open spaces, the bush, the adventure of living there.

Dad loved it. It was a challenge. He was a stranger, going into a different tribal area. But quite early in the piece he was accepted by the big chief, a man named Paketu; he gave Dad a horse, so he was mobile, and that was the sign that he was accepted into the area.

Dad negotiated the cutting rights for Fletchers in the bush there. It had an upside in bringing money into the area but the downside, as local elder Mac Temara saw it, was different — the cash ran away like water and the farms were allowed to degenerate again.

I suppose some of the things about Ruatahuna that made it seem a hard place for Mum were what made it seem an adventure for me. We had our daily chores but again Dad had that way of making them seem a challenge, almost a privilege.

Mind you, Dad was fanatical about doing things properly, of finishing what you started. Everything had to be right before you could relax. He could be a hard taskmaster that way, give you a clip over the ears or a boot up the bum if the kindling and firewood wasn't chopped

Sing? I can remember Howard singing from the time I first knew
the family. I used to ride past the Morrison house and hear
Howard singing while he was milking the cow. The first time I
heard it, I got off my horse and went over and looked in. There
he was, head under the cow, milking away and singing his head
off. I remember thinking: 'My, that is a golden voice. One day it
will take him a long way.' I guess you could say it all started
under that cow!   — **John Tahuri**

for the next day; if the stable where I milked my cows wasn't properly
cleaned up; if the billies we delivered the milk in weren't scoured clean.
Nothing must be done 'half-pie'.

But the important thing is that we knew as kids why the chores
were important and had to be done correctly. If you didn't cut the firewood, you didn't have a fire and you froze. And if you didn't milk the
cows, apart from the distress to the cows, you didn't have a business!
Those cows were my introduction to the commercial world; Dad taught
me how to milk them and from then on I used to sell the milk to the
Mission House — Sister Annie — to the head teacher and the ranger,
to the postmaster and the Indian shopkeepers.

You wouldn't expect that the way of life in a remote bush settlement would produce influences which set anyone on the path towards
a career as a performer. But I can think of two aspects, in particular,
of those childhood days . . . three, actually, when you consider the
positive influences handed on by Dad's example. Things like 'If something's worth doing, it's worth doing well; no shortcuts.'

Because we had only limited use of electricity, our radio was bat-
tery operated, used sparingly, and Wednesday nights were something
to look forward to: the *Lifebuoy Hit Parade* with Selwyn Toogood.
Because we were starved of entertainment, that communication from
outside stimulated me to listen more intensely to what people were
singing on the air.

I used to get so into it that I would mimic whoever was singing,
male or female. I knew all the hit parade songs by heart.

More than that, it gave me a sort of subconscious knowledge of
what people wanted to listen to. And what the majority of people still
want to listen to is middle-of-the-road popular; specialist areas like jazz
and classical were never part of my childhood influences.

The other aspect, or attribute, of those childhood days in Ruatahuna that came back to me years later in my professional career was
an ability to imitate accents, specifically the accent of the Indian family
who ran the store.

I mentioned before I used to deliver milk to them. Charlie Kalan and his father and family were from the Punjab and we became very close to them. Often we would share Sunday dinner. Mum would prepare the traditional roast with steamed pudding and the Kalans would supply the Indian food. So at the age of 10 and 11, I was not only getting exposure to cosmopolitan cuisine — in little outback Ruatahuna! — but I was surrounded by their dialect, their intonation.

I actually profited from it 25 years later, when I had my first professional engagement on the Asian circuit, in Singapore. Shall I tell that story here?

What happened was that I was trying to establish an identity for myself. It was 1968 and no one knew who the hell I was in Singapore. I was billed as an international singer, which at that time I wasn't. I had no musical arrangements; I just used the band, or the quartet, and away we'd go. It was all in our head.

So it was a real 11th-hour adjustment for me. But I had enough cheek, enough ego, to carry it off. I was helped a heck of a lot when, trying to identify myself after the opening couple of numbers, I said: 'Not that you know me, but perhaps you'd like to request a song from my country, New Zealand . . . ' I was really fumbling my way. In a Singapore audience, of course, most of them just looked blank. But somebody yelled out *'Po Kare Kare Ana.'*

It happened that some guys from the RNZAF, then based in Singapore, were in the audience with their wives. So straight away there were people I could identify with, and I was off to a good start.

And then, in trying to identify who I was to the other people, I made up this story that perhaps the Maori people originated in India. And I switched to the Indian accent.

Well, there was an instant reaction: gales of laughter.

Many of the merchants in the East are Indians and they strike their share of antagonism from other people. But Singapore and Hong Kong are cosmopolitan. There's no room for anything but business and they've really got neither the time nor the reason to hold racist or bigoted views.

They're all immigrants, anyway!

So when I switched into the Indian accent, it went over not as a putdown but as something they could all identify with. Immediately I had a rapport with the audience, and I was on my way.

My patter went something like this (don't forget I'm in the Indian accent now):

'About the year 1300AD there was tremendous over-population in India and the Chief Maharajah gathered all the peoples together (and the populace, too) and said: Over-population is a terrible problem and you Maori Indians are the worst offenders!

'Furthermore you persist in washing your bulls in the Ganges.'

'Therefore you must hop in your canoes and get the hell out of here!

'Well; all my Maori ancestories paddled into the Pathetic. After many t'ousands and t'ousands of paddling and piddling, we dropped all the tired Maoris off in Hawaii, Tahiti, Wallace Islands and so on through the Antipodes. More and more were jumping off the canoes until we reached Rarotonga, where some stowaways jumped on the canoes.

'The first canoes arrived in New Zealand in the Waitemata Harbour and they eventually opened up some dairies and vegetable shops in a place now called the Bombay Hills . . . '

How was that? I actually tell the story much better than I write it. But, oh well, please yourself. So back we go to the past, because my first singing engagement in the East was a long, long way from Ruatahuna . . .

Twice a week, on the way back from school, I would call in to chop wood for Sister Annie and co because they were, well, spinster ladies.

Saturday was Town Day, when everybody would come in to shop from out of the hills, the maraes, from all over the valley, into Ruatahuna. Funniest sight you've ever seen, some of them. The big chief sitting on the horse, the wife walking behind holding the horse's tail, and all the kids walking behind her. Talk about male chauvinism . . .

Then all the women would sit outside the shop on one side, all the men on the other side.

Going back a bit, I remember that on the first Saturday we were there, Mum went into the store to buy groceries. Because Mum was fair the locals were amazed, when she got a greeting, that she responded in Maori and carried on the conversation in Maori. They said, in Maori, that it was quite outstanding that this pakeha could speak fluent Maori.

Ruatahuna may have been a one-horse town — well, it wasn't; there were lots of horses — it may have been small but it was still an occasion going into the store once a week — on Town Day.

Once a month came Big Town Day, when we'd go in to Rotorua on a Friday afternoon. We had a Buick Straight Eight. There were two Buicks in the town, Sister Annie's and ours; the red one.

It was my job to clean the Straight Eight, and once again Dad's psychology came into play. I could start the car and move it 15 yards to where the hose was. And then I'd clean it. Clean it? I'd wash it, wax it and polish it until you could eat off the bonnet. Just for the privilege of moving the car those 15 yards.

When we left on those once-a-month trips to Rotorua, our car would be shining like a new pin. But you're talking about metalled roads from Ruatahuna, and the car would soon be covered in dust again. At Waiotapu we'd come off the dust road onto the tarseal for the last 18 miles into Rotorua. We'd stop at the little lake there and us kids would get out with the buckets, the cloths, the shammy and clean the car again, all over. And then drive proudly into Rotorua.

That was Dad; he taught us to be meticulous about looking after things and keeping them clean. The car, yes, but little things too. The rifle, the rods, the shovel and other tools; the things that we throw into the corner these days or replace with disposables. Those were the days of necessity. You had to make sure that what you had was looked after; it had to last.

It was a good life, a real good life, out there. Quiet people; very reserved people; hard-to-get-to-know people. But when Dad finished his tenure there they paid him the ultimate of all compliments. They gave him a huge farewell and presented him with a cloak made from the feathers of native wood pigeons — which, incidentally, were protected then as they are today. But that was overlooked for certain special occasions — like when the ranger wasn't looking!

I still wear that cloak now, with great pride, on really important occasions. I wore it to the investiture; I wore it when I sang at the Commonwealth Games.

When I was getting to the age of not so much fearing my father as looking at him as an example — knowing more often what to do to please him — I was whisked away to boarding school.

For three years, from ages 10 to 13, I'd been learning by example from Dad about farming: when to dag, when to dip, when to crutch, how to milk; about the importance of breeding to improve the quality of stock. Dad improved the level of breeding by bringing in pedigree stock; Aberdeen Angus bulls and a better class of rams.

At that time, it was my expectation that I would become a farmer. But not just a farmer; I'd be a farmer in charge of other farmers. Because when you're growing up you don't see things changing; you want to be like your father. So I'd inherit his job; I didn't know how, but I would.

Of course, things do change. And your life has turnings that you sometimes don't recognise until afterwards.

My life's next turning was when I was rising 13, in Standard Six, and had to sit a scholarship exam to go on to secondary school. We had to nominate the college we wanted to go to; it was a privilege then, not like these days when they're throwing the net out to get kids to go. Well, we all chose Te Aute College because of the mana.

And — great stuff! The two of us from Ruatahuna who wanted to go to Te Aute College both passed the exam, Reti Apirana and myself. From little Ruatahuna, I was off to the big boarding school — and another culture shock.

3

TEENAGE YEARS

WHEN I BEGAN secondary school, because I was going to be a farmer, I took an agricultural course. My first impression of Te Aute was the impressive brick main building, smelling of history and breathing of past great students. Sir Apirana Ngata, Maui Pomare, Tatana and Peter Buck . . . it was easy to be motivated at first. But after a while, you had to remind yourself of why you were there and of the commitment your parents had made to your education.

Going from 'the bush' to Te Aute College was the second culture shock of my young life. Attending Huirau Native School at Ruatahuna confronted me with the fact that I knew practically nothing of my Maori culture or language. Going to Te Aute I discovered the significance of tribe, of tribal differences. I hadn't realised that being an Arawa was any different from being any other kind of Maori, because tribal heritage wasn't part of my upbringing. I learned different when I arrived at Te Aute, because most of the boys were East Coast Maori, Ngati Porou.

I'm not saying they gave me a lot of stick, but they did make me aware of the difference. Mind you, I invited a bit of stick anyway. I wanted to promote myself as being pretty independent; I probably over-compensated in my efforts to show I wasn't overawed by this big, famous school. What didn't help was that I inherited the mantle of a cousin who had been at the school for three years and had left only the year before me. They used to call him 'Blow Bag'. I got nicknamed 'The North Wind' and, when you start off on the back foot like that, you tend to over-react. My reaction was to showboat at every opportunity. And my over-zealous efforts to be noticed met with humour from some pupils and hostility from others.

I got to do a lot of letter-writing home and, though I got supportive letters back, I didn't get lectures from Dad. I guess he thought that if I hadn't learned enough by now, what could he do? But it actually helped me keep my gumption up, that he obviously thought I could cut it at boarding school.

I came from a pretty spiritual, churchy, home background and I used to enjoy it; I was mixing with the older people, playing adults. But at Te Aute, church was a matter of the everyday routine. Incidentally, Divinity was the only subject I topped the class in. I remember coming back from my first term; Dad was driving me to Ruatahuna and I was yapping away, ninety to the dozen. I was telling him that my mate Hapi Winiata was going into the ministry. It seemed like a neat idea. I was leaning over from the back seat, Mum in the front passenger's seat, and saying: 'Dad, I topped the class in Divinity!'

'Oh, good on you son, good on you.'

'Yeah, as a matter of fact I think I'd like to go into the ministry.'

Whew! He almost went off the road!

The irony is that my mate Hapi Winiata did become a minister and still is. He's steeped in the heavy side of Maoritanga; sits on the pae-pae (where they welcome the visitors), knows all the waiata.

My ideas of becoming a minister didn't last. But one aspect of religious education at Te Aute which did stay with me was the musical influence.

We all looked forward to the visiting clergy. Men like the Rev Henry Northcroft, Canon Wi Huata and Rev Sam Rangiihu all made us feel better, less intimidated by the challenges of succeeding; kept things in perspective. But Sam Rangiihu and Wi Huata in particular were, without knowing it, my first mentors not only in music but in the art of entertainment.

Rev Rangiihu in particular would always relax his audience and put them at their ease with humour and timing. Then when he sang 'straight' you appreciated his vocal qualities all the more.

Every holiday when I came home, Dad started treating me differently, like an adult. I'd go out with the head shepherds and put in a man's day. After showing me the rudiments of looking after a rifle, he'd say: 'Right, now go out and do your own hunting.' So I would go out the back of the hills; I'd miss more than I hit, because I used to pull at the rifle instead of squeezing the trigger. But practice makes perfect — or at least competent.

Dad didn't go hunting much in Ruatahuna. He was an admin

Ancient custom is observed: the focal point of the investiture.

Raewyn Saville

Embraced by my baby sister Linda. The korowai (cloak) I wore with pride; it was presented to my father by the Tuhoe people nearly 40 years before.

Raewyn Saville

Approaching the marae past a contingent of the Territorials and (below) the 'Maori Territorials'.

A welcome from Hamuera Mitchell, paramount chief of Te Arawa.
Raewyn Saville

OVERLEAF: With Sir Paul at prayers after the ceremony. Kuia and I both look pretty damp-eyed; Mum is holding up better than either of us.
Raewyn Saville

With my whanau, my extended family, outside our meeting house, Tamatekapua, after the formalities of the investiture.
Raewyn Saville

The wild Urewera country I came to love during my Ruatahuna childhood.
Looking over my horse's head as the track takes us into the dense bush.

The 'official' wedding photo.

The Quartet in the Showtime Spectacular days.

man, getting more pleasure out of setting up meetings around the tribes. In his tenure there, a lot of things happened. About five or six marae, for example, had tennis courts laid. Clay, mainly. We had a very healthy competition, too. Dad stimulated all of that. One marae against another; tennis tournaments amongst ourselves. All in whites, too! Oh, yes. Flash! But it was a great way of getting around all the marae. Dad loved organising people. You can't organise people when you're out in the bush. So it was: 'You guys go out — I'll help you eat it when you bring it back.'

So it wasn't Dad I went hunting with when I came back on holidays, but with Dad's shepherds. On a few occasions I went in with Internal Affairs ranger Jack Henderson and, later, his replacement Rex Forrester and a couple of his offsiders. Rex would give me ten bob and a couple of bullets per tail. I wasn't a member of his gang, as it were; I just used to go for the pleasure of hunting and being in the bush. It was part of the old self-sufficiency thing, too, being able to look after yourself in the bush. I thought these fellows were quite amazing until I found out they were using a compass and a map. If I took a compass and a map with the Maori fellers I used to go in with they'd laugh. They were brought up in the bush. I was never too adventurous. I'd only go with somebody who knew the area.

But the joy of being in the bush is relating to people you know, anyway. Not too many; just a couple, or three. You can spread out, enjoy your silent moments of appreciating nature to its fullest; then enjoy the comradeship afterwards.

The bush, of course, was holidays at home. Back to Te Aute College, my four years there. In the first two years, Third and Fourth Form, I was starting to appreciate that education was a must. But in the Fifth Form . . . The headmaster at Te Aute at that time did not encourage us to sit School Certificate in first-year Fifth. First year, for

---

We got to the camp where there were two fellows hunting. The experienced hunter was Bill Le Gallais; his 'apprentice' was a well-known Rotorua fellow called Harry Bimler, who was then in his first job as a deer culler. In his spare time Harry was reading a book on hypnotism and Howard said, 'Hypnotise me!' Well, Harry went into his routine and Howard's eyes started to close, then his head fell on his shoulder and he was out. I forget what Harry told him to do, but Howard's head suddenly snapped up, his eyes opened, and he said, 'Stick it up your jumper!' and roared with laughter. Well, we all did. We'd really thought he was in a trance!
— **Rex Forrester**

The whole family near the end of Dad's time at Ruatahuna. Mum (with baby Linda in her lap) and Dad in front; at the back, from left, Laurie, Rene, Judy, Adelaide and HM.

Morrison family collection

experience; second year, sit School C. Now that, to me, was an open invitation to cop out.

I believe I had only average intelligence, average aptitude, but I was pretty quick on the uptake in 'the comprehension department'. I think I would have got School C if I'd sat in first-year Fifth, maintaining the momentum of Third and Fourth Forms. Instead of which, two things happened in Fifth Form. I was made head farm boy and I was also one of the main workers assisting in refurbishing our assembly hall. The carving of the pou-pou was done by two master carvers, the Taiapa brothers, Pine and John. They were both trained in Te Arawa, so there was an association there again. I felt proud because, even though they were from the East Coast, they had been trained by my people, were part of me. And I found a new acceptance because my Ngati Porou schoolmates were proud of these masters from the East Coast. John married a girl from the north and he later became a huge influence in the district while master carver at the New Zealand Arts and Crafts Institute.

So I was their sort of handy boy and, along with my farm duties, schoolwork almost went out the window. We made a great job of refurbishing the assembly hall, in preparation for our 100th anniversary.

I got pretty clever, too, in how to run the farming operation as head farm boy. I used to milk the herd of 60 cows, so it was machine milking and I was pretty fast — although a bit of a sleepyhead. Sometimes the cows were being milked while everyone else was having breakfast. Between the farm work, the refurbishing of the assembly hall and sport, I didn't have much input into day-to-day classwork. By then I was too clever anyway — or thought I was.

Rugby-wise, I was good enough to make the Third XV out of six teams, out of a roll of 140 kids. That's how strong our rugby was, because I turned out a pretty good player, though I say so myself. But I wasn't good enough to make the top teams at Te Aute. Apart from anything else I didn't have enough meat on my bones; I wasn't as physically mature as a lot of the boys.

The class of football at Te Aute in those days was so strong. Our First XV played Senior B in the Central Hawke's Bay club competition and the Second XV played all the other schools' First XVs. The last year I was there, five of our First XV were nominated for the Maori All Black trials.

Apart from rugby, tennis was my main sport and I considered myself the best tennis player at college. But I didn't make the top team . . . there was a bit of jealousy, I think. I was told I was a bit of a Casanova, trying to win the hearts of girls from our sister college, Hukarere. And when we used to go to Hastings, for our weekend breaks and so on, funnily enough the other guys would follow me around because I had more cheek than they did; I was buoyed by their confidence in me. But what success I enjoyed with the young ladies of the time didn't endear me to some of my classmates. It was Bighead Morrison again.

It was on a trip to the annual A&P Show in Hastings that I met my future wife, Kuia. We grew up as youngsters in the same village; her dad Hiwaroa and mine were great fishing mates. But when we moved to Ruatahuna we lost touch. So it was a surprise to see that she was at Hukarere, and a bigger shock to see how stunning a young woman she had grown to be. I don't know why but I felt that she was my girl; I'll tell you how things developed later.

Howard was 13 months younger than me. We had a fair bit to do with each other as kids but became close friends when Howard came back from Te Aute. While we were still at Rotorua High, I remember a Sunday church service at St Faith's when there was a loud boom! from outside. Howard was shooting shags with his dad's shotgun! Howard's family relished curried shag — I never tried it myself. But I can tell you that blasting off with a shotgun right outside the church service wasn't appreciated by our minister.
— **John Morrison**

The one example of sporting success at Te Aute which does stick in my mind was in the finals of the intermediate 440 yards at our school sports. I was dawdling along at the back of the big field, my right hand in plaster after an accident, thinking . . . well, nobody expects me to do much as I've only been out of hospital a week. Anyway, going down the back straight four or five pupils yelled 'Go Morrison!'

The feeling of exhilaration when I realised that perhaps some of the guys did accept me urged me to take off right round the outside of the field. I caught the race leader and favourite, who I thought was too good for me; I came to his shoulder and he dug it in, so did I and, beggar me, he caved in and I swept past.

It was quite a humbling and enlightening experience to be congratulated and slapped on the back. From that day I think I felt less the outsider, more confident in my environment. But having no spectre of School Certificate hanging over me in first-year Fifth didn't do much for my scholastic achievement.

I enjoyed my sport, the farm work and the work on the assembly hall. But academic work and I were just about strangers. And at the end of that year — and Dad never interfered, either — I decided that I didn't want to go back to college.

In hindsight it was a mistake. But if I hadn't made that decision — well, it would have changed the rest of my life. Who can say what would have happened? I'd been given a veiled promise that the next year I'd be either a monitor or a prefect, which was a big deal, because we're talking about a college that reeked of history, reeked of mana. Te Aute has probably produced more knights than any other college, Maori or pakeha. Sir Apirana Ngata, Sir Maui Pomare, Sir Peter Buck, Sir Henry Tatana, Sir James Carroll — there could be as many as 10.

I bet no one thought, when I left Te Aute College at the end of first-year Fifth, the name of H. Morrison would one day be added to the list. I certainly didn't! (But I had high hopes, as the giraffe said to his guidance counsellor.)

4

RUGBY, MUSIC
AND MARRIAGE

BY 1953 the family had returned to Rotorua and I decided to go to Rotorua Boys' High School to finish off my schooling. Dad had a good job; he'd been elevated in the department to take over some of the areas around the lakes. He was very good at his job.

Dad got a bit harder on me at this stage. I think he was disappointed that I didn't go back to college and he wasn't going to let me cop out. He'd suddenly become very strict. OK, you're a young adult — but don't get too carried away.

I'd decided to carry on with agriculture and animal husbandry as two of my subjects for School Certificate. It was a silly decision, because there were no courses at Rotorua High School. I had to do it by correspondence.

So that year, 1953, was a waste of time. I was in the First XV at Rotorua High but was dropped because the coach reckoned I wouldn't tackle. He was probably right, too. I remember at that time I was prone to the flash, minutely late shoulder charge. It wasn't rated a dangerous tackle in those days. I ended up playing senior club rugby that year, though not every game. I was sort of first emergency; first man on when the old fellers got tired.

After I left school, in early 1954, I went back to Hawke's Bay. I had a job in the Apple and Pear Marketing Board, as a storeman; then

I went to the Whakatu freezing works. That was another part of my education. Still didn't drink, still didn't smoke, hadn't been tempted at all. And in the hard school of the freezing works, that was pretty tough. The guys there made me feel grown up and were good to me. I learned a lot.

I should say here that I'd always felt more comfortable with adults. Why? At Ruatahuna, from age 10 to 13, I didn't have mates my own age. They were too shy to come round to our place because Dad was the 'big boss'.

So my recreational and conversational company was with Dad's shepherds, the local storekeepers, the ranger, Sister Annie and teachers at school.

That carried to Te Aute, where again I was a bit of a loner. So at the freezing works I was right at home with the grown-up men, grown-up language, grown-up topics. In fact, some of the guys still had a lot of growing up to do and at times I felt more grown up than them — especially in terms of future horizons; a lot of them had no ambitions outside the works.

Our aspirations are governed to a great degree by the people we look up to. My father's example gave me a positive focus. In the case of a lot of the freezing workers, their sons had no greater ambition than to follow them on to the chain. This happened over three generations.

A consequence was that, though skilled in their work, they were the first casualties when technology replaced them. I think it's no coincidence that this is the time span when gangs of various sorts emerged into prominence, finding co-existence within themselves and at odds with society.

The real significance of that year in Hastings was that it introduced me to singing in public, to the concept of training and practising singing. I'd been singing from the time I was a kid; milking my cows at Ruatahuna, in the bush when I came back on holidays from Te Aute. But this was my introduction to singing in a disciplined way, in public. I owe that background to the people in Hastings, especially to the Whatarau family. The Whataraus got me to join the church choir, then the Awapuni Concert Party. And from that, two Whatarau sisters, Isobel and Virginia, and I formed the Clive Trio — the first popular singing group I was ever involved with.

I actually replaced the late Kahu Pineaha, who went solo as a singer, impressionist and exotic dancer and based himself in Sydney.

I'd first met the Whataraus while I was still at Te Aute College and Isobel and Virginia had visited the school with their mother who'd come to take the choir for the anniversary celebrations. We showed them around the place and they sang us a few songs. It was marvellous; everyone fell in love with these two kids. They were only about 11 and 12 in those days and had beautiful voices. I was one of the people who

The Clive Trio . . . HM with the Whatarau sisters, Virginia (left) and Isobel.

sang solos in response to them, part of the little get-together we had.

Mrs Whatarau said that I had promise, that any time I was in the area she hoped we could get together again and do something with my voice.

That came about when I was working at the freezing works during the Christmas school holidays, before I came home. We used to sing a lot on the floor of the small goods department, where we worked on contract. There was my big cousin Taui and an ex-Te Aute College pupil named Star Renata. He was a very good musician and played piano for our school dances at Te Aute. So to keep ourselves and the other guys on the floor amused, there was constant singing. Real extroverts the three of us. We were actually encouraged by the guys at the works and we'd sing at the drop of a hat in those days. Here we were, still wet behind the ears, in this den of hard-working, hard-living, hard-drinking men. Yet among these rough diamonds was that sensitivity to helping young people like myself who were trying to find their way in the world.

One of the guys at the freezing works who heard me sing, Chocky Chadwick, a friend who married into our family in Rotorua, asked me to come along and join the Kohupatiki church choir in Hastings. And it was while I was there that I met Mrs Whatarau and the girls again. Naturally enough I linked up with them when I returned to Hastings after leaving Rotorua High.

From there we joined the Awapuni Concert Party, with the idea of touring the South Island. We thought we could make a few bob and see the country at the same time. So my first experience of touring came from that time in Hastings. Trevor King was our manager, one of the original entrepreneurs. He's retired now but still does one-off promotions; he did one for me last year and another the year before that — a real doyen of entrepreneurs and dead straight and honest, a real gentleman.

The Awapuni Concert Party developed a really tight act, and when I say 'act' that group was ahead of its time. We were the first group to mix contemporary music with traditional cultural music — a practice in those days considered heresy. But the question has to be asked: How traditional is traditional? We were singing *Hoki Mai*, a song that came out of the East Coast, to the tune of *Gold Mine in the Sky*. A lot of the songs of that time were pakeha songs with Maori words.

The first half of the show was all traditional, all culture. I'm stripped to my piupiu, like everyone else, but we couldn't wait till the second half, because that was when we could have a 'lout'. For the uninitiated, including the people who came to see us, it was a bit of a shock. They were expecting a full Maori concert party programme and out we'd come in the second half and do entirely modern, contemporary music; songs of the day. It was the last thing they were expecting.

There were two brothers in the group, from the Waipatu area, who played guitar. They were our backing instrumentalists, and very good guitarists, too. In the second half they'd come on and do *Guitar Boogie*, which was big at the time. And the anchor of the second half was the Clive Trio; myself and the two Whatarau girls. We did the thing right, too. The girls were in ball gowns, I was in a double-breasted suit and bow tie. It made a nice change from the cultural renditions of the first half.

Well, we went around the South Island; we were right on the breadline and taking very little at the box office. I don't know how we existed. But we had help and hospitality from a lot of good people and stayed at a lot of marae. Some of my relations, the Gillies families, were good to us in Lyttelton and I remember getting great hospitality from people in Temuka.

On my Ride For Life I went back to Temuka, which was a very emotional experience for me because all the memories flooded back. In my mind's eye I could see us back then; innocent, raw, not doing very well, plenty of energy and living off our wits — and the help we got from good people along the way. It was a very nostalgic visit.

The concert party tour got to the stage where it was too difficult so I drew out all my savings from the Post Office Bank, accumulated in my time at the freezing works, and we made our way back to Rotorua.

That was my first experience of touring; a great learning curve but not a financial success. And that was when Dad picked us up off the bones of our bum and introduced Howard Morrison the performer to the public of Rotorua.

I'd been playing rugby in Hastings for MAC, a club pioneered by one of the great Maori All Blacks, Tori Reid. After training with them for the first time, I ended up at first five-eighth, a position I was quite unaccustomed to. I was still only 18½, a baby, really. But I was put in among the big boys and I did very well, good enough to get a game in the Hawke's Bay trials.

Mum and Dad came through to watch. I played a good game; solid, good distributor, backed up well — the whole bit. After the game Dad came down to the bottom of the grandstand where we got changed, sat down and put his arm round me and said: 'Good game, son. But one of these days you'll be a better singer.'

He wasn't knocking my rugby-playing ability; he was letting me know he had confidence that I had a future in singing. It was where he was unique; he had an instinct. At that time I hadn't even thought of singing being anything like a fulltime career yet that was the man's foresight. He always promoted me to his brothers, that singing was where my success would be.

After he died, I made sure I honoured that faith. Maybe it was his belief, his saying that to me after the rugby game in Hastings, that influenced what came to pass. But even at a young age, I could see that football was a seasonal thing. The days of glory ended in September! My vanity and ego even then was such that I felt there was something different about me. I wasn't a 'seasonal man' — I was a man for all seasons! Not what I would have said then, of course.

Anyway, after the South Island tour with the Awapuni Concert Party we came back home and Dad promoted a show for the Clive Trio in Rotorua. It was a big show, in the old Civic Theatre, which was the Regent then, and we were very popular.

I was going with one of the Whatarau girls then, Isobel. The parents really wanted us to get hitched but I had no desire. We were too young, anyway, to even think about it. It was just the romance of the time; you're touring together, everybody's clapping you when you sing, they say you look good together and all that.

Just the same I might have gone back to Hastings, back to the MAC rugby team, the Awapuni Concert Party and the Clive Trio; my relationship with Isobel might have continued, might have deepened.

But that all fell to pieces on New Year's Eve, 1954, with the event that shattered our family as we'd known it during the carefree years of my growing up.

Dad had not been experiencing very good health. He was a robust man and they were diagnosing everything from yellow jaundice to gallstones. He'd had a bit of a rough time of it. In the afternoon, following a lunch of fish which he really enjoyed, he got into a bad sweat and became very ill. That night in hospital they diagnosed leukemia; he died at eight o'clock the next morning.

It must say something for the constitution of the man. He'd gone through that year with not much time off work; to be admitted to hospital at two in the afternoon and die within 24 hours — from leukemia!

Dad was only 45 and, for all of us, it was a stunning blow.

Laurie was 23, I was 19 and the four girls were still at home, still at school. Dad had been very much the head of the family, in the old style. He was our provider, our decision-maker, our navigator. Looking back, I don't know how Mum managed.

It was one of those extra sad twists that in the January *Public Service Gazette*, where they ran new appointments for Government positions, they listed Dad's appointment to a position of high importance in Maori Affairs. It must have gone to press before they learned of Dad's death.

As I've said, Dad was a great organiser. He was the main front-line troop when they organised the Maori reception for the Queen and Prince Philip when they came here as 'young marrieds'; he was in the forefront of rebuilding Tamatekapua, our meeting house. So the accolades that went out to him during that funeral time, that he went before his time, were an understatement.

It was a huge tangi and a huge tribal shock.

This was the time when, obviously through the death of Dad, I settled back in Rotorua. At that time my brother Laurie took over the mantle of head of the family. He was a young married man then. While I believe I had Dad's flamboyance and entrepreneurial skills, Laurie inherited Dad's administrative skills.

Laurie was very bright at school, very diligent. We had little to do with each other while growing up, brother to brother. He was being educated at high school in Rotorua while I was at primary school at Ruatahuna. Then he went to Ruatahuna to teach while I was at Te Aute College. So we were never really close as brothers; we were almost embarrassed by the fact that we were brothers but were clumsy in relating to one another.

He could be pedantic at times; he liked to dot the i's and cross the t's. But he really was very bright. He left teaching to work for the Ministry of Works in the survey section and did very well — passed all his exams and he became a surveyor, later an engineer's assistant.

After Dad's death we became closer. Laurie got me work on his survey team in the bush from time to time, when he could get me in. My position didn't have a name. You had to sit exams to be a chainman, to be able to operate a theodolite, to work out the angles and degrees and everything that goes with it. So mine was mainly labouring work — cutting tracks and running the chain . . . and sometimes breaking the chain! Laurie was a hard taskmaster; there was no brotherly love as far as getting work done was concerned. Nobody above him in the Ministry of Works could complain they didn't get a good day's work out of Laurie.

This was early in 1955, which was to turn out a very eventful year.

With the taste of public performing in Hastings behind me, and the concert that Dad had financed for us in Rotorua, I'd started getting different groups together to sing at football clubs and the like.

Laurie was baritone in the first group; at that time it was always who was available. It wasn't the Howard Morrison Quartet, it was the Ohinemutu Quartet . . . any name. At this stage I was still doing survey work in the bush but in Maori Affairs under my uncle Martin McRae, ex-sergeant major in the Maori Battalion.

I heard Gerry Merito play at a family gathering and I couldn't get over how strong an acoustic guitar player he was. We started singing together and I realised here was someone who could accompany me. My father had always reckoned that if I was going to be a singer I should get someone else to play the instruments and just stick to the singing. That was the pragmatic way he had of distinguishing how things should be done.

Gerry was out of work and staying with a relative of mine so I got him a job with me in the Survey Department at Maori Affairs. I'll never forget Martin McRae . . . a real gruff bugger. Talk about Windsor Davies; Uncle was the epitome of the sergeant major, gruff as hell. I took Gerry in to work and said: 'Oh, Uncle — this is Gerry; he's going to be working with us.'

Gerry was limping; he had osteomyelitis. My uncle took one look at him and said: 'What the hell's wrong with you, boy? You got a broken arse or something?' Gerry's affectionately bestowed nickname around the Waikite football boys is still 'Brokie' — Broken Arse!

While Laurie was in the Quartet we had a lot to do with one another, making up for the growing-up years we'd missed. The early Quartet comprised my cousin John as tenor, myself, Laurie and Gerry. When John wasn't available, Tai Eru came in. But the first photographs show Laurie, myself, Gerry and John.

> The bush was our butcher's shop. There were so many deer and pigs we never had to worry about meat. I had two terrific dogs. When Howard got sick of deer and pig he'd go down the river with a rifle. Boom! and back he'd come with a couple of trout.
>
> — **Ray Keepa**

I was working on survey for Maori Affairs with Ray Keepa, Maori All Black at that time; with Huri Maniapoto, now one of the chiefs of Tuwharetoa in Taupo; and with Henry Parkinson, another football mate of mine and a Maori All Black. Those were the days.

I was chainman for Ray Keepa. I was young and fit and single. And when we weren't out surveying, at lunchtimes and after work, I became quite a good ball-handler because I had to run at full pace while Ray practised his pass to me. I was as fit as a buck rat. You couldn't stop me. Didn't drink, didn't smoke, my high was singing.

And I was courting Kuia, so I was really in love with life. I couldn't work hard enough so the week would go fast enough to get back to Rotorua. At night, after working all day in the bush, we used to go right to the headwaters and sleep in the truck. And sing! I'd sing my head off.

Our diet in those days was the Italian tenors like Beniamino Gigli and Tito Scipa. Not Mario Lanza; we thought he was a bit of an imposter. I remember one evening I overheard Ray saying to Huri: 'You know, one of these days that young bugger is going to be someone; he's going to go places with that voice. He's a bloody gun!' They thought I was asleep; they wouldn't tell me that to my face because I had a big enough head as it was. But it gave me a hell of a swell of pride.

One outlet for singing in those days was talent quests, and in 1955, at the Rotorua soundshell, we won one. There were six in the group: myself, Terry Morrison and Wi Wharekura on guitar, Gary Rangiihu, Chubby Hamiora and John Morrison. Laurie wasn't in it; this was before we started singing more regularly. In the semi-finals we came second to an old fellow who came out with two walking sticks and sang *The Lord's Prayer*. We never had a bolter's show!

To my own credit, I was very quick to pick up trends. Even though I wanted to sing what I saw as decent songs, the way to go was straight to the vibes of what was in at the time. As this was when rock 'n roll had hit New Zealand, the group put together a medley of *Rock Around the Clock*, *Blue Suede Shoes*, *Shake Rattle 'N Roll*. Well, the crowd never stopped screaming and in the final we pushed the old bloke with his walking sticks and *The Lord's Prayer* back to second place.

That was my first taste of recognition outside football club singing. It was very whanau. I worked with whanau, I played sport with whanau, I sang with whanau. And I now started to court a member of extended whanau.

> The boys used to sing around the campfire nearly every night. Gerry Merito brought in a zither — it was easier to pack than a guitar. Huri and Scar and Gerry and Howard would sing and it was as good as any of the later Quartet stuff. — **Ray Keepa**

It turned out, though they never said anything to us, that our dads had both hoped Kuia and I would make a match of it. I never found out until we were engaged, when my mother told me how happy my father would have been; that he'd always hoped for this. All of Dad's brothers, when we were going steady, were holding their breath and hoping that it would happen.

Funnily enough, though our two houses in Rotorua weren't that far apart, I didn't know Kuia existed until we were both at college in Hastings. I was smitten by this lovely young lass from wherever — and it turned out to be my dad's mate's daughter. But Kuia couldn't stand me at first; she thought I was a real big head Casanova.

She was right, too. I must have really given an impression of arrogance, of conceit.

I remember an incident from my young days, before I was anybody, that really hit home to me the impression I made on other people. There was a fair in town, a show with all the sideshows and merry-go-rounds and what have you. I was by myself, down near the merry-go-round, when I noticed these two guys and a girl about 20 yards away and they seemed to be fighting, arguing. The girl was holding on to a guy and he tossed her away and I moved towards them in case I could help the girl out.

I said: 'Anything the matter?'

This guy said: 'You're the matter, Morrison!'

He didn't know me from a bar of soap, I'd never spoken to him, but he came up to me and was wanting to fill me in.

He said I was the most stuck-up, show-off, b-x-y-z — the language was something terrific. I didn't know his background, I'd never met the

---

I remember one time we were working in the bush between Tokaanu and Taumarunui, opening up all those lines, and a school was being opened at Whaitikuranui, right in the middle of nowhere. I said to the headmaster (who I knew through rugby) not to worry about meat for the do; we'd bring it. Howard and Huri and Scar went shooting while the rest of the gang kept working, and came out with half a dozen pigs, a couple of deer and a wild cattle beast — there was enough for a feast. I don't know where all the people came from, but there were over 200 there; about half pakeha, half Maori. I think a lot had been balloted farms after the war. After the feast Howard and Gerry and the boys started singing and they brought the house down. The people wouldn't let them sit down. It must have been just about Howard's first public performance, apart from the singing he'd done with the Clive Trio, at that little school in the middle of nowhere. — **Ray Keepa**

guy. I let him have his moment, I kept my hands down and asked him if he really knew me. He admitted he didn't and I calmed him down.

It shocked me a bit, that someone I'd never met could take such a violent dislike to me. But a lot of it I brought on myself. I'd started this over-compensating at boarding college, to hide my vulnerability. And I'd come to really believe it, to believe I was something special and was going to do big things — even though I had no real reason for it. I was working at a labouring job; singing at a few footy clubs was no big deal really. Certainly Kuia was probably justified in her opinion of me.

Nothing much happened until after Dad died. Kuia was nursing at Rotorua Hospital and it was a gradual process getting her to come out with me.

When we married I'd had my 21st birthday about six months earlier; she was only 19. All the laws of averages would have said that that on its own would have made it pretty unlikely for the marriage to survive, let alone the impact of going into show business three years later.

The credit of 35 years of marriage is hers. I've never met, before or since, a more decent and loyal person in my life. And, looking back, how she endured the traumatic changes of my going from bush cutter to meter reader to, in 1960, the leader of a well-known group, while in the process of starting a family . . . In hindsight, I think one of the main pitfalls in relationships with the opposite gender is habit. You get to the stage where you take your partner for granted.

My marriage was never like that; I used to look forward to the homecomings. But really it was a very 'man's world' type of arrange-ment. Kuia didn't, and doesn't, see it that way. She just thinks everyone else is abnormal if they don't act as she does. But that's why I give her all the credit for the survival and health of our marriage.

Anyway, we were still courting, not married yet, when we won that first talent quest. I was looking for better things in my life. The survey work wasn't going anywhere; I was just a glorified scrub-cutter. It was a healthy life, trudging over the hills and through the bush. I was doing more training than the average rep footballer. Ray Keepa didn't train twice a week. He had me running with him every night, and practising every night. I was lucky; I got extra-curricular training! And that's why Ray Keepa was a Maori All Black and should have been an All Black.

But I'd got to the stage where I wasn't enjoying the survey work because it was too far from the spotlight. I wanted to be in town more. So after we won that talent quest, I applied for and got a job as a meter reader with the Tourist Department. It was a job which attracted me because it meant you weren't a labourer any more. You got to wear a collar and tie! There was a lot of snobbery in those days about what job you did. These days you're just happy to have a job. Back then it was a definite step up to have a collar-and-tie job.

I'll never forget going in for an interview. The head of department was taking me through what I had to do. There was not only reading the meter, which was easy enough, but working out what was owed and subtracting whatever discount there was. I'm talking pounds, shillings and pence days. Now this is where you get found out for that missed education; the things that you didn't do at school. I had always managed to dodge arithmetic; my skill was sub-standard. The department head was right there beside me doing additions, subtracting discounts, and I couldn't follow him, couldn't work it out. He thought I was such a personable, well-spoken, intelligent young chappie that I was just having him on. He didn't have to teach me that, for goodness sake!

He just told me where I had to go and, for the first month, somehow some way, I struggled through. You were supposed to read the meter, then give the bill: Thank you, Mrs Brown. But I was reading the meter, then taking some of the bills back home and getting Kuia to help me out.

I'd started the job as a single meter reader and became a married meter reader. Kuia and I married on May 11, 1957.

Before I go into detail about the wedding there were a couple of significant events in 1956.

I've mentioned the financially unsuccessful South Island tour with the Awapuni Concert Party. Well, in 1956 I also toured Melbourne, Sydney and Newcastle with what was called the Aotearoa Maori Concert Party. The group was chosen by national auditions, and so it was multi-tribal. You wouldn't have thought at the time that a group composed of different tribal representation would get on, but we did.

The promoters lost a lot of money, we made zilch. But it was a great experience for me in realising how unique our culture was; something we took for granted here, because we grew up with it. I can still remember talking to people before and after the shows we did in different parts of Australia, and how enamoured they were of the fact that our culture was alive and well, and naively comparing us with the Aborigines over there.

They couldn't understand how, even though we were 'coloured', how much progress we'd made in western civilisation, I guess, compared with the Aborigine. But of course that's their huge problem; I took umbrage that a comparison was being made. On occasions since, I have smugly suggested that we were the only indigenous people colonised by the British not through the power of the musket, but by the pen — i.e., the Treaty of Waitangi.

Members of that group included Tamati Reedy, thirty-odd years later Secretary for Maori Affairs during the infamous Maori Loans episode, Bill Gray, who later that year made the All Blacks, and Isobel

The Aotearoa Maori Concert Party tour to Australia in 1956. Bill Gray, 1956 All Black, is next to that Maori Rudolf Nureyev. (Yep, that's me!)

Another couple of 'notables' on that 1956 tour to Oz. That fella on my left is Tamati Reedy, who was to become Secretary for Maori Affairs some 30 years later.

Whatarau, engaged at that time to a chap named Peter Cowan. It was nice to meet up with a familiar face and we formed a duet as part of the concert party. The crowds over there really loved us — not just the cultural aspect of our performance, they were intrigued by our modern songs and our very well articulated speech patterns. Of course, we laid it on a bit thick with the correct diction bit.

After that trip, pre-Christmas 1956, I had to answer the call for Compulsory Military Training. I was in the 16th Intake. I adapted very easily because I guess I was used to the discipline, through past training from Te Aute College, and because of the independence I'd developed in looking after myself. I was well versed with firearms and my experience in the bush made the camping-out stuff a breeze.

I did well enough to earn a lance-corporal's stripe, which put me in charge of my own section, and I also made the Company B rugby team, at second five-eighth. When we played the grudge match against Company A, there was this tall, skinny bugger in the opposition team. He turned out to be Colin Meads.

One of our locks was Ivan Sapich, a big and usually genial guy. He was marking Pinetree (only a Tea-Tree in those days) and Meads was pushing and shoving him around. Sappo remonstrated and warned this skinny upstart: Any more of that and I'll drop you. Pinetree grinned, and a little later Sappo was legless.

Sappo later became a good mate, in my Station Hotel days, and my path crossed with Pinetree's again, too. I captained a team he played in. Yes, it was a rugby team. No, I'm not kidding you.

I enjoyed my time in the army. I guess everybody who did CMT had some funny experiences and a couple stick in my mind from the time we were in Papakura Camp.

During the first week of training, the Regimental Sergeant Major was explaining about how you form up in companies to make a battalion. He was explaining in a loud voice how, on the command 'Marker!' the guy he'd nominated to be Marker would march out briskly and come to a halt about 10 yards in front of him. And on the command 'Fall In!' the rest of us would take up positions in companies on that Marker.

So it came to the parade ground. He belted out this loud command: 'MARKER!'

The soldier he'd nominated snapped to attention and marched out very correctly, very briskly, and snapped to a halt at the appointed mark. Which I guess is why they called him a Marker.

But hang on a minute! Walking slowly across the parade ground is another soldier, wandering behind the appointed Marker towards the RSM. Picture this Maori guy, not marching but walking slowly, looking very confused. So were we!

He finally reaches the Marker and stops beside him. The befuddled

RSM roars: 'What the hell do you want, soldier?'

And the feller replies: 'My name's Maaka, Sir!'

Here's another one about the same guy. On morning parade one day, our platoon was assembled for inspection and our sergeant major came to — guess who? — Private Maaka. Maaka hadn't shaved.

The sergeant major roars at him: 'Did you shave this morning, soldier?'

'No,' comes the reply. Not 'No sir' — just plain No.

'No what?' screams the sar' major.

'No razor,' says Private Maaka.

If that wasn't enough, the sergeant major also noticed that Private Maaka had his bootlaces tied criss-cross, not the accepted straight-across army fashion.

As clearly as he could, the sergeant major said: 'Maaka, you will come on parade tomorrow with your laces done up in the approved army fashion. DO YOU HEAR ME, SOLDIER?' All but spitting in his face.

Well, the next morning Maaka turns up; he's had a shave but his laces are still criss-crossed. The sergeant major says: 'I thought I told you to do your laces up in the approved army fashion. WHY HAVEN'T YOU?'

'Well, I prefer them this way, Sir.'

They sent him home within the first 10 weeks of training, poor bugger. We didn't know whether he was a Simple Simon or what. I like to think of the funnier possibility, that he conned the whole lot of us and got out of his military training.

So that was the 16th Intake; sixteen weeks plus a couple of weeks' territorial training in the next two years.

Cousin John, as a school teacher, was one of those specially selected for officer training. Us lesser souls, of course, weren't considered. That hurt a bit, because on my driver's licence was 'unskilled labourer'. I knew I was as bright as the next guy, but it was all coming back on me now, after copping out at school.

It was easier to gauge a guy like John because he had done well at school, was training to be a school teacher, and they figured he could be a leader of men. But I gained two stripes during the territorial training, held at Tihoi and Waiouru. At the same camp I had the stripes taken off me because I was caught running the two-up school; a carry-over from the days when I used to put the pennies on the kip at the Whakatu freezing works. Those guys there, gambling for big money, paid me the compliment of being a person they felt they could trust to make sure that a double-tailed penny wasn't slipped onto the kip.

The following year, 1957, I not only got my stripes back but I also gained another one. I became sergeant of my platoon and I was acting sar' major for the Hauraki Regiment. Our colonel in charge was Ray

Smith, then the editor of the *Daily Post* in Rotorua and named in the 1992 New Year Honours.

Back to the land of earning a living, after my time in camp with the 16th Intake, I returned to my job with the Tourist Department as meter reader. And after work, except Tuesdays and Thursdays, which was rugby training, and Sundays of course, I also worked as barman at the Palace Hotel — the only 'sobersides' barman in town.

So I was slogging away at the two jobs and we were still singing one-off shows around the place; up in Auckland, over to Cambridge,

The Howard Morrison Quartet's first recording session. It's the original lineup: from left, cousin John, brother Laurie, HM and Gerry Merito.

wherever we were asked. We were developing a reputation by word of mouth and this was allowing our interest in singing to be sustained. The group formation was still myself and Gerry, Laurie when he was available, Tai Eru and John.

By the time the Christmas holidays of 1956 came, my courtship with Kuia was starting to intensify. We'd been going together now for six or seven months. Everybody, the uncles, the extended family, were hoping that something more serious would be the outcome. They were hoping that Kuia and I would get married, I guess, and they were all very happy when we announced our engagement.

Mum helped me pick out the engagement ring and that's when she said to me: 'I'm sure your father will be very, very happy.'

I guess everybody convinced us that it was a good idea, and we set our marriage down for May 11, 1957. We had no forward planning. I didn't have any money of consequence saved; I guess it would be true to say we were not very responsible. We were in love, we wanted to get married . . . stars in our eyes about the white picket fence and we'd live happily ever after.

However, nobody talked to us about these things. I asked Kuia's father Hiwa for Kuia's hand and he accepted me; Kuia's mother Lola accepted me. They were fine people, independent, minding their own business . . . and they brought their daughter up the same way. Lola died on June 19 this year, just as this book was going to print. She was a wonderful, caring person with a wicked straight-down-the-barrel attitude and sense of humour. We got on really well, perhaps because we were both Leos!

At this time I was still right into my football, too. I was playing now for Waikite club in Rotorua and our coach was none other than my uncle Martin McRae, ex-sergeant major of the 28th Maori Battalion. You never knew who the hell was going to be in the team. My cousin John was confident he'd be in — he was the captain. Nothing fazed him and he was an exceptional rugby player. He also captained the Bay of Plenty reps and might have been All Black material if he'd been more dedicated. But nobody else would dare put on their jersey until their

Howard had his limitations as a rugby player (he wasn't as gifted as his cousin John!) but he loved the game. And he was still the entertainer. I remember a game we played in the mud and Howard hadn't even got his shorts or jersey dirty — as someone pointed out from the crowd at the top of his voice. Howard planted his hands in the mud, turned to the crowd and sang: 'Get a little dirt on your hands, boy!' Everyone broke up, including the players! — **John Morrison**

name was called out, and Uncle was usually writing it down as he went on the back of his Park Drive packet.

We had this huge Maori feller, Tutu, a relation of ours, with a hell of a physique. A lock, he was about six foot four and 17 stone, hard as hell, but he didn't have much football skill. Young and keen. There was this other guy called Peter James. He was a big guy, too, but past his best. An ex-Maori Battalion boxing champion, he used to be put on to make the other teams behave — do what was required and then limp off and be replaced. Martin McRae had got to naming the locks and he says: 'Tutu! Have you got your gear?'

Tutu, eagerly: 'Yes, Uncle!'

Martin: 'Give it to Peter.'

That's the way he was. Anyway, I was playing No 8 now and was going to be the next Alby Pryor. Uncle Martin used to say that if I wasn't at the back of the scrum it lost its sting and that went to my head a bit. Halfway through the season my position was starting to become a bit suspect.

Uncle Martin's reading the team out and he comes to No 8. In front of the whole team he says: 'Nephew, I'm going to give you another chance. Now here's the rules. Stop playing to the bloody gallery. And if I give you the signal, if I don't think you're doing any good, you take a dive.'

Then he turns to Peter James, the knuckle man, and says: 'And if I give the signal, Peter, make sure he takes a dive!'

That was the day my nose was glued to the ball and I reinstated myself in his eyes as being a team regular again.

I took my rugby seriously and I've been told by guys who should know what they're talking about that I could have gone on to higher things. Rep level, who knows? Maori All Blacks? I don't regret now that I didn't go further with rugby, that music and performing took over. But I often did then.

I was as macho then as they are now to prove yourself physically, to prove yourself as a sportsman. I wasn't unique; I was just like my contemporaries. We were all competitive swimmers, we were all competitive tennis players; we all fancied ourselves, the Morrisons in particular, that we were or could be above average. We were all very fast. I was about a yard slower than most of them. But so was my dad, yet he was the one who made the Maori All Black team.

Some of his techniques I inherited. Like skipping with hobnailed boots on, like going to the match at a fast walk. Fast walking is all the go now; I'm talking about 35 years ago. No riding a bike to the ground, or getting a lift with your mates; no, a fast walk in hobnail boots. Then you put your rugby boots on and man, you can fly. You feel as light as a feather.

But whether I could have gone on to rep level, or it could have been

NZ Maoris: No 8, Howard Morrison, well . . . I don't think so.

As the winter of 1957 approached, bringing the football season and our wedding set for May, I began to think about the grudge match with our main rivals. In those years Waikite teams knocked over six premierships in a row. I played in about four of them.

So we were real hotshots, and our main rivals were our Maori cousins, the Tuhourangi subtribe — or Whakarewarewa. The name of the football team was Whaka. Bitter rivals we were, and crowds and crowds of people used to turn up for these matches.

I was trying to anticipate, without telling Kuia, when we might be playing Whaka, so the wedding wouldn't fall on that Saturday. Well, the best-laid plans of mice and men . . . When the draw came out at the start of the season, there we were playing Whaka on May 11. I thought it might be a bit much to ask if I could play the footy match after our wedding and then go away on our honeymoon. So I was gallant; I never even brought it up. But I have to admit the thought did cross my mind!

Let me tell you about the wedding now.

It was a right royal occasion, as most of our family weddings are. We had about 300 people plus. Cousin John was my best man and I borrowed my tuxedo for the day from my cousin and meter-reading mate, Peter Paul.

It was a beautiful setting. We were married in St Faith's Church, on the side of the lake, and there was a big crowd of people there. The wedding breakfast was held in the old whakaturia. My uncle Duncan McRae, Maori Battalion veteran and a brother to Martin McRae, was in charge of the social activities and he said to me the day before the wedding: 'Well, son, you must have at least 500 pounds saved away for the future, at the moment?'

Lying through my teeth, I said: 'Yes, uncle.'

Then he said. 'Well, what are we going to do about some liquor and refreshments for the party afterwards? How much do you want to spend on that?'

'I don't know; you tell me.'

'About fifty quid should cover it.'

Unbeknown to him, I gave him fifty pounds with my left hand after taking it from his right hand. The day before, Uncle Duncan had given me 50 pounds as his wedding gift; he figured I'd get enough pots and pans and blankets to start us on the way. So here I was, the next day, giving him his 50 quid back to buy refreshments.

The bridesmaids were two cousins of Kuia's, Emily and Dorothy, and they really looked beautiful. Kuia was in a wonderful lace dress which the family made themselves, as they had the bridesmaids' dresses in pink. The occasion was marked by the usual embellishments; wonderful speeches, acknowledging the union that a lot of people in the tribe had hoped for. It really all came out that day; how they were so happy that Tem would be looking down smiling. Hiwa, Kuia's father, replied in the same way — that he couldn't have wished for anything better in his life to have happened.

Wedding bells for Howard and Kuia. Cousin John Morrison, at left, was best man and brother Laurie groomsman. Bridesmaids were Kuia's cousins Dorothy and Emily.

Morrison family collection

So it was a joyous occasion. Wonderful singing, wonderful food which came from all over the place — seafood from the coast, wild pork from the bush . . . something we'll never forget. It was nice at that time, being so young, after participating in a number of occasions in the same dining room, to suddenly look at my bride Kuia, the blushing bride as they say, and be able to say: 'Well, sweetheart, here we are. It might not happen again but today we are guests of honour!'

After the wedding breakfast we didn't stick around. Kuia packed her gear, I packed mine, we hopped in the little old Volkswagen and headed off towards Otaki, where my auntie, my father's sister, lived.

A very bad oversight — we never told her about the wedding.

When we turned up on her doorstep the next day she thought we'd eloped! Actually, she was just the right recipe, because we were a couple of young people trying to act like adults and didn't know where to start. So Henrietta Gray and Uncle George, bless their souls, took us through a whole lot of life's pitfalls and promises that was invaluable to us. We didn't know how to talk about what the future meant, or might hold, Kuia and I. We were just two young people in love, and whatever will be will be. That week we spent down at Otaki was very important.

We came back and I started work again the following Monday. Incidentally, we beat Whaka on the day of our wedding. And without me. Yeah.

We stayed at first with Mum. Kuia and I had a room at the house. It was fairly crowded but it was just like having another person staying with us, except that I was sleeping with her.

Looking back, it was pretty naive of me to expect Kuia to fit in, no problems, with Mum and three teenage sisters in the house. Kuia must have felt stifled but didn't complain. The reality was that we couldn't afford our own place.

After a while at Mum's we moved to the bach at the back of the house we're in now; the front house was occupied by Hiwa and Lola. Kuia felt more comfortable being in her own patch. We stayed in the back bach for about six months while I continued with my football and my work. We were doing quite a few trips to Auckland at that time, doing some singing over the weekends and staying with the Bidois family, Grace and Eddie. They were wonderful to us.

Rock 'n roll was really hitting its straps then. There were dance halls right around New Zealand that were full every Friday and Saturday. Johnny Devlin, billed as New Zealand's answer to Elvis Presley, had just finished a very successful tour round New Zealand. I went to see him, to have a look at his show, and I was really in awe, and envious. He had all the gimmickry including girls hired to scream in the right places then jump on stage to rip his shirts off; all of this was backed up by publicity photos (one with a well-known Labour MP of the time, Mabel Howard). I thought gee, maybe one of these days I could do a tour, too. That would be neat.

There was music all over the place. Also hitting the big time was Toni Williams and his Tremelloes and it was the days of the show bands: The Diplomats, the Quin Tikis, Herma Keil and the Keil Isles.

The younger people were going for rock 'n roll and jive. They were getting away from the foxtrot and the waltz, from the palais glide and the three step; all the dances of that era were starting to die out.

It was in this time span, late 1957, that we entered another talent quest, in Hamilton, with a prize of 250 pounds. And I had to make my mind up about this music business.

We lost to Bennie Craig, a jockey later killed, in a fall. He sang and played guitar, and he was good. The catch was that the winner had to go on a tour of New Zealand. And in all honesty, I believe we could have won if I'd told a lie. That restriction made me look at the group a bit more closely. We had John, who was a school teacher; Laurie, who was a professional surveyor and doing very well in his job; and two 'loose' people, me and Gerry. I came to the decision that the group had to change if we were going to be professional.

When I say that Gerry and I were 'loose', I mean in terms of not having jobs that offered a long-term career. While Gerry and I were really keen to become professional entertainers, in 1957 there wasn't such an animal. It was, to quote the song, an impossible dream.

Nevertheless, the dream was beginning to stir in me. I was a young married, I had a child on the way, I had two jobs, I had my football. And I still wanted to sing, to be a performer and entertainer.

THE HOWARD MORRISON QUARTET

THE EMERGENCE of the Howard Morrison Quartet has to be looked at in the context of the times. In the 1950s, fulltime professional groups were unheard of. I've always believed we were the first.

Of course, it didn't happen overnight. We had a long apprenticeship to serve first.

The events which began to push us towards a professional musical career happened in 1957. At that time I still had my meter-reading job. Once I got my act together as far as my sums were concerned, and I could leave the account with the consumer instead of taking it home to Kuia, it became a very good job. It was actually a public servants' retirement benefit. They'd stop to have a chat to Mrs Brown, have a cup of tea . . . what took them a day took me, once I got into the swing of it, a couple of hours. What would take them two days would take me half a day.

So my diet of daily working activity allowed me time to take up golf, it allowed me to learn to fish properly, to take in the pictures when it was wet . . . it was a great job!

Kuia at this time, about a year after we married, was carrying our daughter, Donna. In those days, of course, when you married young they thought your wife would already be in the family way. When relatives found out this wasn't the case, they started asking questions: Was there something wrong with her, or me? Was she barren, or was I dry balls? To be straight, that's exactly what her father asked me. What's wrong with you boy?

I mention this because Kuia was overdue with Donna for eight or nine days, really overdue, and I was meter reading out in the country areas. I had a jeep for that part of the job and on a narrow metal road I came across this car — a stock buyer who cut the corner on me and went straight into the jeep. It later turned out he was blind in that eye and hadn't seen me.

A chap gave me a lift in to see the doctor and we called in on the way to see Mum and Kuia. Well, I didn't realise how bad I looked. There was a fixture on the dashboard which went straight into my knee. I hadn't seen it through the pants but it opened my knee right up and was bleeding like hell. On top of that I hit my chest on the steering wheel and buckled it and whacked my head against the window. So I was pretty sore and groggy; the doctor had me admitted to hospital but the sight of me had been enough to get Kuia going and she was taken in too.

The next morning, after an operation on my knee which they had to do twice, I was wheeled into the maternity ward to see my wife and new baby. I remember the sister in charge thought they were bringing me into the wrong ward!

Our first born, Donna Mariana. As the song goes — I hear babies cry, I watch them grow; and I say to myself: What a wonderful world!

I was a father.

Incidentally, my brother Laurie's first four children were all girls. My sister Judy's first-born — she was married about a year before Kuia and I — was a girl. When Donna Mariana came along, that made six granddaughters for Mum.

We were quite puzzled by this. I remember telling Canon Wi Huata — godfather, by the way, to all my children — that it was becoming a bit of a joke in the village, that our side of the family couldn't produce anything but girls.

Wi Huata gave a naughty chuckle and said to me: 'What you fellows have to do is, you must make sure the woman climaxes first. Usually it's the man who climaxes first 'cause he's greedy, and when that happens it's nearly always a girl.

'You've got to wait until the woman is ready; when everything is right she'll always let you know. Then you make sure she climaxes first. Then it will be a boy.'

Well, you may laugh at this story but I used that recipe. And I know when my son Howard Junior was conceived and I know when my son Richard was conceived.

By the way, Canon Huata was hardly a pea-shooter himself. He fathered five boys and four girls.

Wi Huata was quite a man! And he came into my life more frequently from about this time. He was always close to us, but from this time on it would not be exaggerating to say that he became a guiding light for me, a mentor. And it was at a time when I needed it, when I was in a world of indecision.

At this time, a young married, new father and struggling a bit financially, torn between show business and my new family and wanting the best of both worlds, I guess I was stressed, to use the modern term. I started packing on the weight; I got up to 15 stone, which is a stone and a half above what I should have been, and I developed asthma. I remember that when we were performing in Auckland one weekend, staying with the Bidois family, I had such a bad asthma attack that I couldn't dry myself after getting out of the shower. They had to call in a doctor to give me an injection.

It was a time of 'where am I going?' and I valued Wi Huata's counsel.

The original Howard Morrison Quartet. From left: brother Laurie, Gerry Merito, HM and cousin John Morrison. Morrison family collection

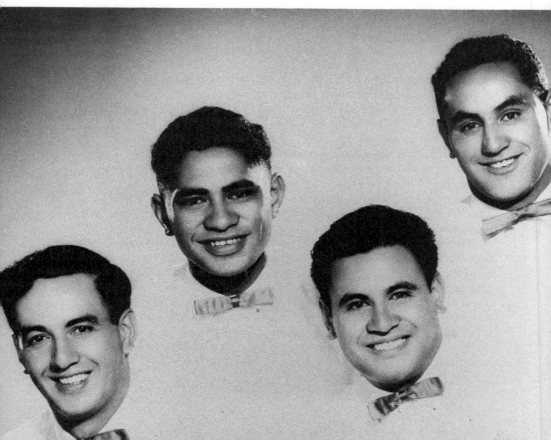

Laurie and I were with the Quartet in the fun days and still there when we made the first records, *Hoki Mai* and *Diana*, for Stebbings. Right after that I got the position of phys ed teacher and sports master at Rotorua High School. That was also the year the Quartet was offered the trip to Melbourne. I asked for leave but the head said the job wouldn't be open when I returned. I was mad keen on my sport and I chose to leave the Quartet and go teaching. I was a tenor but in the Quartet I was just the doo-wah man. Laurie came to the same decision, job ahead of music, but I think he would have made it; he had a beautiful voice. Laurie was a straight singer, Howard was a performer and an entertainer. And Howard was always a perfectionist. You'd see him in front of the band and practise, practise, until he got it right. Near enough wasn't good enough. Even back then, when I'd worked it out that the Quartet couldn't go on indefinitely, I said that Howard was the one who would go on with it and make a career of entertaining. And I was dead right. — **John Morrison**

Later in 1958, when Kuia was still breast-feeding Donna, we went on a goodwill tour with Wi; the family and a few of the gang just traipsing around the central North Island and the East Coast and Hawke's Bay. Even though he was based in Hamilton at that time, Wi always used to go back to his roots, as it were, Ngati Kohungungu. We also went right throughout the King Country and put on shows in country halls and churches, singing and praying. Collections were taken to pay for the petrol, otherwise we got by through the good will of the extended tribal whanau.

Touring around the dioceses — I don't think Canon Huata had any set demarcation area, we just trundled around everywhere — my health improved. I guess I found some comfort in this caring and giving atmosphere.

I never lost the asthma, which was to recur time and time again. And I still have it. But my health improved and my weight went back to normal.

Wi was an amazing man. He had an unpretentious charisma. Now there's a quality that every entertainer would kill for. His sermons were always entertaining, always humorous, but the message came through and left you thinking.

I remember I'd get worried, because of my spiritual upbringing, when I felt that I'd done something wrong — in the old-fashioned term: I'd sinned. I remember saying to him: 'When you commit sins, Wi, it really worries you. The Catholics have confession, but when we do something wrong, who do we have to talk to?'

He said: 'You talk to God, that's who you talk to. Anyway, son, you keep having a conscience. The day you lose that, that's the day you're gone.'

I used to observe the man a lot. By watching how he worked, I guess he helped to take away the fear of fearing God. It would be true to say that Wi Huata's influence on my life helped me tremendously in later years. It helped me place an emphasis on sharing the joys of entertaining not only with the audience but with the people working with you. Sharing, or, as it was later put to me, taking the impact of the show beyond the footlights.

Canon Wi Huata died in December of 1991.

Kuia and I now found our own little house in Panui Street, a one-bedroomed place with a little porch, for ten shillings a week. Mum bought us a portable stove and we had a coal range in there; the toilet was an outside long drop. It was pretty run down, but we were a young married couple then and it was tough times. I was trying to combine singing, the job and football, and we actually found ten shillings a week quite difficult. But I didn't go to pubs, didn't drink, didn't party around with the boys. And that was the difference.

I heard Howard and the boys at the Ritz Hall in Rotorua over the Christmas holidays, 1956 I think it was, and started bringing them to Auckland for one-off shows at the Auckland Town Hall. They quickly became popular; they already had an above-average stage presence. They used to come up to Auckland for eight pounds a night — for the whole group! And they'd drive back home the same night; no accommodation thrown in in those days. Mind you, that was only for the first couple of shows. It went up smartly after that.

— **Benny Levin**

The rock 'n roll era had arrived, music and entertainment were on the way up and we got a chance to sing in Auckland, the big time. Benny Levin was the catalyst, as he was in so many things in my career.

Something that sticks in my mind from that time . . . I asked my boss for half a day off to do a singing engagement. I was worried about losing my job, so I told him the truth. And I'll never forget this fellow; his name is not as important as what he said: 'Well, Howard, I think we'll have to get used to the idea that one of these days you're not going to come back to work here because you'll be too famous. You're going to be singing full time.'

We all laughed about it, but he was serious.

There was an enormous amount of rock 'n roll events going on

around the country at that time, including 24-hour stay-on-your-feet
rock 'n roll marathons, and Benny Levin, through someone else's
recommendation, hired us to sing for five guineas (all up!) at the Ritz
Hall in Rotorua. Then he was convinced. He started to find us a few
engagements up in Auckland, where he was playing — St Seps Hall,
one or two other venues. Not too many, because we weren't well known
outside Rotorua.

Benny was always interested in promoting the culture so he had
Mum and Guide Kiri's concert party perform at Carlaw Park, an open-
air show. It was another way to debut us. What we didn't know at that
time was that the word was getting around about this group from
Rotorua, and a lot of people came out of curiosity. It was a huge crowd
for us, about 4000.

Our repertoire was mainly our versions of hits of the day. I
remember one of my first songs with the boys was Paul Anka's *Diana*.
When I got to that 'Please stay with me, Diana' and I drew the 'Diiiii-
aaana' out, the crowd in the grandstand cheered and whistled and

Belting out Diiiii-aaana at Carlaw Park with Laurie, John and Gerry.

clapped. I'd never heard anything like it before in my life! We were like pop stars! I couldn't wait to get to the 'Diiiii-aaana' part again. And they cheered and yelled and screamed again. I think we were sort of reflecting what people had been seeing in the movies . . . and the crowd's reaction made us feel we were those people in the movies. But really we were just, in the flesh, bringing the people closer to the rock 'n roll phenomenon.

The group at that time was my cousin John, Gerry, my brother Laurie and me. Not long after the Carlaw Park show, Benny Levin put on a jazz concert at the Auckland Town Hall and we were guest artists. We were no more jazz performers than the Neophonic is an indigenous cultural group but, maybe because we were such a contrast to the rest of the programme, we brought the house down. We sang *Diana* again, we did The Diamonds' *Lil Darlin'*, I did a song called *Because of You* with impressions of Nat King Cole, Billy Eckstein, Jerry Lewis. The crowd roared and screamed . . . it was totally unreal.

I often play the tape of that show. It reminds me of the way we were then, both the audiences and the group. It was a significant benchmark, really; it signalled a new direction.

I think that was when Benny thought: 'These boys are going to make it!'

He introduced us to Eldred Stebbing with the idea of making records and a new phase began. As I said before, Benny was the catalyst in so much of what happened in our career. This was, in fact, the birth of The Howard Morrison Quartet.

Even at this stage, the Carlaw Park concert and the Town Hall concert, we still hadn't settled on a permanent name for the group. We were the Morrison Quartet, the Ohinemutu Quartet . . .

When we went to do this record with Eldred Stebbing, he asked us: 'What do you want to be called?'

I threw in this name and that name, my brother threw in another name . . . we were all around the Morrison Quartet, the Morrison Family, the Ohinemutu Quartet, things like that. After a while Eldred Stebbing took me aside and said: 'Look, you're the lead, you're the main man. I suggest you call it The Howard Morrison Quartet. Because if and when the quartet breaks up, there will always be Howard Morrison, entertainer and performer.'

I can still hear him saying it now. With that advice, I went back with a bit of a lump in my throat because I wasn't sure how the boys would take this. My brother, who was a professional man and my elder, my cousin John, a school teacher who could be pretty intimidating . . . Gerry was my mate and I didn't have to worry about him. I was more worried about the other two.

I went back and said: 'I've decided to call the group The Howard Morrison Quartet.'

They looked at me and . . . 'Yeah, very good!'

So that was it!

Eldred was a young technician who had founded Zodiac Records and was keen to promote New Zealand artists. He didn't know quite how, but he had the will and the technical know-how. He had this very flash machine called a Grundig tape-recorder, reel to reel. Very high-tech for those days.

He came down for a weekend in Rotorua and we recorded a whole lot of 'covers' — surfing songs, because they suited our harmonies, and Platters numbers. And I suggested that *Hoki Mai*, to the tune of *Goldmine in the Sky* and with an upbeat tempo, might be commercial; might get air play as a single.

The EP with *Hoki Mai* on wasn't our first record. But it was the one that took off.

When *Hoki Mai* was released, an announcement appeared in the Rotorua paper that it was going to be released through this one music store. I'm sitting in my Holden, with Kuia beside me, looking at the

Tai Eru joins Laurie, Gerry and HM in the Mk2 version of the Quartet.

Morrison family collection

queues of people lining up to buy the 45 by the Quartet. They're all listening to the speakers out in the street, 'Hoki mai e tama ma . . .' and saying: 'Gee, neat eh?' The thought came to me, 'That's me and the boys that's knocking them out!' It was my first foretaste of stardom!

There was another phase before we moved up to Auckland to take on 'the big time' — our first overseas experience, a six-week stint in the Chevron Hotel in Melbourne.

A local friend of mine, Brian Fleming, met someone who had a bit of influence in the Chevron. On the strength of our initial success with the records and those early Auckland concerts, I asked him to further the inquiry about a New Zealand group going over to his hotel to be a support act.

The deal was struck and we were taken on at sixty pounds a week all up, for the whole group — Laurie and myself, Tai Eru and Gerry. We had to find our own way over there and back.

That was our first international experience. We were on with an American who played the harp. Unbelievable . . . he was a great showman. We never profited economically from the trip but it was great experience. On the show biz side, this American harpist took a bit of his own time to show us techniques of showmanship — getting our moves in unison (choreography, you might say), taking our time, introducing our songs properly, taking our bows in unison, working on our timing.

We didn't make much money from our trip but we learned a lot and that really fired me up. When we came back it really hit me that we had to get some permanency in the group.

Gerry and I were lucky enough to get jobs back surveying. Tai had a farm to work, and a good job; Laurie had his work in engineering and surveying. So there we were, languishing away, waiting for the next opportunity — with whoever fitted in.

It was at this time that Benny Levin decided to take a punt and take us on tour. That's when I had to tell the boys the fun times were over; we were deadly serious. Laurie and Tai Eru dropped out. Gerry and I were the anchor, and on that tour with Benny Levin we took Eddie Howell and Wi Wharekura.

The tour didn't make any money at all — another one! But during it Gerry wrote *Battle of the Waikato*. We recorded it live somewhere along the line. And, by New Zealand standards, it was a smash hit.

The records we'd done up to then, apart from the odd *Hoki Mai* and *Po Kare Kare*, had been covers of overseas hits, none of them very wise choices. We weren't discouraged from doing anything we wanted to do, which is the difference between a tough, shrewd manager like Harry Miller, who would have said: 'That's not going to do any good, you're only doing rehashes' and people like Eldred Stebbing who were so nice that if we felt comfortable doing those songs, they'd record them. The truth is, of course, that you can't beat the original.

The parodies, though, of which *Battle of the Waikato* was the first, were a different story. One thing we had in our favour on the New Zealand market was that we had an undeniably down-home, Maori sense of humour. Gerry had — and still has — a very fertile imagination and he and I were compatible in this way.

When Lonnie Donegan came out with his hit *Battle of New Orleans*, we thought his voice was so bad but the song was so cute! It didn't take us long to transpose it into *Battle of the Waikato*. I did the intro vocally — 'Doom dicka doom dicka . . . This here's a story about the Battle of the Waikato; it was fit between the British and the Horis . . . ' We parodied all the Doneganisms. As a matter of fact we thought that Lonnie Donegan's record was a parody itself. Our version got a tremendous reaction from audiences when we first did it live, so it was a natural for a record.

I should also mention that going to Melbourne and then going on tour with Benny were the first two occasions that I left Kuia at home and went to work. Neither occasion was memorable for financial reasons. But they were a taste of things to come: separations and pursuing the goal of achieving recognition in show biz.

Back home after the tour, while *Battle of the Waikato* was making waves, I went into a Rotorua store one day and a guy was demonstrating Electromet cookers. He was very good, too, an excellent salesman. There he was, talking flat tack to all the potential customers and demonstrating the versatility of the cooker. He was in commanding form and position; all of us had to look up to him. It was a tactic business tycoons use; the old power game.

Anyway, I was standing in a ten-deep crowd, mainly women.

He recognised me, came over and said: 'Look, I want to talk to you. My name's Harry Miller.'

Then he turned to the crowd and said: 'Well, folks, here in your midst is your very own talented Howard Morrison. Now this guy and his group, they are really going to go places. And I am going to be their manager!'

He threw back his head and chuckled and he said: 'Yeah, I'm not joking. You just wait and see.'

I thought, you cheeky bugger. At the time I was more embarrassed than anything; I didn't know whether to smile broadly, make some sort of response or just slink off. But Harry asked me to stick around till after the demo, so I did . . . and I had my first chat with Harry M. Miller.

6

ENTER HARRY M.

HARRY MILLER says in his book that he'd seen the Howard Morrison Quartet performing at The Colony, which was run by a mate of his, Bob Sell, and 'was amazed that such a talented group was working for peanuts. My mind danced with the recording and live performance opportunities they offered to an enterprising manager. Me.' Harry also writes that he knew I had rejected previous management offers because I was wary of contracts and agents.

That was right. I was very wary. But Harry was plausible, very plausible. He was also an intimidating bugger; he'd come right up to your nose to talk to you. But the man couldn't be denied, and he came up with the magic formula as far as I was concerned. He guaranteed us at least 2500 pounds worth of work for the first six months and we'd go from there.

In reaction to my saying: 'Where's your guarantee? Put your money up,' he signed over to me the ownership of his Mark 7 Jag. It was on a piece of paper; I suppose I could have asked for the ownership papers as a guarantee. But I liked his style. I suspect that, one, he never had the money and, two, the car was still being paid off.

But the long and short of it was that in the six months' time frame I gave him to act as an agent for the Quartet — we didn't sign a management contract — we never fell below what he'd promised. The deal was that up to X amount of pounds, his commission was 10%.

Harry Miller, at the time of the Everly Brothers tour.

Above a certain amount, his percentage was 20%. From the time we shook hands on it, he never went below 20%.

Harry was a pressure-cooker man. Once we had a deal, he didn't give us time to sit back and smell the flowers. We were working very hard around Auckland, where there were any number of clubs and entertainment places. The Sorrento is one of the few survivors from those times. Others were St Seps, The Arabian, The Colony, Trillo's place down by Westhaven . . . we played them all. Harry kept us busy every weekend. We were doing three, sometimes four shows a night. It didn't worry us, because we weren't boozers, we were doing what we enjoyed doing. But for it to be possible we had to live in Auckland. So we rented this huge house in Penrose, which gave us a bedroom each, plus a big dining room and a good-sized lounge.

The group now, the Howard Morrison Quartet in its final form, was Gerry and me, Wi Wharekura, who I'd plucked out of training college by telling him he was going to be a star entertainer, and a young chap named Noel Kingi, who I'd heard singing in Rotorua and he'd knocked me out with his big bass voice.

Gerry had children, Wi had just got his first, Kuia and I had Donna. We all moved to Auckland, wives, children and all. Three families plus a young single man under one roof; looking back, it's a wonder it lasted a week. The advantage was that we all had children, our first-born, about the same age. It was probably hardest on the wives. Every young married woman wants to be the mistress of her own

It could get pretty tiring, gigging at night at the weekends and then working a fulltime day job in the Penrose factory. I remember Howard nodding off to sleep on the job one time and falling out of his seat onto the floor. He woke up with a bang and quick as a flash, before I could even chuck off at him, he said: 'What about you at The Pines?' That was a nightclub where I went to sleep backstage and went arse over kite off my chair.

— **Gerry Merito**

home, her kitchen. Everyone has different ways of doing things, arranging things, where they put things.

But the women all got on very well. We'd have family meetings when there was friction, and my memories of that time in the big Penrose house are not of fighting and squabbling but of a big, happy family. Sharing our hopes and aspirations with our women made for team involvement and planning.

We were all home for tea, sitting around the family table, and at night we'd rehearse, practise new material, do a lot of polishing. We weren't just playing at the musical side; we were taking a professional approach.

Even though the Howard Morrison Quartet was the first fully professional musical group in New Zealand and were in demand, at this time we were still only working weekends.

Harry had suggested that he keep the money we earned as performers and put it away for us; if we didn't have it, we wouldn't spend it. I trusted him to do so, and he put our early earnings away for us in trust with accountant Bob Wright (after 30 years still my long-time friend and financial counsellor).

We pounded the streets looking for a day job through the week and we ended up all working at the Wicks muffler factory, about 400 yards from the house we were renting.

It got hard to get up to go to work on Mondays, because we would have done two, sometimes three jobs on the Sunday. But we were very keen; we were inspired by Harry's enthusiasm.

Again, we were all reluctant to tell him how good he was. And that was unfair on Harry, because he was good. Like the rest of us, you like to be acknowledged sometimes and get a pat on the back. We never did that to Harry, maybe because he was a guy who came on so strong, who always seemed so full of confidence. So we took the attitude: Well, that's what you're paid for.

It wasn't until later that we saw the softer side of Harry. Sometimes we'd be doing shows back at Rotorua and staying at the family home. Mum would say to him: 'Give me your singlet and underpants; they're going in the wash.' And Harry would sort of put his head down, like a little boy. I think he actually enjoyed being scolded by Mum and treated just like one of the kids, instead of like a big-shot promoter.

Harry kept us busy and we sharpened our skills. He was building up our image; we were doing a lot of performances and riding on the success of the record of *Battle of the Waikato*. Harry then pulled off the coup which resulted in the Howard Morrison Quartet becoming fully professional. He approached Kerridge Odeon and his deal was simple: 'I'll provide the show, you provide the theatres, we go half and half on the promotion and half and half on the profits.' (So I found out later, much later.)

Taking on Harry as manager meant cutting our ties with Eldred Stebbing and Benny Levin. Well, not with Benny; though he'd so often been a catalyst in our earlier career, he'd never been our manager and had actually encouraged us to sign with Harry. Benny stayed very close friends; we still are.

But Eldred was another matter. Harry had formed a record label called La Gloria which at first just re-pressed overseas artists under licence. When he signed us he naturally also wanted to record us, and this is where business can trample on sentiment and even on what you may feel is morally right. We didn't have a signed and sealed deal with Eldred, but he was very close to us. Harry wasn't interested in that; it was just business. If we had him as our manager and agent, and he had a recording company, it made sense to keep all our eggs in one basket. I don't think I ever got round to saying to Eldred, look, we're no longer with you, because I was so embarrassed by it. But he confronted me and I had to sort of be strong and say, well that's the way it is, Eldred; it's a business thing and not personal. It caused me a lot of pain.

Eldred was pretty incensed and he said, well, I am going to really show this deal with Harry Miller up for what it is. And he promoted the tail off *Battle of the Waikato*. All he did was do Harry a favour; it was promoting the Howard Morrison Quartet.

We re-recorded *Battle of the Waikato* on Harry's label; it wasn't as good as the original but Harry liked it. We didn't because we were taking advantage of our popularity and fobbing it off on the public.

Harry's next step was to take us on the road with Showtime Spectacular, in association with Kerridge Odeon. I was a bit nervous about it because of the experience we'd had with Benny Levin. But we were green then, and not as well known. I hadn't realised how much better known and more popular we'd become.

Harry pulled off another masterstroke at this time, which showed the enterprise of the guy. He approached the National Film Unit (this was before television) and they filmed us in their Wellington studios doing two segments of three songs each. We charged them no fee, and these segments — a sort of forerunner to the video clips the pop groups do for TV these days — were played as shorts in all the theatres. Since Showtime Spectacular was touring through all the Kerridge Odeon theatres, it was obviously in Kerridge's interests to push this 'trailer' of the Howard Morrison Quartet.

Posters would go up for, say, *The Man From Laramie* and they would add: 'First-half feature, New Zealand's own Howard Morrison Quartet!'

Well, if I thought we'd found fame when people queued to listen to *Hoki Mai* outside the Rotorua record store, imagine the impact of having this film showing in theatres around the country. We weren't just recording and performing artists; suddenly we were movie stars!

Harry's timing and instinct were great. Mind you, he and we had some luck and some coincidences on our side, too. The fact that he negotiated his deal with the National Film Unit and that they would have to come back through the Kerridge Odeon chain wasn't actually thought of at the time, because the two deals were separate, and made at separate times. But it turned out a masterstroke anyway. Naturally Kerridge Odeon pushed the HMQ film through their theatres because it promoted a stage show for which they were getting half the profits.

It would still have shown imagination and enterprise on Harry's part even if there hadn't been the tie-up with Kerridge Odeon, because the National Film Unit had never before done anything remotely like the 'promo' they did of us.

So there we were, ready to go on the road with Showtime Spectacular. We had another big record on the way — again thanks to Lonnie Donegan; our movie clip was playing in theatres; Harry had us all togged up in Anthony Squires suits which he got through an associate who managed the company. We were really 'up to speed' in appearance, attitude and discipline, all due to Harry.

I'd always put a lot of emphasis on appearance, on showmanship. But Harry turned us up a notch. It was so much easier having a manager who could take care of the fine tuning while we concentrated on getting our performance spot on. And Harry could be a sort of whipping boy; Harry and I would get together and discuss what was good for the group and then I could say: 'Harry says we need to do this.'

However, it wasn't right to use Harry this way so I felt the need to define roles more clearly. I didn't want Harry to intrude on the personal side; I wanted to keep him away from that.

So the way I put it to the boys was: Right or wrong, I'm right. There's only one boss and that's me. If I made a wrong decision, then I would be man enough to clear the air by apologising — and I didn't want to have to do that too often. There only had to be one mongrel in the group, if anyone was going to be called a mongrel, and that was me. And for that I needed their loyalty and respect, right or wrong, as boss. I got that that day and it stayed right throughout the time of the Quartet. That kept us clean, as it were, on the personal side as against the business side with Harry. I didn't want to bring him in to sort out things that we could sort out ourselves. It worked very well.

The record which launched the first Showtime Spectacular tour was *My Old Man's an All Black*. We were on our way to Wellington with Harry about four weeks before the tour began and he mentioned wouldn't it be good to do a parody on the All Blacks going to South Africa. This was in 1960 and there was huge controversy over the All Black touring team excluding Maori players.

Lonnie Donegan had a hit out at the time called *My Old Man's a Dustman* and that became our vehicle. Gerry wrote most of the words.

An early publicity pic of the Howard Morrison Quartet, dapper gents now in our Anthony Squires suits. Clockwise from bottom: Wi Wharekura, Noel Kingi, HM, Gerry Merito.

My main contribution was 'Fee fee, fi fi, fo fo fum — there's no Horis in that scrum' and that's how we bounced it around in the back seat of Harry's Jag.

It took us going down and coming back to put it all together, and we recorded it at the end of a live show in the Pukekohe Town Hall. We used a tape recorder at the side of the stage with a long lead and a little plastic microphone attached to our microphone. That's how bad, how primitive, it was.

Harry wanted us to do it over and over and over. He exaggerates a bit in his book by writing that he said: 'Close the bloody doors and lock everybody in!'

He might have said that to the audience but more in fun, sort of 'Look, we have to get this song down.' I was getting a bit embarrassed by having to do the song twice, but Harry wanted it again.

In fact, though, the crowd suddenly became enthused by the whole thing. I was feeding them lines like: 'We could create history here, folks . . . remember, this could be the biggest hit of all time! And you in Pukekohe could be part of it.' So they were laughing on cue, in the same places as in the earlier attempts, but it got louder and louder.

It ended up probably the worst-recorded song in New Zealand's history — and the most successful. It sold 60,000 copies, unbelievable by New Zealand standards.

We set off on the road to do Showtime Spectacular on the back of that runaway hit record. The Howard Morrison Quartet headed the bill and Harry engaged various other artists as support acts. The show opened in Wellington, at the St James Theatre, and it was a smash hit.

One of the things that worried me was the money; what the Quartet, as the main act, should be getting. I really had no benchmark. Before going on the road, Harry had been booking us for fees ranging from 40 pounds to 60 pounds a show. He usually aimed at 60 pounds, which was 10 pounds for each of us and 10 pounds for expenses and Harry's commission. At that, it was more than we'd been earning on our own.

Harry says in his book that Bob Sell, at The Colony, was the first to feel the effect of the new management contract. He wanted to be the first to re-book us under Harry, and Harry said it would cost him 40 pounds. Bob had used us previously for 15 pounds a show!

On Showtime Spectacular I felt we were doing all right at 200 pounds a week for the group. It seemed like a king's ransom. But in show business, because what you're worth is directly linked to the number of people who pay to see you, and popularity goes in waves, what seemed good money wasn't, in terms of box office turnover. It was, after all, the Quartet who generated that turnover.

After the outstanding success of that first tour, I thought we'd have got a bonus. But we didn't. There was quite a fortune made on the first tour but in retrospect I felt I let the boys down, that the Quartet didn't get an appropriate share of the financial rewards.

The trouble was, we loved entertaining so much that I couldn't quite grasp the facts in front of me, which were that *we* were putting the bums on seats. Twice a day, six o'clock and eight o'clock. Three times on Saturdays; two o'clock, six o'clock and eight o'clock. I didn't have the aptitude to pick up the value of what we were, in monetary terms. I was carried away by the fact that we were superstars. That permeated through the group; we were all full of our own importance.

When we opened the tour, in Wellington, we actually blocked off the mall and the surrounding streets with people going out of the six

Showtime Spectacular on the road (in Nelson) during 1961. A strong lineup, this one — from left: Gene Blazer (bass), Brian Biddick (trombone), Dave Adams (sax), John Daley (compere), Robert Walton (piano), Wi Wharekura, Bob Paris (guitar), Jayne Paris, Kim Krueger (vocalist), HM, Bruce King (drums), Don Frearson (trumpet), Gerry Merito, Trevor King (tour manager), Noel Kingi, Brian (bus driver), Brian Lehrke (stage manager), Hugh Richards (manager Majestic Theatre), Jon Zealando (ventriloquist). Trevor King collection

o'clock show and coming in for the eight o'clock. There was a huge billboard outside the theatre which showed head shots of the Quartet. Harry took us to the front of the theatre. At this time we weren't well known outside the Auckland region in terms of being recognised by the public; we were just a pakeha fella and four Maori guys there in the street, in front of the theatre.

'Look at that billboard,' Harry said, 'isn't it fantastic?'

There were these huge caricatures of our heads, ten times lifesize.

'Yes Harry, yes Harry; it's fantastic.'

'Well, that's how bloody big your heads are!'

That hurt, especially when we had a show to do. But we needed the reminder to keep our feet on the ground.

I mention it because we were getting carried away. The ego had plenty of food, our vanity was well nourished. And we lost sight of the basics. Not only the group; our families could have been better treated. So, moneywise, I wasn't able to look after the group as well as I should.

When we did another tour, after a three-week break, I still wasn't a hard enough bargainer to insist on an increase. Actually, Harry preempted my approach to negotiate a better financial deal by saying to me: 'Look, I notice you're not getting any extra, despite the fact that you produce this damn show.'

He massaged my ego beautifully by saying I should get extra, not as leader of the Quartet but as producer-director of the show. Morally that made me feel OK, that I wasn't screwing the boys. But the boys, though loyal, said that they wanted to ask for more money.

'OK,' I said. 'I think it's up to you guys to get together and confront

Harry about that. I'm happy with what I'm getting, and it's more than you're getting.'

This was in Blenheim, where we'd decided to open because it allowed me to do some pig hunting on the side with a mate down there, a day before the tour started.

The whole cast confronted Harry . . . they wanted extra money. Harry pranced around like a demented hen with its head chopped off, his voice rising to the high squeak it reached when he got excited. 'No way am I going to pay you buggers more, etc, etc, etc' and I wasn't giving him any support.

So he felt let down, because he had to pay extra. That sort of thing used to stick in Harry's craw. He had no conscience about paying no more than he had to, even if it was merited — which is a pretty good business philosophy. In other words, if you agree to do something for me for that amount of money, I'm not morally obligated to give you any more. And if you want to do it for the next ten years and not ask for an increase, well that's all right too.

But if he felt he was being blackmailed — and the confrontation came the day before the tour started — then that wasn't on, even though I believed the boys and the band and the rest of the cast were right.

The second Showtime Spectacular tour opened on the back of another hit record by the Howard Morrison Quartet. This time the song was based on George Wilder, a famous, or infamous, prison escaper of that time. George wasn't a violent guy; I don't remember what he was originally in for but it wasn't anything heavy. He obviously couldn't stand jail and kept escaping; he'd go bush and it took them ages to catch him. Because he wasn't a violent guy, there was actually quite a lot of public sympathy for him. We left poor old Lonnie Donegan alone this time and wrote it to the tune of *The Wild Colonial Boy*. 'There was a wild New Zealand boy, George Wilder was his name . . .'

I negotiated with Harry about improving our royalties from the records. He hummed and hah-ed. There was a business meeting, where there was to be no mucking around, about a week before we went to the studio. Harry sort of agreed, but nothing in writing. We were doing the recording in segments; there were parts when we had the full big band, and parts where it was just us and the guitars.

Before we went in to do the last segment, when we had all the musicians — about 12 of them — ready to go, I pulled Harry to one side and said: 'What about this deal?'

He looked at me blankly, and I said: 'Well, let me put it this way. Unless you agree, we're not going to finish the record.'

Harry had to agree and we did the song; he didn't like being put on the back foot — being 'blackmailed' as he saw it — and this may have influenced what happened later. The long and short of it was the record was another hit and the second tour was another sell-out.

Through this period I know how The Beatles must have felt, what they went through, being thrown into the studio to churn out records to meet the demand. We weren't much good in a studio anyway. The comparison with The Beatles is only that we had to get stuff out to meet the demand. The technical quality of The Beatles, of course, was far ahead of ours. Ours was barbaric by comparison. Essentially we were live performers, and you couldn't capture the Quartet in a sterile studio situation.

I'm still not the same performer in a studio that I am live. My biggest solo hit, *Whakaaria Mai (How Great Thou Art)*, was done live . . . I could never get that feel, that timbre in my voice, that emotive feeling, in a studio. No way. You can't react to a microphone in the same way. I can't, anyway. I need to communicate with the audience, to build up that empathy, that two-way action.

In the early years of Showtime Spectacular the artists with us were Toni Williams, still a dear friend; The Tremelloes; Noel McKay, the female impersonator, he was a superb entertainer; Bob Paris, a very good guitarist, and other fine musicians and solo acts.

It was a great show — it was actually top-heavy. We had too many artists on; we bombarded the audience with talent. But there was so much talent out there. Our shows were a vehicle for a lot of the acts that have come along since. Too many, in fact, to try to mention them all in despatches; it was 30 years ago and I'd be sure to leave some out.

I remember once, with the Quartet, we were doing a record appearance at James Smith's in Wellington and this guy in a trench coat came up to me and very politely introduced himself as Bill Cate. A very polite, very correct guy, he told us how much he enjoyed our music and how he hoped that one day he could be a professional entertainer. That guy turned out to be the Bill of Bill and Boyd. We reminded each other of that occasion on *This Is Your Life*. We gave Bill and Boyd their first big national exposure by taking them on the road with us.

At that time, when we were doing two tours a year and could do no wrong, Harry pulled off what was a big deal at the time and booked us into the prestigious Tivoli circuit in Australia, with a vaudeville show called *Nats in the Belfry*. That meant lengthy seasons in Sydney and Melbourne.

This was a new experience and a new discipline. It meant signing in at the side entrance of the theatre at 7pm every night; you were fined if you were late, you were fined if you missed a cue, all those disciplines. I learned a lot about the theatre.

Doing the same three songs night after night was frustrating. Where it was good was being able to practise every day and, now and again, getting the opportunity to do late shows, especially in Sydney.

Some pundits asked why, when we were running so hot, Harry

A new discipline . . . gaining vaudeville experience on the Tivoli Circuit in Australia with Nats in the Belfry.

Harry Jay Studio

took us away from our New Zealand fans for 18 to 20 weeks, but I didn't doubt his judgment. For a start, I was intrigued by vaudeville and the opportunity to be associated with real theatre professionals seemed a step in the right direction.

Furthermore, for performers of our inexperience to be associated with the theatre at this level, at such an early stage of our career . . . well, many would have paid for the opportunity.

That show was great for discipline but we had a few hilarious experiences. My daughter Donna was about three years old at the time and walking. One night, amid the spectacular sets and all the show girls, the floodlights and the packed audience, I walked on stage — and she walked on behind me . . . I hadn't put her safely in the dressing room!

The audience, sensing that this walk-on was not a planned part of the show, erupted in laughter. The audience reaction frightened Donna, who ran to me crying. I took her to the stage manager and returned to the stage. I was later fined but, in good humour, the stage manager put it down on the books as baby-sitting services!

I was starting to feel the pressure during this time in Australia. We were a young married couple with a young child, I was suffering more and more from asthma, a stress-related condition, and was putting on too much weight again. I had been refused medical insurance before we went to Australia because of the asthmatic condition; they were very strict then. It came to a head when we got to Sydney, after we'd driven all the way from Melbourne in a clapped-out Vauxhall Velox with Kuia, Donna and a TV set and all our gear. Climbing up to the room we were staying in, trying to carry the television set, I almost collapsed on the stairs with wheezing and shortness of breath.

I said to myself bugger this, I'm going to have to do something about it. I started going to the gymnasium and went from 15 stone to 12st 7lb in three months. I was training twice a day, every day. I was super fit and hard; still didn't drink, still didn't smoke. I also started martial arts training at that time, with a private instructor who was part of the show. That helped my singing a lot, and it encouraged me to start having some singing lessons.

I was now 26. Professionally the Quartet was only a year old, but I'd had a long apprenticeship before that in public performing — and I now decided to have my first singing lessons.

I had my first lessons with a German teacher and she picked me as a baritone. Once I got to know her well I invited her to come and see the show. At my next lesson, as I waited for all the praise, she walked right up to me, gave me a more than gentle slap on the cheek and said how dare I hoodwink her by letting her think for more than a month that I was a baritone when I had the vocal equipment for the full tenor range.

But at lessons, I'd been in an unnatural situation. I'd been hitting tenor notes in the show, but at lessons there had been nothing to require me to hit those notes. Even when she was trying me on the scales, I was only singing half-pace, you might say. There was no reason to sing higher notes than she'd asked me to sing.

She was quite intrigued by some of the things that I told her, that all made sense — that I'd been brought up on a diet of Beniamino Gigli, that I'd aspired to be New Zealand's 'Maori Lanza . . . ' She taught me a lot and with the training I was doing, and being so fit, that was the start of the years that I was the fittest, the most confident, that I could ever hope to be. I was really on top of everything.

After I'd invited my singing teacher to see us perform, she asked me to bring our bass singer Noel Kingi along for lessons, but Noel went only twice. The teacher was disappointed for, as she put it, Noel had the most incredible untrained voice that she had heard. To this day, Noel, my sister Judy and Isobel Cowan (nee Whatarau) stand out as the most natural, exciting, untrained voices I have ever heard.

That time on the Tivoli circuit was very important in another respect. Before we went on the *Nats in the Belfry* show, we did a tour with Lonnie Donegan. Wasn't that a coincidence — back-up artists for a guy whose records we'd covered in parody form. Donegan actually felt complimented that we had. As a person he was easy to get on with.

The critique in the Sydney *Daily Telegraph* of the Lonnie Donegan show (I still remember it vividly!) said '. . . the first half featured the Howard Morrison Quartet, a group that must have been formed to allow the leader the opportunity to show off.' Full stop.

Now any artist will at times get bad reviews. Sometimes they're ill-informed, by people not really qualified to criticise; sometimes they're straight-out personal attacks by people with an axe to grind. But sometimes they're justified. Not only justified but spot on the mark. Ouch! That one really sat me back on my heels.

My ego had got me a bit carried away at that stage, because I saw myself as being *the* star of the group. I'd got out of hand and I wasn't seeing the actuality of my over-the-top manner showing through. I was over-zealous, to say the least.

Also at that time, I was fancying myself as a comedian and the group was standing in the back while I was out front telling all these stories! I'm thinking I'm cool and here's these talented guys behind me, too polite to say anything but feeling embarrassed about what was going on.

It was only the odd astute critic like this who was brave enough — because we were going so strong, were so popular — to say: What's this group trying to achieve? The basis of the group is that they're a good-looking group, they're well groomed, well respected, they sing beautifully — so why this preoccupation of the leader to pontificate and tell old jokes or new versions of old jokes?

Things like that buck your ideas up. I believe I was a realist; I can say that now, knowing that my ego was my achilles heel. But I was able to recognise the truth when someone pointed it out to me, even if it came as a slap in the face. When we got to the Tivoli circuit, and had time to rehearse outside of our set vaudeville programme, we sat down every day and combined our ideas and began to utilise all our voices properly. Then we started to grow as a group.

In other words, if Harry Miller hadn't booked us into the Tivoli, we mightn't have struck that second gear which was necessary to catapult us from being above average to excellent. We might never have made that giant step.

The audiences in New Zealand might have put up with it for another two tours, maximum. As it was, when we came back in 1961 we had a brand-new act but with our basic philosophy still intact; the humour and the nitty-gritty of what the people loved about us were still there but we were more polished. And I was less the prima donna; I was more absorbed into the group and was using their talents much better.

We'd reached, I think, international standard.

The New Zealand tours continued to be a success. As a welcome home, Harry put us on the same show as the Everly Brothers and I know we made life difficult for them.

Harry makes the point in his book that a lot of the international artists he brought out were the product of the record studios and the Top Forty. They weren't really at home performing live. In contrast, we were live performers first, second and third; the stage and the audience were our meat and drink.

The Quartet during our season at Andre's Nite Spot in Sydney. From left (in the flesh): Howard, Wi, Noel and Gerry.   Morrison family collection

It might have seemed silly, more or less co-starring us with the Everly Brothers; we could carry a concert without any international acts. But the Everlys had a bit more mystique than us. They had some very big hits at this time and Harry saw it as a chance to reintroduce us to New Zealand audiences in a high-profile situation. So we did a main-centre tour with the Everly Brothers, getting very good reviews, and then turned around and did it all over again in a full tour of New Zealand with just the Quartet.

Similarly, later the same year, Harry put us on with Shelley Berman, the American comedian. This time he saw it as an opportunity to introduce us to the big audiences in Australia, in the Festival Halls.

Mind you, he also put us on with the Kingston Trio, which seemed stupid because they were a similar type of group to us — in earlier days we'd actually covered some of their material. But we got on well with the Kingston Trio, there was no conflict or one-upmanship, whereas the Everly Brothers stayed on their own and we stayed on our own. We were hoping to stick it to them anyway — and we did.

I knew no fear of competition in those days. In fact, I probably never had the respect for international artists I should have had. Back in 1959, we were engaged by Phil Warren to tour with Stan Freberg as his backing singers. I was so full of my own importance, and so was the group, that we felt this task beneath us. We did the opening show in Dunedin and one in Christchurch before we got up to Wellington, more in our own territory. I went into the dressing room at halftime, before Freberg was to go on, and said we'd rather not back him any more because it was no good for our image.

Jeez! Now if any young upstart said that to me, could you imagine what would happen? I'd probably fire him out physically! I think I took Freberg so much by surprise, by sheer cheek, he sat there like a stunned mullet and just nodded his head and agreed. It could have caused an international incident — or at least got us fired.

With the Showtime Spectacular success and Tivoli polish we had more grounds for feeling some confidence in our standing. We still had a take-no-prisoners attitude. I wanted the Quartet to believe that nobody could live on the same stage as us. Nobody. If that sounds arrogant, then I was. But that was my drive, and I'd run all over anybody who tried to take away our gloss or overshadow us on stage. By now we had a bit of professional finesse in our demeanour and I'm sure I'm not exaggerating when I say that the Quartet had reached a unique plateau of popularity as performers in those days.

Our popularity, for instance, made us an automatic choice to be the first New Zealand performers on television. On the first night of public telecasting in New Zealand, June 1, 1960, the Howard Morrison Quartet co-starred with Robin Hood and His Merry Men! I feel I've been the Invisible Man as far as New Zealand television is concerned in subsequent years. But they can't take that away from us — the first group to perform live.

As 1960 and 1961 rolled into 1962, the act had now got to the stage of being appreciated by people in the Establishment. We weren't long hairs, the National Programme, the String Quartet. But we were getting invited to morning and afternoon teas by the mayor and city councillors! Profiles of the Quartet were also being featured in national magazines and on national radio.

Mind you, there were still some raised eyebrows when a pop-oriented — for that time — group like us were chosen for the Royal Command Performance in Dunedin, to mark the royal visit in early 1963. You got your exes paid and your hotel and your meals, and you did the show for love of Queen and Country, to be patriotic. Of course, anyone would have walked on broken glass to be invited. We felt honoured and humbled. I mean, we were loyalists, royalists to the core. This was the Queen, after all.

What did we sing? We sang a traditional Maori fishing chant,

Meeting Her Majesty the Queen after a Royal Variety Concert in Dunedin in 1963. Wi Wharekura and Noel Kingi await their turn. Morrison family collection

Karu, unaccompanied. I think we sang *The Virgin Mary* also. We were very well received.

And, of course, it was a charge waiting in the lobby after the show to meet Her Majesty and Prince Philip. Standing alongside was my cousin Maureen Kingi, the current Miss New Zealand, who had performed the double long poi. I can still remember the scene. When the Queen came to Maureen Kingi, the flashbulbs of cameras from around the world just illuminated the place. Here was a Queen meeting a Maori Princess. Good line, good story, good picture.

When the Royal couple came to us there was another flourish of flashbulbs — not as many as for Maureen, I have to say. But it was the photo which put us into the upper echelons of High Society. Well, we thought so at the time.

The Queen didn't say anything to me but Prince Philip, who obviously had a keen eye for a good-looking woman — bless his soul, that he's human! — spoke to Maureen and then shook hands with me. In fact he dallied a bit because the Queen had finished the Quartet and he was still talking to Maureen.

He paused when he got to me and said: 'You chaps want to get this girl into your act so we don't have to look at your ugly mugs!'

I said 'smart aleck' — but under my breath, of course.

As there was no fee, Harry, like a good manager, wanted to salvage something financial out of our God Save The Queen act. So he contacted the southern entrepreneur Joe Brown — in fact, I think Joe had heard a fair bit about us and it may have been Joe contacting Harry. Anyway, we did a show for Joe down at Balclutha and then did his Dunedin Town Hall dance on the Saturday.

That was our first encounter with Joe Brown, of Miss New Zealand fame, and his son Dennis. It was, as it turned out, a significant meeting . . . it was at this time that Harry began to show a strong interest in spreading his wings.

7

EXIT HARRY M.

THROUGH HIS YEARS of representing us, Harry had no real base. Wherever he as an entrepreneur and promoter could succeed, that was his base. He was fascinated by seeing stars, promoting stars. But we, as individuals and as a group, had a base; we had our homes and our families. We had no ambition to go any further than Australasia, where we were known and successful.

Harry frightened me with his grandiose plans. He was setting up headquarters in Australia, getting involved with overseas artists like Sarah Vaughan, Ella Fitzgerald and Oscar Peterson. His plans for us were worldwide. But in spite of the attractive possibilities for inter-national fame, we felt the personal cost would prove too great.

What was obvious was that Harry would have to work through other agents, and that would lead to a lessening of our ability to make decisions. I know I influenced the boys' thinking by suggesting that signing contracts with international agents was tantamount to signing away our independence.

I saw Harry in September of 1991, and asked him to think about how he felt at that time, when we were turning down opportunities to go to England and America.

He faxed me the following, dated 13 December, 1991.

Dear Howard,
You asked me about the sadness that I had when I could never get the group to go to America and Europe and the reason that I was sad was because at that time, you will recall, I was putting on six or eight shows a year in New Zealand and Australia and our contacts with the entertainment leaders in America and Britain were really fantastic.

I knew the style that you boys had at that time would, of course, absolutely lay them in the aisles in America and, on a number of occasions, I spoke to agents about this.

It was, in fact, Henry Miller (a well-known agent based in Los Angeles) who wanted to get you guys jobs, probably starting in the lounges of Las Vegas, working on the Ed Sullivan Show, Johnny Carson Show etc. It was the kind of thing that could have happened instantly.

You guys had all the talent and I had the contacts and they were ready to roll. I guess all of that would have led to a very different kind of success in the United States and onwards into Europe.

Remember Howard Fielding, who ran those huge Palladium-type shows — Tommy Steel etc, etc? We were close to him in Britain because our London agent was a man called Ian Bevan. There were many opportunities — alas, you turned your backs on them.

It is not something to be in despair about, but for reasons best known to you, you didn't want to go forward.

There is no doubt in my mind the group would have been huge. You guys would have been world famous and probably still singing and making millions of dollars. Such is life!
Talk to you soon,
Harry.

Indeed, such is life. I have never regretted influencing the Quartet's decision not to take on the international market. It's hypothetical, of course, what the costs would have been, in personal terms, and what the benefits would have been.

But, in short, I am both happy and grateful for the way things turned out. If we'd gone to America and become superstars, who knows how we'd have coped with the pressures, how our families would have coped — whether our families could even have survived?

When you look back over your life, there are occasions you can remember, achievements in which you can take pride. But how real, how lasting, are they as time goes by? What you really give to the world and to the future are your children, and your children's children.

Just before I narrated this section, I was watching the television production of the Aotearoa Polynesian Festival, at Ngaruawahia, in

February 1992. There was my son, Howard Junior, coming up to receive the award for Best Male Group Leader. The camera panned to Dad in the audience and yes, there was proud moisture in the old brown eyes. A lump in the throat, too. You bet.

That's what it's all about.

Harry's letter confirms that he could see us being international stars. I had visions of us being consumed.

At the time that these discussions with Harry about our future were taking place (1963), I'd contracted severe tonsilitis. I was having a lot of throat problems, mainly through the strain of what was expected from me as the lead singer and through the Quartet's programme of two shows a day, six days a week, especially on tour. It eventually took its toll.

We decided that I'd get my tonsils out, which, including time to recuperate, would take about two months and there would be a hiatus for the Quartet. It was a straightforward operation. I did have an adverse reaction — I don't know how it compared to other people's — but it wasn't a really big deal. I was recuperating at Harry's place a few days after I came out of hospital and, much to my amazement, Harry — always looking for a chance to get some hype and some headlines — fed to the innocent media that I was gravely ill. Those were the exact words the newsreader used.

My ear, nose and throat specialist wasn't pleased and nor were my family. That was Harry, taking advantage of every situation to keep people in the headlines. But it wasn't a very nice way to do it.

If I had fears about the international market, they were soon realised. Harry, without coming to me or the Quartet first, decided that to mark our comeback we would do another tour. This was fair enough; the only problem was that he farmed us out to another promoter and his associate.

The guy's name was Jim Haddleton and his associate was a friend of ours at that time, a guy called Doug Elliott.

Haddleton was the money man and Doug was the entrepreneur. Haddleton was just starting out; he was fascinated by show business and wanted to get involved. That didn't sit well with me. Why would Harry do that? Well, he was starting to move on to other things so it was his way of keeping us occupied by letting someone else do the promotion.

We were to do a tour under this guy's banner, Jim Haddleton Presents, which I was very reluctant to do. It annoyed me because it didn't have the gloss of the Howard Morrison Quartet, Showtime Spectacular, Kerridge Odeon and Harry Miller. It seemed a downgrade.

On one hand, Harry was telling us we were stars, that we'd make it big in Europe and America if we'd only take the leap. Yet on the other hand he was farming us out to a novice promoter.

I couldn't understand — that was my naivety — why he would

give the show's rights to another promoter to make all the money while, on the face of it, Harry was only going to make 20% of our fee. Yeah, a real dummy I was.

But I still smelt a rat and Harry, by not telling me the way it really was, didn't make it any better. It would have saved a lot of heartache a little later.

I was giving this Haddleton chap a hard time about the deal, letting him know that I wasn't happy with it. Perhaps he saw a way of wooing us away from Harry Miller, because he was besotted by the entertainment world; really keen to get amongst it.

He showed me the contract that he'd signed with Harry. Haddleton and Harry were actually partners in the tour. They were to go half and half in the up-front money. I can't remember whether Harry was on 50% or 60% of the profits, but of course he still took 20% off our fee.

Obviously Harry felt he'd be giving too much away if he'd waived the 20%. But if he had waived it, he might have allayed my fears. Well, Jim Haddleton couldn't show me the contract quick enough and I just folded the document and put it in my pocket. Haddleton was leaping up and down because he wanted the contract back. But he wasn't about to try and take it off me physically because I was a very fit and strong gent.

I said to the boys: 'We've been rorted. However, we must do this tour, to fulfil our commitments. And then we're going to have a look at things.'

Well, we did that. Our next gig was at Checkers night club in Sydney, supporting Nelson Eddy, and I had a meeting with Harry. At that time he was negotiating with Viking to sell his record company, La Gloria.

Harry said: 'I've done you a fantastic deal.' And on royalties he had. But I didn't grasp the business meaning of that; that we were the carrot for Viking to buy La Gloria. My business skills hadn't yet been sharpened sufficiently. I was learning all the time, learning by every mistake. I'd like to say that if I made a mistake, I learned from it and it didn't happen again.

I said: 'We're talking about this deal, Harry?'

'Yes, and then you'd be independent, free of my management and all that.'

'You wouldn't screw us, would you, Harry?'

'Of course not.'

'And have you ever?'

His voice went up, in affronted despair. 'Me? Whaddaya talking about?'

I handed him the Jim Haddleton contract. 'What's that, Harry?'

Well, the blood drained out of his face. In hindsight, it was almost as if he'd been paying us back for putting him on the rack once or twice. The smart thing for him would have been to have told us, and put us in the partnership deal with Haddleton. But Harry had no guilt pangs at all. If you were prepared to carry on, not ask for a rise or anything, he certainly wasn't going to offer one.

If he had said, this deal with Haddleton, why don't we work it a third, a third, a third, that would have brought the group into the business side as well as the performing side. We wouldn't have felt like the hired help.

It took Harry only about six hours to recover from being exposed like that, and then he started getting aggressive with me again. Where's your loyalty, and all that jazz. He chose a bad time to do it, as we were in our dressing room warming up to go on before Nelson Eddy.

As an aside, Nelson Eddy was a lesson for me to watch. He was someone I'd admired as a young fellow, when he was singing with Jeanette McDonald. He wasn't any chicken then. And now, here was this stooped old man, walking in the back entrance an hour before the show, muffled up with a hat and scarf and heavy overcoat. And then suddenly he'd be on stage, back straight, elegant in a tuxedo, silver haired, sophisticated — marvellous, a real pro! I watched the man every night and I learned what style was about, and how you could be one person for yourself and another for the public.

So there we were, in our dressing room at Checkers, and Harry was coming on like the Roaring Forties. I said: 'Harry, I've told you. You screwed us; there's no deal with the record company. Forget it.'

He was panicking; he must have had the Viking Record Company people ready to sign. So he tried another way, he tried to get to the other guys, in front of me. And this was about quarter of an hour before a show! Well, he did the wrong thing. I'd always kept the boys away from Harry, because he used to really get under their skin. I'd been the buffer between them. So when he appealed to them for support, said that I was being uncooperative, the boys gave him real verbal barrels. At that, the blood went out of his face again. And I knew OK, now's the time to get rid of him.

So I said: 'Harry, we've got a show to do; get out of here.' And I threw my arm out in his direction; it connected with his well-endowed nose. That backed him out through the door, and as I slammed the door he was trying to come back in — and it connected with his nose again!

The next day I was full of misgivings. Harry, with his face down, said, 'I never thought I'd see the day when you'd take a poke at me.' I had, even if it was by accident, and I felt bad about it. Harry was able to hold his feelings and get onto the business side, just like that. He took advantage of the fact that I was feeling pretty down; we'd had some good years and I didn't want our association to end like that. 'OK,' he said, 'our contract is now null and void. But in return I need you to sign

An advertisement Harry Miller's La Gloria record company ran in the Everly Brothers programme.

the transfer contract for the recording company.'

Well, I could really have stuck it in. But because he had me in a vulnerable moment, I chose not to. And that was virtually the end of our association with Harry M. Miller.

Before we leave the Harry Miller era, it's probably worth looking at the Quartet, at the act, as it was at that stage.

The Quartet was very professional. We'd gained a lot of discipline and showmanship through that season of vaudeville, with *Nats in the Belfry*, and from the wide range of venues we played. Theatres one week, cabaret the next, night clubs, football clubs . . . we got a very broad spectrum of opportunities to entertain. Different audiences, different age groups, different social levels.

We could perform as a group with two guitars, or a quartet plus rhythm section, or a quartet backed by a 12-piece or 16-piece or 21-piece band. That's how versatile we were.

We were always well turned out, always reliable, very much in demand. It would be true to say that we were no longer in the business purely and simply for enjoyment. It was a business. We loved the tours. They allowed us to extend our association with people beyond the stage. In every town there's another story. In every town we had built up a following. I have reservations about the word 'fans', to me, it's too pop-oriented. I'd prefer to call them followers and friends.

If we were playing Invercargill, I'd know we'd be looking for the McRae family; I'd know we'd be meeting up with Colin, and we'd always have a hangi after the show. In Dunedin, there'd be another group of people, like the Cassidys and heaps of mates from Mosgiel. In Christchurch there'd be Sandy Dacombe and her friends. Sandy goes back to coming to the show with a group of people when she was only 14 and she has been an ardent follower, first of the group and then of myself, ever since. There were many others in that category throughout the country — the Tomoanas, Huatas, Rangiihus and others.

So we had a following, up and down New Zealand. It was like when you go on holiday and you always drop in on friends in certain places. We used to meet our friends on our territory; they would come to our shows. And they weren't bludgers, either; they weren't the ones who hung around looking for free tickets; they always came to the show and paid their own way.

It was a good aid for us to keep our feet on the ground; to keep 'the common touch' and not try to be something we weren't.

But on stage we were very professional and took our work seriously. We never played to just those friends; we played to the whole of the audience. We'd learned the lesson that when you're performing you have to be unselfish; you have to give a lot of yourself.

What the group lacked was substance, in terms of musical appreciation. None of us could read music. Most of our repertoire was covers, or covers of covers. You'd barely recognise some songs by the time we finished with them. But we didn't have our own, fresh material. All our ideas were based on current songs and records, or something we'd conjured up from the past.

From the outset, before we went on tour, the Quartet was a self-contained unit, not needing anything from outside. Our instruments were two guitars, maracas and tambourines, which we played ourselves. We didn't have the time and wouldn't make the time to sit down and learn the ABC of music.

The bands we chose were of the same ilk — Toni Williams and his Tremellos, the Quin Tikis . . . all 'ear' musicians. At rehearsal we'd go over and over and over things until we got it right. If we'd had knowledge of musical theory, we'd have been able to write it down and then have to rehearse it only two or three times.

We should have sung more with professional readers of music. But, without wanting to sound racist, many pakeha musicians didn't have the Maori pulse in terms of attitudinal responses, showmanship and so on.

We wanted our bands to be right there with us, to be able to go

The Quartet, 'semi-professional' days long behind, at rehearsal: a Sunday night ritual. You can imagine Gerry's question: 'How do I tune this piano to my guitar?'
NZ Herald

with our ad libbing and improvisation. We rehearsed hard; we might have had only 'head' arrangements but we were tight. It was part of our act to also have that freedom of approach, to throw in something new in midstream.

One skilful 'reading' musician who was an advantage to us was Robert Walden. He became our official pianist-accompanist from 1960. He was a great asset in teaching us the finer points of harmonies, of part-singing; something we'd previously done just by ear and instinct. Sundays especially, in the afternoons and evenings, were dedicated to allowing Robert to teach us how to sing properly in parts. It was usually to hymns and it was from these sessions that we developed our technique of giving our own version of Negro spirituals. This made a contribution to widening the Quartet's repertoire at that stage. But the underlying truth is that even though Robert was there, we never took full advantage of him.

This was where Gerry could have helped himself, by getting more closely involved with a technically strong, educated musician like Robert. He could have improved his formal musical knowledge. But Gerry, I guess, had developed a bit of arrogance. He was very reluctant to tune his guitar up to concert pitch. He'd prefer the guy to tune the piano to his guitar!

In 1958 and '59 when my brother was in the group, we had to remember what fret on the guitar our songs were. So F was No 1 Fret, F Sharp was No 2, G was No 3 and so on. And we didn't talk about doing a song in G or B Flat; we'd say this one's in Three Fret, or whatever. That's how musically illiterate we were — and stayed — in the technical sense.

I still don't know how to read music. I've kept putting it off and putting it off. Am I saying now that it's too late? Of course it's not! But I have another reason, or excuse: too much to do, too little time . . .

So our lack of musical education didn't help our cause. But there was another facet of our act, our improvising in midstream, that we used to stimulate one another. We all had a raunchy, cheeky sense of humour; our on-stage affinity was sometimes uncanny. We developed this unbelievable sense of timing.

So really, we didn't have to rehearse much with bands. It was more a case of follow us and see what happens. I guess that was part of our appeal.

My excuse when Harry's offsider Graham Dent told us we should learn to read music was: And lose our instinct, lose our naturalness? The truth is, we could have combined both. We should have made time to clean up our act in musical appreciation, learning how to read music,

One of the more frequently used publicity shots from the Quartet's Harry Miller days.

the structure, having charts and hiring bands who could read music. It would have saved a lot of time, hard work and frayed nerve ends.

Yet even after all this I would still prefer a band who didn't read music, a band who would follow me at the drop of an eyelash.

So that was the Quartet at the time of the breakup with Harry.

As entertainers: very professional.

As musicians: technically limited.

As crowd pleasers: out on our own.

We relied heavily on the ever-popular parodies, on our on-stage humour; but we'd started sneaking in better and better material. We did a lot of impressions, and sometimes a 'straight' number would become a comedy number more or less by accident. I remember Gerry and I had a comedy routine with Harry Belafonte's *Banana Boat Song* that could go for six minutes.

One night we went into the very serious introduction to a straight version of *Granada* and Gerry, for no particular reason, threw in a loud 'Ole!' The crowd broke up, so the 'Ole!' stayed in. By the end of the tour *Granada* had become a comedy routine.

At times we went a bit over the top with the comedy side and the crowd would get restive. But I think we usually woke up to ourselves pretty smartly if that happened, and got our act together again.

Doing a lot of work in Australia, where we couldn't use colloquial Kiwi humour, helped us to judge when we'd crossed the line and were talking liberties with our audience.

As an act, we developed to international standard from that first 1960 Showtime Spectacular tour through the school of hard knocks. Our experience on the Tivoli circuit and the variety of cabarets and league clubs we played in Australia gave us a great opportunity to extend our repertoire, sharpen our act and learn how to handle a wide cross-section of audiences. Theatre audiences were our favourites.

We were taking breaks at the right time from our New Zealand audience and coming back with 'new' old stuff as well as fresh material.

I'd realised that I couldn't do 90 per cent of the lead singing, which, driven by vanity, I'd been trying to do and I'd started to farm out more judiciously, and democratically, solo spots to the boys. We were learning to pace ourselves.

It was a bit like the Harlem Globetrotters. They'd realised that every one of them couldn't put a top performance together every night on the road. Physically they'd become blown away. So they'd learned to spread the workload around.

Without saying we specifically used their example, it seemed prudent for Wi to sing a couple of solos, and similarly for Noel and Gerry.

It was commonsense, because audiences were appreciating the particular vocal qualities of all four members instead of just me and

Noel Kingi. Noel and I were the backbone of the group in voice production. Gerry was the driving force in harmonies. He could go anywhere, take any part; his pitch was absolutely marvellous. If Wi went off an alto note Gerry would take it over just on instinct.

I relied on Gerry a lot. We never had any dispute about the material we were using or the way we were doing it, yet my decision at this time to spread the lead-singing role among the four of us probably staved off a passive revolt within the group. Although no one had said anything to me at the time, they'd become a bit tired of just being backing singers.

We now had a successful basic format. A strong opening, a friendly chat to get the audience relaxed and on our wavelength; moving through different elements of music and strengths of the group — we hardly ever did a song without explaining or back-announcing why we did it. And we always wound up with a strong finish.

Certain numbers became virtual standards for us during this time, because the audiences expected them — songs like *Granada* and *Begin the Beguine* from me; *Sixteen Tons* and *Old Man River* from Noel; *I Must Have Been a Beautiful Baby* from Gerry; *Velvet Waters* from Wi; and, from the Quartet, *Where Have All the Flowers Gone, Get a Little Dirt on Your Hands, Virgin Mary* . . .

We used to get a bit guilty about doing these sure winners time and time again, until we learned how to do them in medleys. While having your own style is important, there are always tricks of the trade you can pick up as you go along. When we appeared with the Kingston Trio in Australia we saw how they worked their most popular songs into a medley so they didn't have to do each one all the way through, every time, but retained the impact. In time, we adopted the technique.

A lot of this growth and development in the Quartet came about through Harry Miller's influence; the acts he booked us with and the places he booked us into.

We went through a lot with Harry. There were some hassles, some friction; maybe we didn't make as much as we should have in monetary terms out of the bonanza years of the Quartet.

But there were plenty of good times, fun times and exciting times, too. If we'd never met Harry, if I'd never stopped to talk to that Electromet salesman in the Rotorua appliance store, we may never have become fully professional entertainers. We may never have even reached for goals as high as we achieved.

Harry and I lost contact for a long period of time but I watched his progress and how he became the top promoter in Australia, bringing tremendous acts and shows to that country.

One of Harry's greatest achievements was when he was brought in late to rescue the Australian celebrations marking the 25th year of Queen Elizabeth's reign.

Harry told me when I went over to see him in 1991 that the honour of being given that responsibility far outweighed the financial considerations, and that part of the payback would be that he would be mentioned in despatches with almost a guarantee of going from Harry M. Miller, citizen, to Sir Harry Miller.

Of course, what subsequently happened was that Harry was charged with misappropriating funds from the Computicket operation.

Harry did tell me that he became so immersed in organising the celebrations that he let the day-to-day operations of his own business fall by the wayside. By the time he got back, things were already well in train which brought about the negative result for Harry in his association with Computicket.

This could all come under the title of conjecture, I suppose. Anyway, the long and short of it was that Harry was charged and jailed. I personally felt a lot of distress about this and, about a month after Harry was sentenced, I wrote to assure him that the love and the prayers of the family were with him.

Harry wrote back and anyone would have thought that he was taking a vacation — if hardly in Club Med surroundings. I remember he wrote: 'Do you know that they spent one million dollars to get me?'

That was the end of Harry's knighthood, of course. And the next time I saw him in person was when he was one of my surprise guests on *This Is Your Life*.

Harry was unfairly maligned at times and he is undoubtedly the best impresario Australasia has ever seen. Harry remains a friend.

In our relationship, the only naughty thing he did was not telling me about the deal with Jim Haddleton — and, anyway, from that I gained the freedom from being managed and directed. Ironically, considering all the hassles over that record company deal, we never had a hit for Viking!

This could be a good time, too, to look another big name in New Zealand music who kicked off around that era. It was great for live music, those early to mid-sixties. If we'd had 10 o'clock closing in those days, with pubs looking for live evening entertainment, it would have been a marvellous musical scene. As it was, a lot of groups went overseas to make their mark.

Prince Tui Teka was probably the first and was performing overseas before we made it full-time, back here, as the Quartet. He originally went overseas with a circus. When we became popular and went to Australia, we took in one of Tui's tent shows in the Sydney Showgrounds. I was pretty disgusted, really.

They were billed as 'cannibal Maoris from New Zealand', poking their tongues out and so on; a sideshow act. They were making a dollar, but seeing them promoted that way wasn't something I was proud of, as a Maori. I felt our culture deserved a better platform than a showground sideshow. But what price integrity? It doesn't pay the bills.

When I look back at some of the things I did in pursuit of the market, my respect for the language and the culture wasn't always what it should have been, either.

The best example of how people felt I'd brought disrespect to the culture, and of how themes should be respected, was our recording of *Hoki Mai*. I picked the song as a potential commercial winner. It was the first single we put out as a Quartet and we recorded it at an upbeat tempo, the way we'd heard other people sing it.

Trouble was, I didn't know the history of the song and neither did I bother to do any homework about its background. All I knew was that it was sung to *Goldmine in the Sky*.

The late, great Tui Teka.

As I later found, the song was dedicated to the Maori Battalion and the original title was *Tomo Mai*. Mind you, the words are of victory and pride, hardly dirge-like, and I still don't think our bright tempo was inappropriate. The main issue, I suppose, was singing a song with a strong Maori sentiment without taking the trouble to find out its significance. Some people were offended.

On a trip to the East Coast in 1991 I was reminded of my lack of sensitivity when I visited Ngata College. I really got a broadside and, at age 56, it was taken on board by me with considerable embarrassment. I'd have to say that.

In reply, I said to the speaker, Koro Dewes, the principal at Ngata, 'I think you've waited a long time to tell me that.'

He replied, from across the floor, 'I've been waiting for you to come on my ground,' adding relish with hearty, self-satisfied laughter.

Tui Teka, of course, made huge strides from those sideshow days. He came back to New Zealand and took into his group bass guitarist Charlie Te Hau, a friend who has done a lot of work with me in the years since. He went to a talent quest one time where he saw a young entertainer called Billy T. James and took him on board. At Billy's funeral at Ngaruawahia comment was made in the whaikorero (the speeches) that it was from that same meeting house that Billy was taken away by Tui Teka in what turned out to be a turning point in his career.

Because we grew up in the same little hamlet, in that beautiful valley, Ruatahuna, in the Urewera country, Tui and I became close. We used to love meeting one another; we'd yak away in Maori, recalling those old times.

What Tui never lost was his grassroots nature. A photograph of Tui with the Volcanics showed how sophisticated he could be but he was always essentially that same basic person — with expensive tastes!

Later on, after all his success overseas and particularly in Australia, Tui actually put together groups that had no musical background whatsoever; he taught them from scratch.

I don't know whether that was out of frustration with the idiosyncrasies that go with professional musicians and singers; it could have been. But he trained these people the way he wanted them to be trained; to do what he wanted them to do. Tui then did shows wherever there was a hole in the wall. He didn't do the more sophisticated cabarets; he sought out his people, his audience. He spent a lot of time on the East Coast, where he met, trained and eventually married Missie.

In 1970 he started making New Zealand a more permanent base and headlined Joe Brown's Miss New Zealand tour that year. Then he had a heart attack in Wellington which incapacitated him. I'd just come back from Manila and I replaced Tui to finish off the tour.

That heart attack was brought upon by Tui being terribly obese. And he was working very hard. He would scrape himself together . . . the man must have been suffering. He had diabetes, heart trouble, bad circulation. But he just had a love for entertaining.

Tui also had problems holding on to his money. For a down-home body he loved material things — flash cars and staying in the best hotels . . . then he'd go down to the local tavern which held only 60 people to put on a show. And talk about the entourages of today's superstars — Tui had tribal entourages!

When Tui had his second attack, a bad one, and was in Gisborne Hospital, we went and saw him. He was beyond cautioning then; he wanted to get back on the road and work. It was obvious he had some financial commitments he wanted to meet. So the business that he loved consumed him and his body finally gave up.

I touch on Billy T here, as well, because both Billy and Tui had too short a span in which New Zealand audiences could enjoy their gifts.

Both had served a long apprenticeship in a hard school overseas, and for them to come back and be recognised in their own country was, I know, a great comfort and a great source of pleasure to them. They both left a legacy of love, of endearment, in spite of the short span of time; they were both very important contributors to New Zealand's show business-entertainment scene.

At the time when the Quartet was at its zenith, Tui and Billy T were both making their names overseas. And there were dozens of groups, Maori groups, whose contribution was recognised in the TV series *When the Haka Became the Boogie*.

It was a great thing for Maoridom. Because even though they didn't go under the tag of 'Maori bands', it was Maori names and Maori faces which were leading the charge for popularity at that time.

There was a good spinoff for all of us. While we weren't exactly in competition, we were very competitive. And that rubbed off in terms of lifting the standard and keeping us on our toes. With more entertainment venues and a bigger population, who knows what strength the vibrant music scene of those years would have reached in the '70s?

But fulltime work was simply not available; some groups headed overseas and some simply faded out.

8

HELLO JOE, FAREWELL QUARTET

THE BREAKUP WITH Harry Miller left the Quartet on eggshells. Suddenly we had no manager and I had to assume that mantle. That's when we started doing the tours with Joe and Dennis Brown.

Joe was of the old school — a man of the land and a successful race-horse owner (one of his best was Reformed, who won the 1952 Wellington Cup and ran third in that year's Melbourne Cup). Joe believed in the land. His motto was: Buy land, it doesn't move.

Once we were driving to Mosgiel and came round a corner behind a truck laden with topsoil. I said to him, 'Hey Joe, someone's pinching your land!'

Quick as flash, Joe came back: 'Ahh, but there's plenty more underneath!'

Despite his show business success, Joe didn't abandon his farming interests at Mosgiel. As John Berry recorded in his book *Seeing Stars*, Joe would put a paddock down in potatoes every year and, when the crop was ready, invite people to bring a sack and dig their own. The big attraction was a bonus for families, with the price reducing according to the number of children down to a minimum of one pound per sack. Crafty customers used to swap children at the gate. This tickled Joe, because he was actually quite happy to sell the spuds for a quid a sack.

Joe had a terrific operation down there and he was an over-the-top promoter of Howard Morrison. There was no other act that would live on the stage with Howard Morrison in Joe's opinion. That wasn't the only reason we got on well. I found it easy to talk to Joe. And talk we did, for hours and hours at a time.

Dennis was just a youngster when he came on to the scene, and something of a fish out of water. He also had strong feelings for the land, but inherited the donkey work of his father's show business promotions; entrepreneurial work which I don't think he really enjoyed.

Dennis was and is a mate — very sensitive, very much a home body. I think, underneath it all, he actually despises some elements of show biz — the hype, the BS, the compromises, the tantrums, the idiosyncrasies — but he just got swallowed up in it through taking over from his father.

With Joe and Dennis and Marge, Joe's wife, I shared a wonderful part of my life. Joe was a nice man to be around, and a very moral man. There was going to be no hanky panky with the Miss New Zealand contestants while he was running the show. All the girls, the winners and the losers, from that Miss New Zealand era would still remember Joe, Marge and Dennis with more affection than anyone else outside their own families. The girls were mainly provincial types, suddenly put in the limelight, and they all grew from it. A wonderful part, over the years that I've toured, has been former Miss New Zealand girls coming back stage to introduce their husbands and their children.

The Quartet did a Saturday night Dunedin Town Hall dance for Joe after splitting with Harry in 1963, and we had a handshake deal to do a tour in tandem with the Miss New Zealand contest, which wasn't doing too well at that time. Combining the Quartet with the Miss New Zealand Show made it a success, there's no doubt about that.

Joe may have been more a friend than a promoter, but he was a very sharp businessman, too; his characteristics weren't what you'd expect from a promoter, but he had an instinct about what people wanted. His philosophy was that people will always need food, shelter and entertainment. Joe believed in entertainment directly to the people, and we were part of that.

Joe's concept of the Miss New Zealand Show was always sophistication without too much glitz; middle-of-the-road wholesome family entertainment. He had occasions to pull me aside and tick me off for what would be regarded as very mild these days. Well, even those days!

One night, for example, as I was introducing say Miss Manawatu, I said, 'Now, this young lady loves crosswords. I was sitting next to her in the bus just today and she said to me: "Howard, what is a four-letter word ending in 'it' that you find in the bottom of a birdcage?" I said to her, that would be "grit". And she said: "You wouldn't have a rubber, would you?" '

The crowd loved it and the girls didn't know who was going to cop it next. But it took only a couple of nights for Joe to pull me aside and say, 'Howard, would you like someone to say that to your daughter?' I never put it back in the act.

Joe got very upset when anyone raised criticism of the Miss New Zealand Show on moral grounds. If there was a letter to the editor with an address, he wouldn't just reply to it; he'd go round to the house. Not to tell them off, but to tell them how high the standard of the show, and the contestants, was.

A collage from late in the Quartet's career, during the Miss New Zealand tours.

Morrison family collection

Those girls, for the four to six weeks the show ran, had the greatest experience of their young lives and they learned a lot. They had to be able to communicate, they had to keep up an image and they learned to deal with the media and to cope with hardened professional entertainers. Joe made sure, of course, that we never gave them a hard time.

We felt for the girls when it came to the finals, because what do you say to the losers — except hard luck, I guess. None of us were allowed to show any favouritism at all.

Dennis and I had a lot in common and we still do. He was a keen sportsman, a very good fast bowler whose career was restricted by heel problems. He loved physical sports; I think he thought of show business in terms of people who slept all day and were lounge lizards after the show.

Dennis and I were always close; we were one another's conscience at times. The influence of his father was always there; the influence of my father was always there. The last thing we talked about, on a personal basis, was show business.

In 1979, when I re-formed the Quartet to promote Tu Tangata, Dennis put the tour together and it was a huge success. On a personal basis, of all the promoters and entrepreneurs with whom I've been involved, the Browns and Benny Levin were my closest friends.

Joe died in late 1986 and it was a matter of deep personal regret that I was unable to make his funeral. But I paid my own homage in my heart and visited his grave with my troupe in 1989.

The Quartet, although four people working together and living in each other's pockets, were still very fresh in 1963. When we took up with Joe and Dennis Brown it was another new challenge. And, of course, it wasn't a hardship to have this bevy of beauties going around the country with us. By international standards they weren't a bevy of beauties; they were just natural, homegrown girls.

There was no such thing in those days as feminists placarding outside the theatre; the crowds went along to rah-rah-rah for their local representative. When we went to Christchurch the audience cheered loudest for Miss Canterbury, and so it happened in every town.

Our first year with the show saw the Miss New Zealand winner Elaine Miscall go on to become Miss World runner-up. This created phenomenal interest from the New Zealand public and Joe Brown was fighting off the sponsors wanting to cash in. Joe got great satisfaction from this because in the years before he had found endorsements and sponsorship difficult to come by.

Joe was always passionately keen to promote New Zealand, and he reckoned the best way to promote the country was through its people. The year before the Quartet came on the show, the winner, Maureen Kingi, appeared on national television in the USA doing the quadruple long poi. Now we had Elaine Miscall going on from winning Miss New

Zealand to be runner-up in Miss World. So a cattle market, as some of the extreme feminists were calling Joe Brown's shows, for two years running gave New Zealand a high profile.

On the shows we were the connecting link; the people who kept the show together. But after Elaine's great success, the girls became the focus and we became the support act.

That wasn't good for us professionally. By the time we got to 1964 we were starting to get a bit loose and a bit lazy. There was another attraction on stage with us and, while it was a good, light relief, it took the spotlight and the pressure away from the Quartet and made us a bit too casual.

The climax of the tour was the choosing of a Miss New Zealand. After a tour, the girls were forgotten, Miss New Zealand represented her country for one year — and the Quartet went on. I suppose that used to get under my skin a little; here we were, propping up girls who were going around the country and not making much of a contribution to the show except in that they were representing their province. While it was good for their development, I think it eroded our enthusiasm because we had the luxury of supporting, and guiding, instead of having to lead and be the focal point of the show.

We did get involved. All of us were helpful to the girls to the point where they reached the finals. None of us looked forward to the finals, because we grew close to the whole group.

There were a few of them who were ambitious, there were a few who were obnoxious, there were a few who couldn't or wouldn't be helped and there were a few who were wondering what they were doing there. But all in all, they were a nice, wholesome group of girls.

So those tours were a lot of fun but I think they were a factor — not the final nail in the coffin but a significant factor — in dissipating the enthusiasm level of the Quartet in goal-setting.

The challenge was starting to go. Our families were getting older and the tours too long. On the shorter tours, Kuia and the kids used to come on the road during the school holidays, as did the other boys' families, so it was whanau, whanau. But this one involved such a big touring entourage that it wasn't practicable to involve our families.

We were starting to take short cuts, and we were professional enough to do it. The reviews were always good to the Quartet because we gave good value. And we learned out of some bad experiences.

It was a relief to us, to be honest, when we broke with Harry. But, just the same, there was a downside. Because he was no longer there as a whipping boy, I couldn't shunt the blame for unpopular decisions on to him, and there was a restlessness growing amongst the group.

Gerry and Noel loved parties. Gerry is the first to say he doesn't regret any of that — but he would rather have done it without the alcohol. Gerry and Noel used to pursue those parties with passion. Wi and I would go to a few parties but never drank, so we were in pretty good shape the next day.

I felt my discipline was being treated by the other guys as school-teacherish by now. You know: we're adults, we're grown up, we can maintain self-discipline without being treated like kids.

But why I was so strict was that I resented the boys going to parties and singing all night when other people were paying to come to the show to hear the group singing professionally. The partying demeaned the image of the group and I could never go along with it.

It was funny; after a show, we'd disappear from the stage door in our own directions and mightn't see one another till we came together again for a rehearsal or show. But sometimes the other two would come to the shows a little worse for wear. And that's when I'd get school-masterly; sometimes very schoolmasterly.

I suppose there were rustlings of discontent emerging within the group. I was still the boss, make no mistake of that, but it was getting harder for the others to accept it. And, of course, the more I knew it was getting harder for them to accept it, the harder I got, to resist any inclination to weaken.

Breaking ties with Harry was a relief, but we felt a bit stranded at times. Just the same, though, we got plenty of offers of work in Australia. We worked in most states, in all the top cabarets and hotels.

Australia did a lot to keep elements of professional and sophisticated attitudes in the act. If we'd stayed in New Zealand all the time and not had those breaks away, I think we would have become sloppier and sloppier.

An example comes to mind of the resistance to one another's ideas that was creeping into the group. Before it was: What do you think of this song? Run it through . . . yeah! And in we'd go; we'd all work on it and mould it into the act. At this time when our unity was starting to splinter, a boy called Trevor Wilson sent me some lines on a song that he thought would be good for a parody. Called *Mori the Hori*, it was based on Ray Stevens' *Ahab the Arab*. As it turned out I only used 'Let me tell you about Mori, the Hori, the chief of the Aotea tribe . . .'

On the bus, I said to the boys, 'I've got this great idea. You've heard *Ahab the Arab*. Here's the title sent to me by this young fellow: *Mori the Hori!*' I had this look of anticipation on my face, waiting for a wave of yeah, yeah, yeahs. When the boys weren't impressed at all with the idea, I said OK, I'll write it myself.

I launched it and recorded it with the Quin Tikis, who were touring with us, at the Taihape Town Hall. The audience reaction to it was absolutely fantastic and the record was another smash hit. *Mori the Hori* (or *Howie the Maori*, as it later became) was the first parody we came up with since *George the Wilder New Zealand Boy* in 1962. It was also the last. The episode showed that the unity, that bond, that

The original Quin Tikis.

Dauphine Photographic Services

on-the-same-wavelength approach, was fading.

After the Quartet did the Miss New Zealand tour in 1964, we went back to Australia for a season at the Chevron Hotel, in Sydney. My 29th birthday was coming up and Kuia was expecting our third child. I felt the vibes of the Quartet, how we were going, our lack of fresh goals; I looked at myself, still young, married, a third child on the way. There were also rumblings from Wi and Gerry's wives, Noni and Betty, about us being away from home too often, too long.

But the bottom line was the challenge and motivation was gone. This was the time to break up.

I could see us going on for a few more years and making a lot of money. But I had that feeling of lost impetus, loss of drive. I decided I wanted to set myself fresh goals, as a solo artist, and I discussed it with the boys briefly. Very briefly.

We were in the lift at the Rex Hotel, going up, and I had John Berry, then a show biz columnist for the *Auckland Star*, standing by to tell him the news that we were breaking up, and that we were going back to New Zealand to start our farewell tour. But I virtually told the boys in the elevator, from ground level to the second floor. I got no kickback and the announcement was made.

John Berry was absolutely stunned when I told him the news and, being a good, suspicious journalist, he thought it was maybe a false finish; that we'd be doing a Nellie Melba. But we assured him that this was the decision. Well, I had to assure him. The boys were still pretty nonplussed. I hadn't given them much notice. I told John to hold the story until I'd contacted Benny Levin, as I'd chosen Benny to promote the farewell tour — as a partner.

See how things change! I went from a grateful, aspiring artist, singing for whatever money was given, to an astute business person in the space of four years.

I decided to co-promote the farewell tour with Benny Levin because he'd been the first. And things that go around come around. I know the Browns were disappointed that they didn't have the opportunity and I suppose they had reason to think that perhaps it should have been them. But I also know that for Benny it was one of the thrills of his life to be able to do the tour. He said so on *This Is Your Life.*

When it all came together and the announcement was made, the reaction in New Zealand was one of disbelief.

The good part about it was that we'd agreed, as a Quartet, to do this tour to mark our breakup. It wasn't as if we'd stopped in midstream because we couldn't get on with one another. Our career as a group wasn't just petering out; it was going out with a bang. Better to finish with the public saying 'what a shame' instead of 'it's about time'.

I had to negotiate with the boys, like other promoters had previously negotiated with Harry, as to how much money they were expecting. It was quite sad that I had to talk to Noel, Gerry and Wi separately about how much they wanted. But, emotions aside, this was business. And, in essence, they got what they asked for.

I look a bit of a gooseberry here . . . with Gene McDaniels and Dee Dee Sharp, in my first show as a solo performer. Morrison family collection

Before the farewell tour I'd already spread my promotional wings. I was a partner with Benny, Joe Brown and Phil Warren to do a quick tour with three black American singers — Gene McDaniels, Ben E. King and Dee Dee Sharp — and an 18-piece backing band. I was to be the connecting link.

I felt like a fish out of water at first. We had 18 professional musicians and, while I had arrangements for my part of the show, I missed the ability to adapt in midstream, to go from one flow to the next, which was a practised art with the Quartet. But because I was the only local on the programme, all the friends I had around the country came to the shows wishing me the best. They carried me. In Dunedin, one review said: Three Negroes upstaged by one Maori.

Gene McDaniels came over on the popularity he'd gained through pop songs like *Chip Chip, Goin' to Build Me a Mountain, Tower Of Strength* . . . he'd had some big hits. Then he went on stage and wanted to sing jazz. The critics savaged him.

Ben E. King was a good act; he stuck to all his hits. Dee Dee Sharp was my first real experience of an overseas artist putting on the prima donna act. She was a real old tart . . . well, a real young tart . . . in being demanding and hard to get on with.

That tour was also my first experience of being on a show with people who smoked grass. We were still innocent; I guess pot smoking existed in the cities but it wasn't widespread or open. I saw what it did to Ben E. King and his band in particular — sometimes they'd just do a show from memory — and I made a vow from that time on that I wouldn't have any musicians working with me who smoked pot. And I stuck to it; in fact, I fired a couple for that reason in subsequent years.

I remember bringing Gene McDaniels to Rotorua, and I made him promise that he wouldn't smoke grass around home. He was paranoia personified, away with the fairies half the time. One night I took him for a drive around the Blue and Green Lakes. I took him down to a little creek that exited into Lake Tarawera and I shone a torch and he could see all the fish spawning, coming up the creek. He'd never seen anything like it. Of course, I never poached a couple of fish; future knights wouldn't do a thing like that! I just showed him . . . the fish, that is.

On the way back I stopped on the lookout point between the Blue and Green Lakes. It was a beautiful, still night and the moon was shimmering on the lakes on both sides.

McDaniels started crying, sobbing his eyes out.

I said: 'What's the matter, Gene?'

He said to me: 'Now I know why you don't smoke shit.'

That quick tour was good for me. While we'd been away in Australia for two or three months the Quartet hadn't been seen in New Zealand. And the first reappearance was me, as a solo support act for these three black artists. It was good experience and it also built up the promotional hype for the Quartet's farewell tour. The media was asking are you going solo already? It was a good way to test the waters.

After that quick tour, the momentum built up to promote the Quartet's farewell. It was an outstanding box office success.

From the group's point of view, there was no depression that the tour was the last hurrah, the end of the Quartet's career. We just went out there and had a good time, and we were on stage for over two hours at each show. We sang not just the old favourites but numbers we'd nearly forgotten about; the people contributed to the atmosphere and to the repertoire by screaming out songs they wanted to hear. It was like a long, ongoing party.

The last wave, the last show for the Howard Morrison Quartet; Regent Theatre, Rotorua, New Year, 1965.
OVERLEAF: *How the* Daily Post *saw the occasion.*   Daily Post

The last show

"We felt it would be better to hear people say 'what a silly decision' than 'it's about time'."

The words were those of one of the best-known entertainers in New Zealand show business history, Rotorua's Howard Morrison.

The occasion was the last performance together of the Howard Morrison Quartet, in the Regent Theatre, Rotorua, last night.

The theatre was packed with a nostalgic crowd of fans, friends and those who just came to see the quartet for the last time. An afternoon farewell performance had been equally well patronised.

The selection of songs performed by the group, however, held no sentimental significance for the famed quartet.

"There'll be no nostalgia in the songs we sing," leader Howard, 29, said in the dressing rooms before the show. "This will be treated as just another show" Some of the songs the group sang were their better - known numbers.

But the hit which has never been equalled by any other New Zealand record — My Old Man's An All Black—was not among the farewell songs of the all-Maori quartet.

Manager

The idea for the tune, which smote the New Zealand Rugby Union's decision not to send Maoris on the 1960 All Black Rugby tour of South Africa, came from the group's manager at the time, Harry Miller.

"We laughed at the suggestion at first, but that record has sold 58,000 copies, New Zealand's biggest seller," said Howard. "And it still sells every winter."

The group came to its decision to disband because it "had to break up some time," he said. It preferred to take the course while still on top.

The group was born during the winter of 1955, its members being Waikite Rugby Club players. A win in a Christmas talent quest at Rotorua's Soundshell set the young singers on their way.

Full - time professionals since 1960, the quartet had changed its personnel considerably by then.

As it disbanded, it comprised Howard, Jerry Merito, Wi Wharekura and Noel King.

Payments

In its first engagement, at a so-called rock and roll jamboree in Rotorua, each member of the group received a fee of 15s. The next appearance was worth £12 12s to the quartet.

"Now it costs anybody £50 to have Jerry's guitar case open," said Howard.

Each member of the group now figures on earning at least £250 a month.

Four of the quartet's records have sold more than 20,000 copies and about a dozen have topped the 10,000 mark.

Their first long-player, On Stage, Off Stage has sold 30,000.

As the group prepared to go on stage yesterday, their popularity was well apparent.

Autograph books were brought in to the dressing rooms regularly. When the quartet was on stage, the audience hung on every word and action in a performance that was as humour - filled as ever. A crowd which would have filled the theatre again had waited in vain outside in the night air, hoping to get in.

Nearly flopped

But, Howard had earlier recalled a time when the quartet thought it was going to be a flop.

It was the Sydney Lord Mayor's show in 1960 and the group had just finished a 28-week stand in New Zealand which had left them able to do almost anything on stage and be applauded to the roof.

"After our first number at the Lord Mayor's show we thought we were going to be bombed," said Howard yesterday. "It looked bad. After the second, things weren't quite so bad."

"But it took one of our old Maori numbers to save us." The song was Karu, the fishing chant sung without accompaniment.

The group eventually became so successful in Australia that it has toured every year since and been acclaimed each time.

Now no more a quartet, the group will still be in entertainment, each man on his own.

Howard himself will compere and sing with a New Zealand tour begining in May featuring the Miss New Zealand contestants and the Quin Tiki band. There is also a possibility he will conduct an adult television show this year.

Jerry, 26, a former Whakatane boy who spent 10 years in the Cook Hospital, Gisborne, after being stricken at the age of eight with osteomyelitis, has hopes of becoming entertainment officer for New Zealand's prison farms. Otherwise, he will be looking around for really good talent in the hopes of forming his own group, featuring a girl singer.

Wi, 25, a former training college student who never got as far as teaching before being swept into show business, will start out as a single act next Saturday. At the end of March he will go on the road with guitarist Peter Posa.

Records

Noel, a 22-year-old, who has known no job other than that of a singer, will also go into entertainment on his own. He hopes to cut records before going on an Australian trip next month. Depending on his success, he may then go on to England.

The closing chapter to the Howard Morrison Quartet story was written last night. But it looks like being only the forerunner with many sequels yet to be penned, as each member carves his own individual niche in New Zealand show business.

As we went through the country making our farewells, it was obvious that we could have gone on and on into 1965. But I'd made the commitment that we'd do our last show in Rotorua, where it all started.

It was to have been an open-air show at the Sound Shell but, because of wet weather, it had to be moved indoors to the Civic Theatre, then the Regent Theatre. And because of the demand we had to have two shows on the same night.

I can still remember what we wore: our off-white suits in the first half and blues in the second. We did our two shows and went back to the dressing room afterwards; all changed in the same room. We stood in a row, as we normally did after a good show. I would be in front, clapping my hands, and the boys would be patting one another on the back and patting me on the back. That's how we used to finish our shows when we knew we'd had a good one.

We just said 'Cher!', shook hands and went out of the dressing room into the dark to make our separate ways home. No farewell party, no hullaballoo. And we left an audience which I think, as in the other towns, felt that it wasn't really a farewell tour; felt that maybe it was just an impetuous thought and we'd be back in '65.

For all the success and warmth of that farewell tour, the time was right. The Quartet could have gone on for five, six, maybe seven years. But only if we still retained our enthusiasm, our enjoyment and our closeness. And we'd been beginning to lose that. While there was sadness, it was time to move on to new challenges.

Sir Dove Myer Robinson, the then Mayor of Auckland, attended our Auckland farewell in the town hall and came on stage. His words were to the effect that while the Quartet had brought so much pleasure, our break-up was an 'unnatural disaster' that would blight the happiness of thousands and thousands of New Zealanders. We recorded that show. To this day, those words of Sir Dove Myer's express the affection the country felt for the Quartet.

The Quartet made such an impact that when I tell people we performed professionally only from 1960 to '64 they are amazed. We'd done so much: tours, records, films, television; the first in everything — the best in everything.

Outside New Zealand, one of the memories which gives me greatest satisfaction was an occasion in 1961 when Eartha Kitt had an argument with the management at the Chevron in Sydney, packed a sad and decided she was too sick to perform that night. We were at the Tivoli then, were called in to take her place and had her whole 16-piece band that still had to front up. We had no charts for them, so it was just the Quartet and two guitars, with this huge band behind us that did only one fanfare for us to come on, a chord at the end of each song, and a chaser to go off.

I walked on and, before we sang a note, I said: 'Good evening. I hope you have a good time — and for God's sake don't blame us if we're not what you expected!'

We had them on our side. The Anzac feeling was still very strong. We sang songs like *Maori Battalion* and *Po Kare Kare Ana* and we had the whole place stamping. We took an audience that had paid big money to see Eartha Kitt, international star, and they got four Maori fellows and two guitars instead. And we won them over.

Things that stand out about New Zealand's relationship with the Howard Morrison Quartet is how we were able to sustain, and be sustained by, people who followed us through those early years of trial, tribulation and growth to a high standard of professionalism — yet we stayed the same people in their eyes.

Staying the same, familiar, *their* Howard Morrison Quartet, was important because we didn't want to lose the common touch, the special appeal we had to New Zealanders. Our theatre audience mix was Gran, Granddad, parents and kids. Over the years the mix has stayed the same for me.

At the time the Quartet broke up, the boys never expressed to me how they felt. Gerry, always the closest to me, there at the outset, there at the breakup and still performing as a solo act today, has subsequently said that he wasn't personally ready. He feels, in retrospect, that we could have got a completely new 'script', done a complete re-vamp of the show and still carried on for a good while.

But he concedes that we were all getting a bit sick of each other, the original closeness of the group had dissipated and it was probably time for a change.

I should stress that ties of loyalty and the closeness didn't end with our breakup, as was shown when the boys unhesitatingly came back for two special reunion tours in later years.

Strangers hearing us get together now, nearly 30 years after the Quartet broke up, would be quite baffled because they'd think we were speaking some foreign tongue. I've felt some wry amusement watching Rawiri Paratene on the TV comedy series *More Issues* using a sort of muso-speak. I'm not so amused that he was using it in a gang context.

Rawiri was quoted as saying, 'It's the sort of language the Maori musos of the late fifties and early sixties used to use; the sort of language Howard Morrison might have used.' The plain fact is that Howard Morrison, Gerry Merito, Wi Wharekura and Noel Kingi invented it.

We were socialising after a show one night and Gerry and I were talking in Maori. A woman in a group nearby said we were arrogant and rude for speaking Maori. We were so innocent — I'll use that word rather than stupid — that we apologised. But as a direct consequence of that we started a language of our own.

The original source was ventriloquist Jon Zealando, who was on our show at the time. Jon had this metallic robot puppet for which he

New Zealand Entertainer of the Year 1966. I doubt if even I would have predicted I'd be back to receive the award again, a decade and a half later.

couldn't pronounce the letter 'b'. So boy became doy. Her sounded like twer; so girls became twers. And the vocabulary was gradually expanded.

If a woman was a nice person, we would say: 'Sheed!'

Or not so nice: 'Sheed not!'

Or 'Heed' and 'Heed not' in acknowledging fellas.

No one would know what we meant because we'd just say it very casually. I might meet someone and want to know if I was liable to get into a conversation I'd rather avoid. I'd say to Gerry: 'Woody be?' And he might say: 'Heed,' meaning he's all right. Or 'Heed not!' We had some rude ones; a 'Finbar' was some vulgar-type person. We could conduct a whole conversation in our slang.

The younger guys, especially the other Maori musicians, loved hanging round when they saw Gerry and I and the other Quartet boys and Toni Williams together. They'd be cracking up, listening to us and trying to pick up the language. Billy T used it a lot and he always gave credit as to who started the language.

And, of course, Carl Doy, of *Piano By Candlelight* fame — we call him the Original Doy! Carl remembers when he first arrived from England and came to a session. Everyone was saying 'Hello Doy!' and he was thinking 'What a friendly bunch of people these Kiwis are.' Then he looked around and realised everyone was saying 'Hello Doy!' to everyone.

When we did the *This Is Your Life* programme and they brought the Quartet together for it, we just burst into the old language as if we'd never been away. One viewer wrote to the paper that her one big complaint about the programme was that she thought we were rude — she actually thought our showbiz lingo was Maori! Fancy, 30 years after we created our own lingo, we were getting ticked off again.

Years later nothing has changed. The length and breadth of New Zealand, wherever musicians and singers meet and greet, the greeting is Hello Doy or Twer, with the accepted thumbs-up word being 'Cher!'

Before we move on I'll take a look back at the members of the Quartet as they were in those years when we were blazing fresh trails.

Tai Eru was an on-again, off-again member of the early group with Laurie and cousin John. Tai came to Australia with us for the Chevron gig, for four weeks, but on his return he chose not to stay with the group because of his commitment to his family's farm.

It was a damn waste, really, because he had all the ingredients — tall, dark and handsome and a very good voice; tremendous personality and, like myself, he had the ego to match. Then again, what are you without a little bit of that if you choose the stage?

Tai was an A grade tennis player and a single-handicap golfer so he's an excellent sportsman. He remains a good mate and still sings at some of our social functions and enjoys performing with my band. Tai didn't entirely give up singing; he was host at the Tudor Towers in Rotorua in the late sixties to mid-seventies. Tai is still on the farm and we see a lot of each other, especially on the golf course.

I first met Gerry Merito after he had spent some time in Cooks General Hospital in Gisborne with severe osteomyelitis. Gerry is a personality . . . he's a typical Leo, very outgoing, great sense of humour. And he could pound out sounds from his acoustic guitar that I haven't heard the like of from anyone.

Gerry the irrepressible; Gerry the diplomat.

Gerry the humorist; Gerry for his quick wit and his timing.

Gerry for his huge aroha and compassion; Gerry for his sincerity; Gerry for his dreams.

Some of those dreams were a bit over the top but that's part of his character — the supreme optimist.

Gerry was, and still is, a shy person in some respects, but very relaxed. I don't think he would be ulcer material, ever. Gerry could relax and drop off to sleep at the drop of a proverbial hat. Away back

Howard as a performer . . . the energy the guy created was
unbelievable, and it was infectious. We all used to lift and
support each other, but Howard was the key. If Howard was
down, we could be in for a bad night; we'd be really battling.
But we could be down and Howard's enthusiasm and energy
would lift us up as soon as we got on stage, even if we'd been
arguing two minutes before going on. His voice? Well, I don't
think there was anyone to compare with him in our day. He was
out on his own.   — **Gerry Merito**

in 1957 we were doing a Telethon guest appearance in Melbourne.
Backstage those Telethons were always chaotic, noisy and a hive of
activity.

They'd cued us to go on following a particular act, so we were
standing at the ready. Then came a delay of about 10 minutes while
they went to the switchboards to do some more promotions to drag in
more funds. Finally we got our cue, walked on — and no Gerry. We
had to postpone our performance! We looked everywhere in the studio;
still no Gerry. Not until a studio assistant looked behind one of the
curtains did we find Gerry; standing, in his tuxedo, guitar round
his neck, leaning against the wall, chin on his chest, sound asleep —
Telethon pandemonium all around him! Now how relaxed is that?

At present Gerry is a one-man band show. He has spent some time
in Perth and he does well. Everybody loves Gerry and he loves everybody. A great mate.

Noel Kingi, sadly, passed away after months of ill health at the
time this book was in its final stages of production. Noel joined my
group at age sixteen, a raw, unsophisticated young adult and his vocal
equipment was something that really left the audience spellbound.

As a personality, Noel had a great sense of humour; loved to laugh.
Loved watching wrestling, cartoons, loved playing cards. He wasn't
very energetic on the physical side but loved parties. Life was there to
be enjoyed.

Noel used to get Gerry's goat at times, especially in restaurants.
He'd look through the menu, bring the waitress back, change his mind
and change his mind again. He'd hold everyone else up. One time one
of the gang was having rice pudding with hundreds and thousands
sprinkled on top. Noel said in his deep bass voice, 'I'll have some of that
but without those fiddly things.'

He'd already held us up by changing his mind several times. So
Gerry said to the waitress, mimicking Noel, 'I won't have the rice
pudding but I'll have a bowlful of those fiddly things!'

Five minutes later, that's exactly what he got! His joke backfired.

Noel could get aggressive when he'd had too much of the brown ale, which caused a bit of strife at times. But, for all that, I always found him a very loving and loyal person. And he never let me down when it counted.

Sadly, Noel didn't continue singing professionally, didn't even try, really. He spent his last years in Opotiki.

Wi Wharekura was convinced by me to stop short his training as a school teacher and join the group fulltime in 1960. Till then he'd been on again, off again. Wi was always neatly dressed, well turned out, always on time. He also had a great sense of humour. Actually, combined, the Quartet had this tremendous affinity, one to the other, when it came to bouncing gags around.

Wi had a personality that brought a lot to the Quartet and he provided a steadying balance. He looked the part, sang well, did the job. After the Quartet broke up he formed another foursome called The Sheratons and they did extremely well in Australia and in the East, playing some of the top night spots including my favourite, the Eagle's Nest in Hong Kong. Wi later got into the horse racing game, going training in Australia, and, later, in New Zealand. He loved a punt, still loves a punt.

As four people, as the Quartet, we were a formidable combination.

Funnily enough, in the humour department, the biggest source of mirth at our own expense was me.

One time in the Christchurch Town Hall was memorable. The boys were doing their doo-wah, doo-wahs and I was doing my impression of Johnny Ray; with wet handkerchief, wringing out the tears — I used to really get into it. Towards the end I'd go right down on my knees. The audience always cracked up but this particular night they were really roaring with laughter. It was almost like the laughter struck another gear!

I thought to myself: Howard, you're really killing them tonight!

When I finished the boys gathered around me and, for the audience's benefit, all put their hands to the side of their mouths and, in a loud stage whisper, said: 'You were great but your fly is open!'

9

GOING SOLO, GOING EAST

I MAY HAVE made the breakup sound an easy decision; not much emotion involved. But that wasn't the case. Reaching the decision was easy enough; even announcing it. But absorbing it afterwards was a different story. It was heart-wrenching.

I don't know whether it was better or worse that we didn't have a big breakup party after the farewell tour. It might have released the emotions, instead of bottling it up and dealing with it in our own different ways. But we didn't. After the last show, at the Regent Theatre back home in Rotorua, we went back to the dressing rooms and went our separate ways home.

I decided to take a break, and part of it was heading to the Ureweras, my 'therapy ward'. Ruatahuna has always been important to me when I need some time to myself, and I definitely needed some time at this stage. The impact Ruatahuna had in my early years has never left me and going back gave me the time, and the peace, to evaluate this crossroads in my life. So there I was, down the Whakatane River, tranquillity and history surrounding me, calling out silently to Dad and other important people in my life to guide me.

The peace of this place is so all-embracing you can hear yourself breathe. I didn't come out with the rest of Howard Morrison's career mapped out, but the philosophical wrinkles were ironed out. I came out feeling Jeez! You're a pretty good fellow, you've got talent and your whole life is ahead of you. Relax and enjoy.

I'd agreed to do Joe Brown's 1965 Miss New Zealand tour on my own, after the breakup of the Quartet. And I wasn't sure that it was the right thing to do; I wasn't sure that New Zealand or I were ready for a solo Morrison.

I think my misgivings were right; that first solo tour with Joe wasn't a good one for me. The audiences wanted me to do *Granada* without Gerry Merito, or *My Old Man's an All Black* without the Quartet. I didn't yet have my solo act together. I was pushing too hard. I was trying to jump off the stage right among them and strangle them and say 'You will love me!' I overcooked the 'Here's me, the solo artist and great entertainer' instead of doing a professional show and letting them make up their own minds.

I must say, though, that subsequent tours with Joe were fun as well as successful. I did the Miss New Zealand tours again in 1966 and '67, and we did country and western tours in those years too. They were very popular, especially in the provinces. Among the artists were Paul Walden, Peter Posa, John Hore, Eddie Low, Gray Bartlett, the Quin Tikis, Jim McNaught, Suzanne Prentice. The C&W tours were great for my morale in that the shows were unpretentious and a lot of fun. There were no star spots — everybody on stage among the hay bales, joining in duets, trios and, at times, choruses with the audience.

It was on one of these tours that I created a skit called *The Mail Must Go Through*. Actually I stole the idea from our compere on the Showtime Spectacular shows, John Daley. What we did was involve the whole cast and, as the tour went on, the skit got crazier. There were arrows and tomato sauce all over the stage — it was chaotic. Some years later the skit proved to be the high spot of the Michael Fowler Theatre opening when I did it with Stu Wilson as the Pony Express rider and Bernie Fraser as the chief of the Blackfeet. As well, we had 17 dancing girls acting out the war whoops of his warriors.

Some of the send-ups among the cast of the C&W shows were a real break-up and often quite spontaneous.

One night our compere, Neil Collins, who did a mime to a record, had the speed changed on him two or three times during the song — from 45rpm we flicked the speed to 78rpm, to 33 and back again. Like a good trouper, Neil managed to cope. The audience thought it was part of the act and screamed with laughter. It was a one-off only. Neil wasn't amused.

There was another one-off, at Eddie Low's expense. He sang the beautiful song *Maria* from *West Side Story*. The opening lines are 'The most beautiful sound I ever heard . . .' The audience were hushed and attentive, when suddenly, before he could sing the next word, 'Maria', over the speakers came the sound of a toilet being flushed. Someone

There was plenty of fun and no superstars on Joe Brown's C&W shows . . . spots ranged from joining Paul Walden and the Quin Tikis, being demoted to halftime ice-cream boy to appearing in full cowboy rig.

(I wonder who?) had put the off-stage microphone down the toilet bowl. This was in Balclutha, where the town hall toilet was conveniently, if you'll excuse the pun, situated close to the stage.

In 1965, my first year on my own, out of the blue came the opportunity to play the part of Kingi, a Maori shearer, in a low budget movie being made in Melbourne called *Funny Things Happen Down Under*. I got into it by accident; the blokes working on the script were a couple of mates of mine. And that movie introduced to Australia a 15-year-old girl named Olivia Newton-John.

I came back and promoted the movie around New Zealand. It was novelty value again; gee, Howard Morrison movie star! Now I'm not saying it was any great shakes as a movie and I'm not saying I was any great shakes as an actor. I don't know whether Marlon Brando saw it, but I don't suppose he'd have lost any sleep. There I was in a black singlet and black pants, like a dinkum shearer — but with Brylcreem through my hair! I can't say I felt natural performing in front of a camera lens rather than an audience.

My acting debut (with not a Brylcreemed hair out of place) in Funny Things Happen Down Under. OPPOSITE: *The Kiwi effort.*   New Zealand Film Archive

3 Stars of PACIFIC FILMS' Movie
"DON'T LET IT GET YOU"
N.Z.'s FIRST COMEDY MUSICAL !!!

★ **KIRI TE KANAWA** ★ **HOWARD MORRISON** ★ **CARMEN DUNCAN** ★

A Pacific Films Production
"DON'T LET IT GET YOU"

starring

Howard Morrison

Carmen Duncan

Garry Wallace

Special Guest Star:

Normie Rowe

Guest Artist:

Kiri te Kanawa

Featuring:

Rim D. Paul

Herma Keil

Lew Pryme

Eliza Keil

Gerry Merito

Eddie Lowe

Gwynn Owen

and

The
QUIN TIKIS
SHOW BAND

with

Harry Lavington

Tanya Binning

Alma Woods

A comedy with hit music,
produced and directed by
John O'Shea. Director of
photography - Anthony
Williams - Associate
producer, Russell Rankin.

Music and lyrics by
Patrick Flynn

and

Joseph Musaphia

Scenario by Joseph Musaphia.

AND THE FIRST SINGLE FROM THIS SPARKLING MOVIE, IS, <u>NOW</u> AVAILABLE,
2 B-I-G NUMBERS FROM HOWARD!!

"HAERE MAI MEANS WELCOME"
together with
"LIVIN' AND LOVIN' "
REMEMBER – IT'S HAERE MAI YEAR !!

However, it was a new experience and a lot of fun. And I was pretty inspired by it. I thought this could be the new direction! I encouraged John O'Shea of Pacific Films to come up with a script for a light-hearted musical comedy of our own, which we called *Don't Let It Get You*. Joe Musaphia wrote the script and we had a guy named Patrick Flynn do the score. He was a key music man in the background of Harry Miller's big musical extravaganzas in Australia; an eccentric guy, but quite brilliant.

Don't Let It Get You introduced to the New Zealand viewing audience all the acts of that time. We brought Normie Rowe in from Australia so we could have a trans-Tasman release, and we had all the local acts — The Keil Isles, Kiri Te Kanawa, the Quin Tikis (with Rim D. Paul, Eddie Low and a very funny guy, Gary Wallace), the late Lew Pryme — whoever was around at that time.

It was a lot of fun, we involved a lot of people, it had a bit of box office appeal . . . but we lost a lot of money. I did, anyway; what seemed like a king's ransom at that time. All the savings I had accrued over the previous years were out the window. I had to borrow from my own family. We weren't always well heeled in the Quartet years; it wasn't like having a regular job with a regular weekly wage. It was either feast or famine. Getting into a regular plan of budgeting and saving was difficult. It was a haphazard way of life, needing a lot of discipline to adjust to the peaks and valleys of life's testing financial ways.

So what did the movie achieve?

It became another benchmark in New Zealand showbiz history. It gave me my first Entertainer of the Year award because I'd done things which other entertainers would probably have loved just to have thought about — but didn't or couldn't do.

As an experience, *Don't Let It Get You* was very enjoyable. As an investment, it was disastrous! But I suppose, along with the Aussie movie, it helped my transition into a solo act. But no more financing movies, thank you.

Out of it, the Quin Tikis and I started our partnership. We did shows in Australia and Tahiti, shows with Joe Brown. Although they were my backing band it was very difficult to keep them in check. They were a talented band but real scene stealers and it was a totally different feel to performing with the Quartet. This was like a non-stop potpourri. The saxophone player picked up the guitar; the drummer would pick up the bass. Eddie Low, who was playing with the Quin Tikis then, played the guitar but he would pick up the trumpet. They were a versatile, talented bunch of guys.

I started to sink more into the group and just do my three or four solo items. This worked for me, because it took the pressure off becoming a soloist after so long as part of a group; the lead singer, but still part

On stage with the 1969 Miss New Zealand entrants.

of a group. On the other hand, in my close involvement with the Quin Tikis, I found myself falling into the same trap; of having support, as I had with the Quartet. It was really defeating what I was trying to go for as a solo act. Other groups I had were also show bands. It was allowing me an escape route.

Then another lucky break came my way in the form of Lada Ourednik. Lada was a successful restaurateur who did very well in Auckland with El Matador before taking over a small restaurant-night club in Sydney called Spellson's. His rationale was that by having me as the first drawcard, I would attract the burgeoning population of New Zealanders in Sydney — plus, of course, all their Aussie mates.

The result was that the club went over like an Irish satellite. However, a luckier break than the other lucky break that was supposed to be a lucky break (are you still with me?) happened during my brief season at Spellson's.

I was singing one night to about three tables of customers and among them was a promoter I knew, named Les Masliah, an Egyptian and a real sharpie. He managed a lot of the Maori groups in Sydney, including the Quin Tikis, and booked them into places in the East. I'd known Les was there to see the show; what I didn't know was that he was virtually giving me a private audition. After the show he approached me, on behalf of the food and beverage manager of the Singapore Inter-continental, to do a season there.

I'd heard offers like that before, and they'd come to nothing. But this time the offer was exactly what it seemed. More. It was, as it turned out, my gateway to the East.

THE SEXY SAVAGE

FOR WHAT WAS totally new ground for me, a completely new challenge, I had only two weeks' notice. And I still had no arrangements to speak of. So a local boy, Dennis Paul, stage name Rim D. Paul, helped me throw some arrangements together so that I at least had a satchel of music with me. I was hoping that I would get over there and strike a band that could ad lib a bit. That's what I was hoping for; it wasn't to be.

When I arrived in Singapore I met the Intercontinental's food and beverage manager, a Brazilian guy named Danny Cortez. The food and beverage manager in these big international hotels is always the entertainment manager as well. He was about the same age as me, was multi-lingual, very much the entrepreneur and we got on well. He wanted to upgrade the entertainment scene in Singapore, make his hotel *the* place for an evening out, for entertainment. He was very forward thinking.

Cortez, at great expense, had brought out a band from Germany. They were hopeless! I think the leader was a refugee from Hitler's SS Youth. I would count in one, two, three, four — he would repeat the numbers after me in German to his band. The rehearsals were less than adequate. There was one good musician, the pianist, but he was an alcoholic, always drunk. The rest of them were very straitlaced and humourless. So I had a real problem on my first international gig.

Initially I'd thought they were going to be too good for me — all the way from Germany! It didn't turn out that way.

They bugged me so much that one night I suggested to the audience that the band didn't smile much because they were once arrested for loitering in front of an audience. The band leader told Cortez that I had to apologise or they would quit. As it was, Cortez was pretty keen to get rid of them. He told me not to apologise and a deal was struck in that Cortez found them work at a Bavarian restaurant and bar in town. A sad epilogue was that the pianist who was always drunk was found murdered and thrown in a Singapore monsoon drain a year later.

I finished my season with the hotel's resident trio, who were not only good readers of music but were flexible enough to follow my ad libs and unrehearsed songs.

This Singapore engagement was the gig I mentioned away back in the Ruatahuna chapter; about how I picked up an Indian accent from the Punjabi shopkeepers in the village and used that in my Singapore act, and about RNZAF personnel being in the audience on my opening night. Those Kiwis really saved my bacon. What with my first-night nerves and my problems with the band, my opening night at the Singapore Intercontinental could have been two shows in one for Howard Morrison — the first and the last! Not only did the air force fellas and their wives join me in entertaining the audience with a bracket of Maori songs, they also helped create an atmosphere not often seen in cabaret in Singapore.

It has been my experience in cabaret in different parts of the world that wherever there is a New Zealand contingent supporting a New Zealand artist, you can always expect the Maori songs to get full-throated support.

The same thing happened when the captain and crew of the frigate *Waikato* turned up to see my show at the Eagle's Nest in the Hong Kong Hilton. New Zealanders are proud advocates of their country outside the three-mile limit. The Maori haka party from the *Waikato* performed on stage with me, stripped to the waist in full regalia . . . well, actually in full light regalia. The Hong Kong matrons were never the same again — perhaps this was the first of the now-popular male stripper revues!

During my opening week in Singapore there was an international conference and I did the floor show part of it. That was when I first met Lee Kuan Yew, who had been in power for eight or nine years, and was making some really radical changes. At a press conference while I was there he told the American Trade Commission Singapore was a free-enterprise country, they were going to develop their nation and Russian roubles and mainland Chinese money were as acceptable as American dollars. At that time it was pretty provocative language to use, saying you'd go to bed trade-wise with the Russians, the Chinese or any communist state.

What's happened in the intervening years? Well, Lee Kuan Yew turned the economy of Singapore right around. He was pretty dictatorial, but successful in economic terms through that attitude of opening up his markets to anyone who wanted to trade. Just think what possibilities for New Zealand's trade could have developed had we copied the same initiatives in the 1960s and '70s.

These are the things I used to look at. I was an inquisitive sort of bugger. When I got this performing offer, I asked if I could go over 10 days beforehand to get a feel of the place. That's when I realised there wasn't any such thing as a Singaporean. Like there's no such person as a Hong Kong-ian! They were all transient, there to make a quid; they were all merchants. And the majority race, Chinese, had arrived as refugees.

So you basically had a non-bigoted audience, notwithstanding that a few probably accepted humour at their expense through gritted teeth; you could poke the borax at anyone and be pretty safe. I took advantage of this to do a fair amount of lighthearted stirring, and it went down well. I hasten to add that I was just as ready to poke fun at myself. In point of fact, I always started that way. It was imperative that I did so other races didn't feel they were being singled out.

This attitude stemmed from knowing how I'd feel if other people came to our country and were disrespectful to our race and culture. I've found the best groups of people who could take a put-down in the spirit it was intended were the Indians and the English. God bless them, for I soon discovered that in the East one had to be very careful of what one said, to whom and where.

So it was another learning curve for Morrison, in terms of being alert to sensitivities no matter what country you were in. The Indians, as I said, were a different story.

One night a Sikh came in after the show had started and walked across the floor I was performing on to get to his table. He had a white turban on, like Sikhs wear, and a blonde on his arm. I was talking, introducing a number, and the audience did a double take to watch this couple. In those days, that was another unusual sight, even in the free-and-easy sixties; a Sikh with a blonde woman on his arm. I wanted to bring the attention back to my corner. So I said, in my Indian accent, 'Good evening, sir, and who shot you in the head?' Everybody cracked up.

The Sikh? Well, he carried on to his table and I said, still in an accent, 'Thank you sir, for being such a good sport about me suggesting your turban was a bandage.'

His reply, across the crowded room, was, 'It's quite all right. I'm in a very good mood tonight because I've just learned, by telegram from Calcutta, that my wife has died of snake bite.' Well! How would you top that one?

Escorting the Queen Mother of Thailand through the hotel after my show at the Siam Intercontinental.

Morrison family collection

We became firm friends. He was a doctor in Bangkok and when I eventually got there we resumed our friendship and remained good friends for eight or ten years before losing touch.

This was the era of Tom Jones and Engelbert Humperdinck. I was ad libbing most of those songs, *Delilah, Please Release Me* and so on. We had good houses every night. As well as the travelling merchants and the local nightlifers there were a lot of people there either directly involved or on the periphery of the Viet Nam War. So I had very good audiences to perform to.

My contract was extended to six weeks, we had good houses all through and my first appearance on the international circuit was a reasonable success.

The money was OK. But in those days, with the novelty of being on my own in one of the glamour merchandising centres of the world, I bought up large. I brought back cases and cases of clothes and toys for the family, without any regard for the fact that we weren't rich. I always spent a lot of money on the family, and I mean the whole family, mothers, sisters, cousins . . . I was a little extravagant, to say the least. So I burned up most of the money I earned, especially that first time. It was the novelty, you see.

I came back to New Zealand and did the Miss New Zealand tour as well as cabaret at Logan Park. Everything was starting to zing along for Howard Morrison, solo performer.

Still near-fanatical about keeping fit, I introduced the family to squash and running . . . I was an entertainer but I made time to do other things I enjoyed. I started playing football again for my local club, in reserve grade, and got a couple of runs in the knockout finals for the A's. I was playing competitive squash, having a good time.

Also at this time I was Howard Morrison, racehorse owner. I acquired from trainer Eric Ropiha a short-term lease of Con Dios, which I named when she was but a yearling. At age three, Con Dios was tuned up and Eric was confident of her winning at the Otaki Maori races.

All the omens were in our favour. Maori owner, Maori trainer, Maori jockey (Herb Rauhihi) — what chance did pakeha owners have in a photo-finish with a Maori judge named Winiata? And a Maori judicial committee in case of any protests! One start, one win, and Morrison was out. Must be a record of some sort — how many owners have had 100 per cent winners to starters?

Probably it was just as well I didn't stay in the racing game because I was still trying to recover from the financial hiding I got doing *Don't Let It Get You*. Fortunately, it wasn't as hard as it might have been because we inherited a freehold house. Before that, like most New Zealanders, we'd had a house with a mortgage on it, out by the Springs. When Kuia's father died he left her the house at Ohinemutu Village and moving there enabled us to sell the other house and cut our losses from the movie. We've been there ever since.

They were still tough years, but I was starting to realise I had to budget better. I'd work at Logan Park for two or three nights a weekend, depending on the bookings, and the money would come in haphazardly. Luckily I had a very good accountant, who made me send him enough money to make sure the tax was paid and other responsibilities met. I used to insist on getting paid by cheque, so there was no temptation of blowing it. I'd send most of it to my accountant, Bob Wright, who I've been with since 1960. He and his wife Julie are on the short list of my closest friends. Bob guided me (more like directed me) to form a company for which he was made secretary. He made the investments, paid the bills, transacted the business and played golf with me — poorly.

So everything was starting to cook again. I was on every local TV show being given an airing; the *Happen Inns*, the *C'Mons* with Peter Sinclair. I did *An Evening with Howard Morrison* which was an absolute disaster; technically, musically and vocally. But it did introduce to New Zealand a guy who came over as a ten-pound assisted immigrant baker. (I don't know whether he was a ten-pound immi-

*On the road in the Showtime Spectacular days with my good mate
Toni Williams.*

At the Hong Kong Hilton with band leader Romy Posades and his vocalist wife Rita.

With the greatest entertainer of them all, Sammy Davis Jnr, at the Sheraton, Waikiki, 1971.

Maori warrior Howard with Joe Brown and Eddie Low.

Director Sigmund Spath lines up Robin Hood . . . Bic Quic in hand.

Looks like it's been a successful day on the Whakatane River for my mate Pera and me.
NZ Woman's Weekly

The dog Tramp and I sharing a quiet moment by the lake a few years back with my sons, Richard (left) and Howard Jnr.
NZ Woman's Weekly

Kuia and I with Howie the dog on the back steps of our Ohinemutu home a dozen or so years ago.

NZ Woman's Weekly

Community services staff gather in the Rotorua offices of the Department of Maori Affairs. From left, behind HM and district officer Harris Martin, are Merle Brightwell, Henry Pryor, Manu Pene, Trevor Maxwell, Peter Kapua and Mita Mohi. In front is my sister Adelaide.

NZ Woman's Weekly

Taking a break during a Top Town show with Roger Gascoigne (left) and Stu Dennison.

Elmer & Ambrose

grant but it makes a better story.) That fellow is a good mate who turned out to be a very talented comedian and impressionist: Chick Littlewood.

An Evening with Howard Morrison, with Desma and friends, Toni Williams and Chick Littlewood didn't do a thing. Television was still in its black and white days, of course. Essentially I was a live enter- tainer, and the budget for New Zealand television shows was hardly immense. I wasn't a stand-up comic, I wasn't a continuity man, I wasn't a quiz master. And there weren't the opportunities to do full- scale shows because there was no budget. So at that time there wasn't too much room on TV for a person like me.

Anyway, I was too involved in live shows, tours of New Zealand and tours of the East. That's when I started singing at Logan Park and then along came the Station Hotel days. The Station became my New Zealand base. I was still fit and energetic, and quite an innocent in terms of rubbing shoulders with the top-shelf boys, the seasoned drinkers. I used to go to Auckland on a Friday and have a session with my Station mates, and I was so fit that alcohol only gave me a buzz and never affected me at all. I got into a routine which I subsequently regretted; an unhappy consequence of a place which I genuinely enjoyed going to.

But all through my life I reckon I've had a lucky leprechaun on my shoulder. Out of the blue, Danny Cortez, the guy who'd made it happen for me at the Singapore Intercontinental, called me and asked if I'd like to do a season in this brand-new Sheraton Hotel in Manila, of which he was now manager. Of course I wanted to. By then, I had my act together as far as music arrangements were concerned.

That Manila gig was awesome. I was following the trio that made the huge hit *Juan Tanamera* and had opened the hotel. On this occasion, the Sheraton was saying farewell to them and hello to me.

Laser beams . . . that's what us musos called Howard when he wasn't happy with us. If you mucked it up behind him, he'd turn around and you'd cop those laser beams from his eyes. He didn't need words. I'd idolised Howard from the Quartet days and I couldn't believe it when he called me in to work with him — I was playing with a local band at the time — in the early 1970s. I've been with him ever since — Singapore, Kuala Lumpur, Hawaii, all over New Zealand . . . What can you say about the man? He's got a world-class voice and he's the ultimate professional. He'll keep the band rehearsing for as late and as long as it takes, until you get it right.

— **Charlie Te Hau**

The cover charge for the night, including food, entertainment and alcohol, was $US500. This is no misprint. $US500 each!

The guest of honour was Imelda Marcos. They had a fountain, over ice, that had a continuous flow of champagne; candelabra with real crystal; no two rooms in this hotel were alike in decor. We're talking about luxury plus. I'd come from the Station Hotel, an ageing New Zealand establishment and the simplicity of a room with no facilities; within a week I'm staying in a suite in this super luxury hotel.

Danny Cortez had a lot of confidence in me. Me? I crapped myself. Here was this black-tie crowd, shelling out 500 bucks apiece; here was the First Lady, Imelda Marcos, and here was the *Juan Tanamera* trio. Their repertoire was all romantic songs; they dedicated an original song to Imelda and gave her a scroll of it. Everyone was in tears . . . and I had to follow that!

I bowled over two large cognacs and went on. Halfway through my first song this nondescript gentleman with glasses and grey hair walked over to the 'top table' and was talking to Imelda Marcos. I had a microphone with a long lead and I walked up beside him. I tapped him on the shoulder and, steeled by the cognac, I said: 'If you haven't got a reservation, will you kindly get out of here? Otherwise sit down.' But not in an unfriendly tone.

Well, he nodded and the crowd erupted. I found out later why the crowd laughed and applauded *after* he nodded. Their laughter was probably mostly relief that he didn't blow his top. He was the most powerful businessman in the whole of the Philippines. With one finger he could have snuffed out the power for Manila City. And Howard Morrison too, for that matter. Just as well he took it the right way.

For the rest of the night I just went up and up and up; everything I did worked and I finished the show on a high. I did so well that when I went back to my room I was in tears, and I dropped to my knees and said thank you to God. That night remains vivid in my memory. Some of the tears I shed were because my family weren't there to see it. I was on my own. But what happened that night established me in Manila. I became the darling of the Mighty Five Hundred in Manila, the 500 known millionaire families.

Danny Cortez had taken a risk on an unknown and had come up trumps. The newspaper review the next day dubbed me 'The Sexy Savage from the South Seas'. I'd been joking about the sexy savages of New Zealand and they attached the name to me. They're romantics, the Filipinos. Instead of saying 'he's tall, dark and handsome' or whatever, they'd say 'he's tall — and he looks like James Garner'. They'd associate you with a movie idol or something they could get a handle on.

Because of the crowd there that night, and the reception they gave me, I was assured of a fantastic season. My four weeks were extended

Guest starring on Philippines television.

Morrison family collection

to six weeks, six weeks extended to two months and finally to three months.

Imelda Marcos often brought a party of followers. I know she was made out to be a Dragon Woman when the regime was overthrown, but I have to say she was great support to me.

I didn't see the ugly side of Manila at first as I never moved about. Everything I needed was in the hotel and the weather was oppressive. I'd just sing hard, live hard, sleep, go to the gymnasium, get ready for the next show. That was my routine. It was hard on the 'pipes'. Although I was doing only one show, it was never less than an hour and a half, sometimes two hours, because the audiences were so good. But in the early stages I saw only the glitz, the celluloid part of Manila. After two months I saw the darker elements of life in the city.

Many Manila men have a philosophy that your wife or your mistress, if she's good enough looking, is open territory . . . but if you're looking at my wife or my mistress the way I think you're looking, I'll have you shot.

One night I got a request to sing *Impossible Dream*. I made a joke of it. I said a world like the world in the song was an impossible world — and anyway I didn't know the song or the words. I added, still making a joke, that I didn't do songs like that unless I got 50 pesos. Then I realised that someone wasn't seeing the funny side, because the request came up with a 50-peso note attached. I responded by saying, 'Look, I really don't know the song but I'll give the 50 pesos to the boys to have a drink on.' When I asked who'd requested it, a guy put his hand up and I said I'd sing something else for him.

After the show, I'm walking off the stage and I'm confronted by three fellas from this table. What was happening was that a lot of wives and girlfriends were bringing their men to see the show, this 'sexy savage' thing, and the men didn't like attention being taken away from them. So while one guy was saying that I'd insulted the table by not singing this song, which I think was just an excuse, another took a king hit at me. In those days, just before martial law, a lot of guys carried guns and checked them in at the cloakroom, like coats and hats, on the way in. You never knew who the hell had one.

Luckily these guys didn't have a revolver or a knife among them, but I found myself fighting three of the buggers. They were getting close to putting me down on my knees, so they could have done some damage with their footwear. Then I felt one go flying off my back, and then another went flying. Nobody helped me from the staff. No one. It took an American GI on leave from Viet Nam to come out of the audience, and we cleaned the three of them up.

Fun time!

I had a godfather there at the time, a guy called Kelly Segovia. He had one of these illegal gambling dens with two big iron doors — you had to use a password to get in. Kelly had met the Maori Hi Five on their way through to the States and he looked after them in Manila. He became their godfather, their patron, and he did the same for me. He was in a tough line of business; he could have people knocked off.

The day after this incident with the three bullies, he brought a fellow round and introduced him to me and said this is your bodyguard, he'll be with you all the time from now on.

'Look,' I said, 'back in New Zealand if we have a fight like that we forget it afterwards. We shake hands and have a drink.'

'I don't care if these people are my relations, my cousins,' he said. 'If they come back here they're dead, unless they come to apologise.'

Later that day the three who'd had a go at me came back and did apologise. The word was out; guys had been asking around who they were. Their spokesman, who was a lawyer, was very frank about telling me that they hadn't realised I was 'under Mr Segovia's protection'.

The funny part about it was that two of them were distinctly the worse for wear with reminders of the previous night on their faces. They came back to the show that night and we had a good old rave after. I never saw the GI again.

There were some bad incidents at that time. Cabarets, which carried signs that said 'check your gun in here', were often the scenes of shootings. A couple of friends of mine came back from Viet Nam and were at a show in town when this guy and his entourage came in. He was a movie actor and a karate expert, Fourth Dan or thereabouts. He wanted this table, not my friends' but one nearby. He said to the host of the group, 'I want this table.'

'This table is ours,' the guy said.

The movie star said, 'Do you know who I am?'

The guy said 'yes', pulled out a revolver and shot the actor. He got off later for self defence because the movie star had his hands registered as dangerous weapons and had made threatening overtures. Wicked, eh!

Imelda Marcos booked me to do a show at the palace — a Command Performance of sorts, with the emphasis on the word 'command'. A year earlier The Beatles (I'm talking about *the* Beatles) had turned

Final exams after the karate lessons I took in Singapore for four weeks a year over eight years. That's three roof tiles on each side these guys are wielding.

Morrison family collection

down an invitation to go and meet the ruling family. This snub did not go down at all well and The Beatles, who were received in Manila by cheering crowds when they arrived, had to sneak off to the airport by taxi, carrying their own bags.

So HM wasn't about to repeat their mistake.

The Command Performance was a daytime gig in a venue that was beyond my ability to describe. It was vulgar indulgence to an unbelievable degree. I put on a good show and, later that evening, myself, the band and the 200 or so especially invited VIPs, were escorted to the royal yacht for an evening cruise in Manila Bay. We moored at that well-known citadel of World War II history, the island of Corregidor.

All this showed me the disparity between the haves and the have-nots, terms not strong enough to describe the immense differences. These people were the ones who were actively engaged in screwing as much as they could for their own financial gain. By contrast, I met a lot of the ordinary, simple and naturally hospitable people of the Philippines and liked them immensely. I was introduced to the other side of the Philippines by members of my backing band, who came from 'ordinary' stock.

Manila was full of music, full of fun, poverty, sadness, violence, unpredictability. But the music side was full of beautiful people. I made a lot of friends among the Filipino musical groups. In all the countries in the East, the groups were nearly always Filipinos. They were so good, so professional.

Because my Manila engagement had gone so much longer than originally planned, Danny Cortez generously offered to fly Kuia and our daughter Donna over for the last month of my engagement. Kelly Segovia took me to the airport to meet Kuia off the plane and we actually met her at the gang-plank. We walked right past security and the other agencies — and he had his slippers on! Kuia almost freaked out when I met her at the gang-plank. What was I doing there?

We went back to Kelly's place to celebrate her arrival. He'd had a huge cake made, about three foot by two foot, with a barrio (village) scene on it, just to honour Kuia's arrival. Balloons with 'Welcome Kuia' filled the room.

Kuia and Donna's arrival was timely. In spite of my shows going well and being feted by the elite, I was getting pretty fed up. Fed up with the crass, over-the-top display of wealth on the one hand and the widespread poverty of the masses on the other.

Towards the end of my stint in Manila I got my next 'Eastern offer'; to sing in Bangkok, at the Hilton. I made it huge in Bangkok. There's no other word for it.

The vice-president of Hilton Hotels South-East Asia, Ken Moss, took in a show and offered me a contract to do the Hilton Hotels right throughout the East. So by the end of '69 I had a circuit. And everywhere I went I was creating attendance records and drawing exceptional reviews.

However, while Howard Morrison Entertainer was making it big in the East, there was a definite downside for Howard Morrison Husband and Father.

When I first went to Manila, my children Donna, Howard and Richard were ten, seven and five. Kuia was still keeping the home fires going. While I was enjoying the novelty of the high life the actuality of day-to-day existence was happening back here. I was in fantasy land. It doesn't fill me with too much pride when I look back and say 'and loving it'.

I used to phone home, write home and send money home but it's not the same. I was accepting engagements and extensions of engagements to further my career without any consultation. I'd just go ahead and do it. That's where I'm fortunate, because when I reflect on those years I realise that those were the times when I should have planned better to spend more time with my children. Even though I took Donna to Hong Kong and Manila, and all the kids on a New Zealand tour, it was still difficult for the two boys. They simply weren't seeing enough of their dad.

That's why I reiterate that Kuia would have to be the most decent and loyal person I have ever met. It's not easy for an attractive young wife and mother with an absentee husband, and at that time she wasn't just languishing at home being a house executive. Her outlet from the kids at that time was playing squash, playing in tournaments and things of that nature. Knowing the squash world as I do — well, it's not confined to squash! — there would have been plenty of guys making sheeps-eyes at her, and no one to run interference for her. Not that she needed anyone with her laser beam stare!

Just the same, keeping house must have been very difficult for her. The rest of her age group, her friends and my sisters and so on, had their husbands at home. They had someone to cook for and be there for; Kuia had the children and one empty chair at the table. I used to come home like the all-conquering hero and I didn't want to hear any bad news. It was like honeymoon time all over again. Let's enjoy the fruits of life and love.

While my lack of attention to the realities of life made it easier for me to concentrate on my shows, it was at a big cost to the family responsibilities that I took for granted. I was definitely selfish.

Things were starting to really open up in the East, and there were opportunities I did turn down.

Two Jewish brothers, millionaire jewellers, saw me in Bangkok and they had an open cheque book. They were going to guarantee me money that was massive by today's standards, let alone the standards of '69–70. They wanted exclusive rights to my services for six months.

They were going to spend the first two months based in Los Angeles, refining me, getting writers in, then four months in which to make it. If we couldn't make it in that four months, then I was out of the contract. Why didn't I at least see what would have happened in six months? Maybe I was afraid of succeeding!

I just wasn't interested. It was the old Harry Miller thing all over again. It would have meant a loss of control, of being able to pick and choose; a loss of a lifestyle that I enjoyed.

What I liked about the East, and why I kept going back, was that if they liked you international status meant nothing to them. I was their man. I had influential people supporting me. Ken Moss was in my corner. He would fly in people from all over the East for my gala appearances. He gave me that sense of status. He didn't treat me simply as an entertainer; he knew I was that already. He said I had strengths in other areas, as a diplomat, as an ambassador. He took me to places like the Hong Kong Jockey Club to introduce me to a section of people who could be good for me — and for his hotel. He was very honest about that.

Moss sent a memo out to every Hilton I appeared in. Here's the modus operandi, here's who you invite. You have a gala opening for Morrison and you will invite these people, this VIP list. The list would start with the Prime Minister or Governor's office and work down. All my gala opening nights were in front of these people. So I'm promoting the hotel, promoting New Zealand, promoting myself.

Did it work? Of course it worked. The OBE I received in 1976 was for services as an entertainer and for promoting the country internationally, mainly in the East.

I've mentioned Singapore, where it all began, and my time in Manila. But right through an eight-year period, from 1968 to 1976 when the disco craze spelt the demise of artists like me, I performed at almost every Hilton in the East. In Kuala Lumpur, Singapore, Manila, Taiwan, Hong Kong and Bangkok.

When I went to Malaysia I presented a 12-pound trout to Tun Abdul Razak, the Prime Minister. This was in 1974, when I was doing New Zealand Food Festival promotions in Kuala Lumpur and Singapore as part of my cabaret season. I'd suggested to the Ministry of Foreign Affairs in Wellington that I present a rainbow trout to the Prime Minister of Malaysia. I still have a letter I received from the Secretary for Foreign Affairs saying that our High Commissioner in Kuala Lumpur felt such a presentation would not be appropriate and 'would not be especially welcomed by Tun Abdul Razak'.

A week after I had settled in at the Kuala Lumpur Hilton, I took the bull by the horns and rang the protocol officer at the Prime Minister's office. I identified myself, of course, adding that I was the nephew of the very first High Commissioner to Malaysia, Sir Charles

Presenting a New Zealand rainbow trout to the Prime Minister of Malaysia, Tun Abdul Razak.

Bennett (a friend of Tun Razak's), and explained my reason for requesting an audience. A meeting with the Prime Minister was arranged for the next day and at that meeting I duly presented the rainbow trout to Tun Razak on behalf of the people of Rotorua. The Prime Minister was delighted and passed on his best wishes through me to Sir Charles. (By the way, the trout was stuffed, and was still on the Prime Minister's office wall in 1986.)

Meanwhile, I'd expanded my horizons to Hawaii after further approaches from Ed Murdoch, a chap I'd met in Bangkok. Ed was an ex-army theatrical booking agent — Viet Nam, Bangkok, Philippines.

Hawaii appealed to me because it was Polynesian and was the epitome of tropical paradise. It was also relatively close to home. My first gig there was at the Outrigger Hotel as a support act to The Reycards, a comic duo from Manila who had made it internationally. It was a good mix, their act and mine. Among the headlines I got there was 'Fresh Breeze from the South Seas'. I created my own market in Hawaii on the backs of these guys and was offered the Sheraton Waikiki, to open a room on the 31st floor called the Hanohano Room — beautiful view, supper club, tuxedo job.

I have to say that it looked on for me in the States. My American contacts had things like the *Johnny Carson Show* lined up, and an opening at the Flamingo in Las Vegas as support act for comedian

Cracking a funny as co-host on the Don Robb Daytime Show *in Hawaii. Our guest is the famous trumpet player and band leader Ray Anthony.*

Jackie Green. The deal was on the table. Don Ho had made it big in Las Vegas and John Rowles was on the boil; Polynesia was in. I had a good opportunity, if I wanted, to take my career further. I'd been given the green light, but I backed away from it.

When I opened the Hanohano Room, Sammy Davis Jnr was the main act in the ballroom. Sammy was the first superstar attraction during the Sheraton Waikiki Hotel's opening celebrations. He was the greatest entertainer I've ever seen in my life, and made me wonder what I was doing in the same business. He was on for two nights. The first night he apologised for his voice not being in top shape. He really didn't have to apologise, because for two and a half hours he took us through a programme that included impressions, tap dancing, playing various musical instruments, an incredible repertoire which showed the man's tremendous versatility.

I had a suite next to his, and had the opportunity of spending some time with him and his entourage off stage. After his show on the second night he invited us all out to a late supper . . . partying on, great fun and frolics. Then, after spending a couple of nights with him, I saw the other side, the cost, of that type of lifestyle. When he eventually went to bed, here was a man who was so lonely and insecure that he had to have his uncle sitting on one side of the bed and his musical director, George Rhodes, on the other. And they couldn't leave before he went to sleep.

Two others I met during the opening-week celebrations were Andy Williams and Glen Campbell. Williams was all class, while Campbell was one of the hottest acts in the world at that time.

Whereas Sammy Davis wanted to be touched in return by as many people as he could, Williams was paranoid about his privacy. All three were surrounded by entourages that would have done justice to royalty. What I saw were examples of artists being consumed by their own popularity and it didn't look attractive to me. I guess I'm justifying the decisions I made in not signing contracts that *may* have tied me to a similar lifestyle. I've never regretted the Quartet not going international in 1962, and I don't anguish about turning down two contract offers I received in 1969 and '71. Had I taken those opportunities, it would have been a complete disregard of my family — and might have been the end of my marriage.

At that stage, I was starting to become more aware of the sacrifices Kuia, in particular, and my children were making. We stayed in Hawaii for six months, I finished my season at the Sheraton Waikiki and we all returned home — no regrets.

Before saying aloha to Hawaii, I should mention that I experienced yet another discipline while I was there — television acting.

On my opening night in Hawaii, one of the promoters who wanted to get me under a management contract was a top DJ in Honolulu. He had a lot of grease, to use the American slang for influence, and brought Jack Lord, alias Steve McGarrett of *Hawaii Five-O*, along to my show. This was some compliment as Jack wasn't known to socialise much. But he and I got on so well he instructed the casting director of *Hawaii Five-O* to get me a part.

I had a read for the casting director and got parts in two episodes — both times as a baddie! It was enjoyable, and frankly I would have loved to have done more. Playing character roles was fascinating.

Jack Lord was *the* boss on *Hawaii Five-O*. What he said was law. There is no doubt that his show was a huge boost for Hawaiian tourism. Lord has since retired in Hawaii. A semi-recluse, he is a well-respected painter and his works sell for megabucks.

Meanwhile, back in the green, green grass of home, the C&W tours with Dennis Brown and residency at the Station Hotel kept me busy and I allowed myself a longer time with the family, especially the kids.

My contract with the Hiltons still continued but I became more and more involved with promotional tasks for New Zealand. It was

enjoyable work. I kept close to the Trade Commissioners and appeared at some of their presentations. I attended cocktail parties and spoke to service clubs. Air New Zealand were promoting me and I promoted New Zealand.

Trade Commission staff and travel agents frequently brought potential customers to my show and used that as another way of promoting New Zealand and its products. I never tired of talking about our country and, as an example, most press interviews which started off inquiring about my life in show biz ended up promoting the virtues of our country — flora, fauna, people and culture. Back in New Zealand I was starting to make some noises through the press about the opportunities to expand our promotions in the East for primary products and our country as a tourist destination.

That year, 1971, I was also headline artist with the 'C'mon to New Zealand' promotion aimed at boosting travel from Australia. A couple of years later, I headlined the 'New Zealand Showcase' performance for delegates to the International Association of Air Transport Authorities world conference held in Auckland.

Somebody must have been listening. I have been involved with members of my family in assisting the promotion of our country in the East and North America at least once a year ever since that time.

With Jack Lord, alias Steve McGarrett, on the set of Hawaii Five-O.

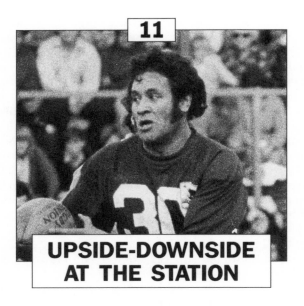

11

UPSIDE-DOWNSIDE
AT THE STATION

FROM ABOUT 1965 to '68, most of my cabaret work in New Zealand was at Logan Park, for Bob Sell. Bob is worth special mention because he set the standard for night life in Auckland. You could say Bob played a big role in changing the way Aucklanders dined out, in introducing some sophistication to the scene. Out of the Cold Duck era into Black Label Lanson. He had a beautiful restaurant, the La Boheme; he had The Colony; he designed the restaurant cum showplace for Logan Park. Another nitespot for Bob, one I opened, was on the North Shore called The Knight Club. Funny, that — a bit premature! Logan Park was a beautiful cabaret and I played seasons there, Fridays and Saturdays. They were always jam-packed.

As an alternative, Tom Madgwick and Bob Wynyard, proprietors of the Station Hotel, decided they wanted to open up their dining room to have cabarets on Fridays and Saturdays also; Tommo's place. When I was approached to open it, I thought it was a little below my dignity to go from the plush decor that Bob Sell had created at Logan Park to a hotel dining room, as it were, at the Station. It proved, of course, to be a different market. This was the time when the 'Howie' tag started. I'd never been Howie before that; it was always Howard.

I remember those early days, or nights, at the Station vividly because the band was led by Morrin Cooper, subsequently Mayor of

Howick. A friendship began, through music, that has stood the test of time.

The Station was good in that it enabled me to spend most of the week at home. Fridays and Saturdays I'd be in Auckland and when I wasn't at the Station, also known as Harbour Lights, I was at Logan Park. Then Bob Sell's time at Logan Park expired, so to speak, he moved on to other things and I became more or less the exclusive property of Harbour Lights.

After Morrin Cooper, we brought in some new blood. Lee Grant, the actress, was one of the first singers there; Bridget Allen, a good friend of mine and a great jazz and blues singer; my pal Ray Woolf was a regular front man for a time. The band was led by a young pianist who became one of Australasia's top musician-composers, Mike Harvey. Playing the drums was Vic Williams, now a culinary and wine expert on television.

Performing in Tommo's Place at the Station Hotel, 1970, with the Billy Peters Band.
Rykenberg Photography

What the Station offered was regular weekend work when I came back from tours to the East, or from internal tours with Joe and Dennis Brown. It was a good mix. The downside was that I was in a hard school there; I mean seasoned, experienced drinkers. Remembering that I didn't have my first drink until the Quartet broke up, it was still novelty time for me. I'd flip up to Auckland on the Friday afternoon, have a few voddies and tonic, tell a few stories and a lot of lies with the gang in Uncle Tom's Cabin. I made a lot of friends.

'Characters' abounded in the Uncle Tom's Cabin crowd. Uncle Tom himself, Tom Madgwick, became almost a second father to me. He used to call me 'son'. Bob Wynyard and I didn't hit it off all that well initially, but we became firm friends. Tom was a publican of the old school, the pioneer New Zealand hotelier. He'd sit on his stool at the corner of the bar and there wasn't much he missed. He'd been a hard man in his day, like any publican has to be, but he had the traditional heart of gold. And I mean heart of gold.

I enjoyed the Station life, mixing with my pakeha elders as it were, and seeing a side of life that was new to me. But the truth is that I began drinking too much — and I was an amateur drinking amongst the professionals. I started smoking at that time, too. After all the discipline I'd imposed on myself, it was almost as if I'd tossed it all out the window . . . party time!

So while the old Station Hotel was a part of my life, and I value the friendships I made there, it wasn't a time that I can recall with great pride professionally. Some of my performances, some of my behaviour, I can't dwell on with great pride. But it *was* a part of my life story.

The Station scene enabled me to expose an approachable side of my personality. Conversely, through sometimes excessive drinking, I compromised my professional standards at times; put on some self-indulgent shows when I was performing to my mates instead of to the paying customers. The upside was the many friendships I made. The downside was not the influence of the place but the fact that it exposed an achilles heel in me — over-indulgence. Nothing by halves!

The hotel was the headquarters of the Auckland rugby team, and I made friendships among the rugby guys which have lasted. The Alby Pryors and Pat Walshes; and Bert Mackie, who introduced live music to the taverns when he had the Thunderbird on the North Shore.

The Station Hotel provided a platform for some of the greatest mental and spiritual challenges I've had to face. I was at a stage where I could have gone right off the rails. There were enough warning signals around as to where that road could take me. Everybody needs a bit of help in recognising when a pleasure has become a problem. I will always be grateful to Bob Wynyard and Tom Madgwick for taking me aside and gently but firmly advising me to pull my socks up.

Over the years, Bob and I have been extremely close. He introduced me into the Carbine Club of New Zealand, an organisation which came to play a big part in my life. In fact, as this book went to press I was the current president. You've never heard of the Carbine Club? Well, it's not a secret society and, while it is fairly exclusive, that's because of the strict limitation on membership numbers. Basically those members are people who share common interests of friendship and sporting involvement, and our half-dozen luncheons each year are associated with a major national or international sporting event.

The club takes its name from the great New Zealand-bred race-horse and sire of that name and it was formed 10 years after the original Carbine Club of Melbourne. Bob Wynyard was one of the founders of the New Zealand Carbine Club, back in 1971. Members of the club were later very helpful in promoting my endeavours in the Tu Tangata programme. They were right behind different fund-raising efforts of mine and, with Sir Denis Blundell as patron, the club was an active participant and contributor to a kohanga reo and homework centre in Maketu, on the Coast. Major contributions were also made towards the now-completed whakaturia community centre in Ohinemutu, 50 yards from my home.

In all, the club has helped me raise over $100,000 for various charities and we did it in a fun way.

The fun way was the Howard Morrison Celebrity Golf Classics. Over the years, those celebrities have included Beefy Botham and other English and New Zealand cricketers, plus luminaries from show biz and the world of politics; the KZ7 team; All Blacks. One year we even had the great country and western singing star Charlie Pride, a single handicap golfer.

Sir Denis and Lady Blundell became very close to the Morrison clan, partly as a result of all these joint endeavours. Make no mistake, the Carbine Club opened a lot of corporate doors for me in terms of supporting my Tu Tangata programme. And, of course, I would never have become involved with the Carbine Club if it hadn't been for Bob Wynyard. In him I found a very strong and effective ally and together we were a formidable team. I was an ideas man but Bob made sure the i's were dotted and the t's were crossed. He is one of the most organised men I have ever met.

The fun-time celebrity golf classics brought me back to the extended family fold in recreation and social spinoffs, more especially with cousin Terry and the old gang, Roger Solomon, Tai Tito and others. Terry and I organised all of the golf tournaments and my personal golf handicap improved from intermediate to senior in a short time.

Another off-stage fund-raising activity in which Bob Wynyard was involved with me was two celebrity rugby games for the Crippled Children around 1970. The first was at Taihape, organised by former All Black Arthur Jennings. Arthur's team came from the central districts

Risking life and limb for charity . . . in action at Waitemata Park for the Howard Morrison All Stars.

and included a number of representative players. The Howard Morrison All Stars was put together for me by Ivan Sapich, a former Auckland rep. It included John Hart, Adrian Clark, 1956 All Black Bill Gray, Gary Inglis and a heap of Dally mates from the Waitemata club.

The match attracted a huge turnout, a bigger crowd than the Fijians had at the same ground the year before. The second match was held at Waitemata Park, where we gave Jack Gleeson's Evergreens their first defeat in years. My All Star team created a bit of history for HM. Here was I, captaining a team with two former All Black captains on my side — Wilson Whineray and the great Pinetree Meads. Again the game attracted a huge crowd and was even shown on television news that night. A lot of bucks were raised for the Crippled Children.

So while my dad's judgment that I would become a better singer than a footballer was right, I reckon I did pretty well as a singer to captain a team containing two former All Black captains! I haven't played rugby since, but my celebrity golf classics still continue as fund-raisers for various causes, Child Cancer, Crippled Children and Life Education being the most recent.

All of these things came about during or as a result of my Station Hotel days and associations.

So it was a good port, the Station, to be able to relax from the pressures of entertaining . . . seriously! I don't think I let my audiences down but I guess I put on some pretty self-indulgent shows. Half the audience were my mates, and the other half were usually three-parts to the wind. I probably sounded better to them than if they'd heard me stone cold sober in a theatre!

It was a great era for cabaret and live music in the early '70s. People were starting to go out more; they were drinking better wines. We were becoming a little more sophisticated about how we wanted to spend our disposable dollar. The country seemed affluent. I didn't see any unemployment around. But then again, I had narrow vision in those days. I could only see the world I was involved in.

At the beginning of 1974 I had another opportunity to perform before the Queen and the Duke of Edinburgh. A friend and a much-admired producer, Dicky Johnston, had been commissioned by the Internal Affairs Department to put on a monumental extravaganza in honour of the Queen and the Duke's attendance at the Waitangi Day commemorations. In those days it was celebrations. This was also to mark the change from Waitangi Day to New Zealand Day, an initiative taken by Norman Kirk.

A monumental extravaganza it was. I think in terms of dollars and cents spent, even by today's standards, it would have been extravagant. The cast was going to be thousands and the whole concept Dick envisaged was a coming together of us as a nation. It would start with the discovery of New Zealand by Kupe (played by HM), the dispersal of the tribes, the coming of the first land agents — the missionaries! — and then seguing (there's a good muso's word) into the arrival of other immigrants. The birth of a nation. Dicky Johnston received an MBE for that effort.

An interesting spinoff was that this was the first overseas trip by a young bride, Princess Anne, and her husband, Mark Phillips, whom we met on the royal yacht, *Britannia*. A quite unremarkable couple, I thought. What was remarkable was the reception we had on the *Britannia*. Everything was so precise. The Queen comes out; cocktails, mingling with people. Later her own band plays *God Save The Queen*. The lights dim, you look around — and she's gone. Time to exit. That's theatre.

I guess Howard Morrison was unlucky that I wasn't an All Black selector in the early 1970s; the form he showed in the charity games at Taihape and Waitemata Park would have meant he was a certainty — if you were looking for a particular sort of player!

I was fortunate enough to play inside Howard — I was halfback and he was second-five. By fortunate, I mean that I was that far away from him he didn't really affect my game.

He was quite a dominating influence on the field . . . then again, he has always wanted to dominate — generally with his voice — and that was the best part of his game in Taihape!

He had very quick hands. So quick we never used them. The miss-pass, which has become a tradition of New Zealand rugby, really gained notoriety at Taihape in 1971.

Adrian Clarke, that brilliant first-five, quickly worked out the only chance we had was to keep Morrison out of the game. And that we did! I remember at one stage we even tried a double miss — halfback to centre direct — but on this occasion Howard's hands got in the road — but, as to be expected, let him down.

I remember the Taihape excursion really well . . . driving down after club rugby on the Saturday in the company of Gary Inglis, Peter Murdoch and Wally Jelicich, staying overnight at the Taihape Hotel, getting to bed at about four in the morning (ideal pre-match preparation!), scheduled to come home on the Sunday night but being talked into staying by Howard. He would take us fishing the next morning, and where he would take us you "didn't need rods, the fish would jump into the boat". We were well equipped (I can still recall at 6 o'clock in the morning Wally Jelicich in barefeet, frost bitten).

I'm sure we did catch a few fish, but it was Monday night before we got home! We were 24 hours late, we had all missed a day's work . . . and Peter Murdoch and Gary Inglis had nearly missed their marriages!

(I never could understand women — after all, we were only 24 hours late; it's very difficult to ring from Lake Rotoaira.)

Thanks, Howard, for a great game. More importantly, thanks for the fishing; and, more importantly again, thank God for your singing ability!　　　　　　　　— **John Hart**

All through my professional life I've always had a major event every five to seven years that sort of catapults me back into the public focus. This time I didn't have to wait the 'five to seven'.

In August 1975 I turned 40. I was working the Miss New Zealand circuit and Dennis Brown had this idea. He said to me: 'Why don't we have a birthday party for you? Why don't we have a reunion of the Quartet for that birthday party? And why don't we put it on at the Christchurch Town Hall?

Why Christchurch, you ask? Well, it has always been my favourite and best show town, that's why!

That loyalty aspect, how the boys were very loyal to me through all those Quartet years, was proven more than 10 years after we broke up. I made three phone calls to Australia, where Gerry, Noel and Wi were all based at the time, and received the same reply each time. Asked if they'd like to come back for this one-off reunion show, with no guarantee of how much but with air fares paid, the unanimous response was, 'Cher! We're over there!'

The show was booked out in advance, not once but twice, with the rest of New Zealand screaming out why wasn't there going to be a reunion tour, covering the other centres. Thinking greedily, Midas-wise for money, this would have been a great coup. So what started out as a birthday celebration ended up as two shows at the Christchurch Town Hall. It was billed as *Return Of A Legend*.

What brought the 1974–75 years together, was that I dedicated the show not only to the Quartet's reunion, but to the memory of my brother Laurie. With that in mind, no expense spared, I took the whole family down to Christchurch. It was a reunion of more than just the Quartet. It included the people who came to the show, because they were the extended family. I remember that when I came on stage, and the applause stilled as the audience waited for the first notes, a lone voice yelled out: 'Happy Birthday!' And from then on the show just zinged along.

We didn't give in to the temptation, and the demand, to make that reunion show a continuing tour. We'd planned it as a 'one off' and we kept it that way. We stuck to the original purpose: to get together for a celebration and a commemoration. And that's what it was. The Quartet came together, put on a show — two shows — full of memories and emotion and warmth, and the next day the boys flew out again to Australia.

Directed by David McPhail, the two shows were taped for television. David and his crew did a tremendous job, considering they had no script to work from. The two shows were edited and a one-hour special was to be shown at a later date. Two days before that later date arrived, some television wheel-nut erased the tape. The only remaining evidence of that show is some rough footage not used on the original

I shared Howard's griefs, as close mates do. Grief at his father's early death (my dad Tupara became his dad) and grief when his brother Laurie died, also far too early. It was me Howard called the night Laurie died. I drove him to Whakatane to bring the body home. At the graveside, the group sang *Three Steps To Heaven*, which was Laurie's song. Hitting and holding the notes was the hardest thing I ever did — any of us ever did. And everyone burst into tears.   — **John Morrison**

master, which was shown in 1991 on the series *When The Haka Became The Boogie*. Sigh . . . to me it's typical of opportunities lost for Morrison on television.

The years 1974 and '75 were marked by tragedy, the death of my brother, and by highlights of the 'life goes on' theme. Yet towards the end of 1975, I went through a period when I was starting to lose direction again. Confusion prevailed as to what I really wanted to do with myself.

After the reunion concert, the rest of the year was like a letdown. I started to regret the decision not to have made the concert a reunion tour. Sure, there was work I could have orchestrated here in this country. But my enthusiasm was blunted and the thought of going back on the road with a cast I'd have to put together, after the tremendous impact the reunion concert had had, well . . . the thought of doing less than that standard wasn't very inspiring.

I started to have thoughts like: What do I really want to do with the rest of my life? It would be true to say that my mind and my moods were in turmoil. The fun had gone out of this 'no business like show business'. It had become too much of a chore.

My brother Laurie had tragically died in a car accident the year before. Memories kept coming back of how we were in those early years, barnstorming around the place having a lot of fun with music . . . Up until then I'd been too busy to reminisce but now, running into my mates Tai Eru and John and Terry Morrison, I seemed to have developed a penchant for wanting to chew the fat about those early days. When we were fearless, when we were optimistic and, even though we didn't have much, we were exceedingly happy and in love with life. If you want to talk all the time about how much fun we had in the past, it suggests that maybe the fun has gone out of the present.

There could have been a deep-seated malaise in that I'd been an entertainer now for so long that inside the entertainer was a person trying to get out — screaming to get out. I can remember wanting to be taken more seriously, to be recognised as having strengths other than entertaining. I'd developed an aloofness which was unfair on the artists and other people who toured with me. At the least provocation I could be abrasive and unpredictable. Now's probably a good time to apologise, not only to those artists I gave a hard time but to any people I disappointed at that stage in my life.

Though I had friends, close friends, I lacked someone to bounce things off. There was no window to my soul and the chip on my shoulder was fast growing into a kauri stump. This period of irrational behaviour was mainly confined to the 'inner circle'. Maybe I was going through an early mid-life crisis! After all, I'd just turned 40. I had great confidence in the way people reacted to me in entertainment and diplomatic circles, which I'd proven for a long time in the East. I actually fancied myself as being a future High Commissioner with an overseas posting. I believed that I could do a very good job. To summarise, I guess, there seemed no more challenges in entertainment. I didn't want to go through the rest of my life being regarded as just a singer of songs and 'jolly good company'. I was ready to do something else; possibly in the public service without being a public servant, and have my singing as a second job. As it turned out, that's the way it ended up in 1978.

So my instincts in 1975, even though I could not put my finger on where the opportunities were or the directions I wanted to take, were right.

In September and October of 1975, I organised another sojourn with hotels in Singapore, Kuala Lumpur and Bangkok. For the Kuala Lumpur part of that journey I had Uncle Tom Madgwick with me. He wanted a trip away and it was nice to have someone like Tom there to actually see how I went in the places I'd spoken about over the years. In Bangkok I took my favourite uncle (by blood this time), Tupara Morrison. What a hit he turned out to be! After a few days all the staff in these international hotels were calling him uncle.

Having Uncle Tupara with me on this overseas trip was not only good for him, it was even better for me. He was amazed at the reception, and the standing, that I enjoyed in the East. His pride made me even prouder, made me stand taller, and together we had the time of our lives!

I finished the engagement in Bangkok and then Uncle Tupara and I came back to New Zealand through Singapore. It was there, while I was doing my final season, that I received a call from the New Zealand High Commissioner's office saying that a diplomatic chappie wanted to come round to see me and could he make an appointment. I said he could come around any time and half an hour later I was presented with an official letter from the Governor-General's office in New Zealand asking me if I would accept the Order of the British Empire. There were no guarantees, of course, but would I accept it? And I was to give my reply to the secretary for the High Commissioner. Which

Proudly wearing the insignia of the OBE, awarded in 1976. NZ Herald

was, of course, in the affirmative.

I didn't tell my uncle this news. I was certainly more appreciative of everything that was going on around me than I had been six months previously. Oh yes, that obnoxious, abrasive personality of a few months ago was now just a complete stranger in my memory banks!

It was coming up to Christmas when I returned to New Zealand, I was booked to do shows in Queenstown, a working holiday gig for Bert Mackie, Roger Solomon, Kuia and myself. While we were there the New Year's Honours list was announced and I was made an OBE. The Morrison clan went wild with joy — an OBE in the family to go with cousin Ruia Morrison's MBE, awarded for her services and success in tennis. (My mother subsequently brought more honour to the family when she was awarded the QSM.)

12

GIVING SOMETHING BACK

I THOUGHT THE OBE was going to be a turning point in my life; I had a responsibility to live up to. I didn't quite appreciate what it meant. I felt more important but it didn't make me suddenly more important, more in demand. It's like being awarded Entertainer of the Year, which I was in 1966. It's nice to be honoured, but tomorrow's a new day. You've still got to get out and hustle.

So really I didn't know what was expected of me. What I did feel, more and more strongly, was the challenge to give something back to society and, more especially, to my people. I looked at the position of Maoridom in society and to me it was sad. The Maori face was showing up in the gangs, in institutions, in unemployment, in under-achieving in schools.

In entertainment, I felt I'd achieved much more than I could have hoped for — I didn't have any more mountains to climb. I was fairly comfortable with my achievements in show business; now was the time to give something back to the people. They were idealistic thoughts, and at that time I was full of idealism. I knew I had something to offer my people, and New Zealand society, outside of show business. It's all very well to make grand statements about our social problems; I wanted to put my money where my mouth was and do something.

So come 1977, there was the announcement of a new Secretary of

Maori Affairs, Kara Puketapu, the first Maori appointed to the position. He was a hatchet man. He'd cleaned out New Zealand House in London, he'd worked for State Services; so he knew the system very well, he knew bureaucracy. And he was very strong on his Maori side because he was chosen by his own people to be a leader. He fulfilled that by becoming Secretary of Maori Affairs.

Kara came out with a statement of policy: he would address education, social services and youth development as key areas. It was just the spur that I needed.

While idealism and civic responsibility might have begun to stir in me, I was still no paragon of virtue. At this time show business was going through some tight times. The cost of putting on the big tours was almost prohibitive and TV was affecting live entertainment. It was virtually turning full circle back to weekend work for entertainers. I still had a fair.amount of cabaret work, including the Ace of Clubs in Auckland for Phil Warren. The Ace was the home of the inimitable Marcus Craig, alias Diamond Lil. Doing a season with Lil and Doug Aston was cabaret in vaudeville; everything over the top. But what an enjoyable hoot, performing at the Ace with a performer's performer. There's no one quite like Diamond Lil.

After a show at the Ace of Clubs one night, I'd had two or six drinks because I'd been driven over from my Takapuna base, the Mon Desir, and had no intention of driving myself. But I deemed that the group of people who'd brought me over from the Mon weren't sober enough to drive back. Guess where their car was parked. Up at the Auckland City Council, right outside the Transport Department office. There were cops around, checking this and that, and Morrison says: 'I'll drive.'

I backed up and hit the kerb.

A guy yelled out: 'Hey!'

I wound down the window. 'Yes, officer?'

'You just hit the kerb!'

'Well, it's not marked. You can't see it.' Very chirpy; I was in complete command of my faculties.

Would you blow in this bag, sir? Certainly, sir!

Half an hour later I was having a blood test. That was an indication of misjudging the fine line between social drinking and what the law requires. It's the sort of thing that has happened to a lot of male Kiwis, including plenty of mates of mine. Excuses aside, what is clear to me is that a lot of virtues can become vices when practised to excess. I felt real shame and disgrace. My state of mind went back to the depression I'd wrestled with in late 1975. So when I read Kara Puketapu's statement of philosophies and directions, I felt a surge of excitement. I could see a possible new direction for me.

Next door to my house lived a respected rangatira called John

Rangiihau. John happened to be one of the people Kara Puketapu had approached for some counsel, guidance and support. John was doing tutorial work for the Waikato University and it was a smart move by Puketapu to bring him on board. John was very well respected by all tribes and was a superb orator in both languages. I say was, because we lost John. He died, in his own house, in 1987.

I had a chat to John and said that I was very interested in the youth development side of Puketapu's philosophy. He said that I would be very valuable; he gave me more than just encouragement and became a strong advocate for me. I'd told John that I had strong feelings for many years to eventually do something 'on the coal face'. It was a commitment I'd made to my father and also to my uncle, Dad's eldest brother, that eventually I would come back and do all I could for and with our people. So John Rangiihau set up an appointment for me with Kara Puketapu at a hui in Rotorua, part of a tour Puketapu and his head office team were making to explain the new direction the department was taking.

My brother-in-law Trevor Maxwell and I had a meeting with Kara. He didn't give too much away but he was quietly thrilled as it turned out. And the long and short of it was that, with State Services approval, he appointed me as a consultant in the youth development area. Appointing someone as a consultant was a safe way to go. Then, it meant 'You're on trial'. In the 1990s, a consultant is a guy who borrows your watch then tells you the time.

Anyway, I was on trial and Trevor was to join my team. We were to work with the local office in Rotorua to set up a youth development programme.

How's this for a coincidence? The day that Kara Puketapu announced that I was to join the Department of Maori Affairs was the same day that I went to court and was reported in the *Auckland Star:* 'Howard Leslie Morrison, drink-drive charge'. The new Howard and the old! I started the job and I was immobilised; I couldn't drive.

The announcement of my appointment drew heavy media attention; the editorials were complimentary and supportive. But I was careful not to try to answer questions I wasn't qualified to answer. To help me to glean ideas about what direction I should take in terms of youth development and what the problems were with Maori kids in education, I talked to my cousin John, a teacher at Rotorua Boys' High School. He and his brother-in-law, Dave Dorset, were able to obtain for me the statistics of achievement and non-achievement; the statistics about Maori school leavers. What a revelation! We'd suspected it was bad; we hadn't realised it was a disaster area.

After looking at the figures for Rotorua, I obtained the stats for all 21 secondary schools in the Waiariki district, from Tokoroa, across to Taupo, down to Te Kaha, including Whakatane and Opotiki, across to

> A lot of people think that Howard's social involvement in more recent years, his work with kids and towards the advancement of his people, is a part of his maturing. But to me it has always been there. Religion has always been an important part of his life, despite the way the times were when we started our careers, and he has always been deeply family oriented. He used to tread more softly on social and cultural issues but I saw it coming a long way off.
> — **Gerry Merito**

Te Puke, and all the schools in Rotorua. Statistics available in 1978 showed the rate of Maori pupils leaving school without qualifications averaged 77 per cent! We had the evidence of the problem, the extent of what we were looking at. After the Shock! Horror! the question remained of what to do about it? These statistics, obviously, were faceless. There were young people out there who were streaming out of the schools with no skills, adding to the unemployment list and in some cases presenting ready candidates for gangs, which were starting to reach frightening proportions in terms of numbers.

Trevor Maxwell and I sat down with the district community officer Powhare Te Maipi, in charge of community services in Rotorua, and worked out a strategy. Very simply, it was to go into the schools and interview school leavers (first, because that's where the immediate problem was) to ascertain where we could help them as a department, through grants, through our vocational training programme, or through encouraging them to stay at school. That information was filtering through the guidance counsellors in the schools, but the Maori kids were not fronting up to the guidance counsellors. We wanted to approach the kids directly.

Well, the resistance we met in the schools as up went the cry of 'separatism'.

I said to the critics: 'Separatism is already there. In your own statistics it says: scholastic achievements — Maori, non-Maori. Maoris have already been separated from the rest. How can we be anything other than helpful, when we're bringing you something for nothing? Bringing the resources from the community staff in our office, bringing in people like the Maori Women's Welfare League and other resource people out there, to talk to these kids on a one-to-one basis? To see how we can help.'

Some of the principals were in favour, some weren't. The first reaction from the schools when they heard I wanted to visit was: Crikey, Howard Morrison! We'll have him here to sing a few songs and generally amuse us — and get him for nothing . . . then they heard the type of things that I was saying. Without any fear or favour, I was saying to the Maori kids that they had to do better, that they had to support themselves better, that we wanted them to hold their heads up high, that we recognised that we (not just them, but the entire race) had a problem and had to address it.

To try to cut down this resistance to using the Waiariki district as a 'test area', through John Morrison we went to see the then senior inspector of secondary schools for the area, Noel Scott, subsequently the Member of Parliament for Tokoroa. Noel had Kara and myself as guests to a Waiariki district secondary school principals' conference in Rotorua. I'd had a talk to Noel beforehand and he put me through the grinder as I explained what we wanted to do. After knocking some of the rough edges off our strategy, and curbing my thunder-in-one-hand and lightning-in-the-other attitude, he could see that the resources we had were going to be valuable. He asked the principals to co-operate.

Though reservations were still there, we now had entree to Waiariki district schools. Kara Puketapu and the newly appointed Director of Youth Development, Wishy Jarram, Powhare Te Maipi and his community services staff in Rotorua all worked together and formed a task force. This also brought in Maori resource people from the community. There were volunteers from Maori wardens, Maori Women's Welfare League, Maori Women's Health League and elders.

A Tu Tangata school visit. It looks like I've found the funny bone of these Kawerau College kids.   Morrison family collection

It was quite a sight. We would turn up at some of the schools with an entourage of 20–25 people. My job was to address the whole assembly and that's when I brought my show biz talents to bear. At that time, even though I wasn't on the hit parade, the kids certainly knew me from my 'Bic Quic' ads. The power of TV!

I felt the best way to get their attention was to do the things I knew best. So I sang, and I introduced some of my task force people. These included Irirangi Tiakiawa, who had been brought on to assist me in my work, and a chap named Peter Kahukiwa who was an ex-president of the 'Filthy Few' gang. My nephew Temuera, already prominent as an actor, and my future son-in-law Anaru Grant were also members of our team. Mita Mohi also came up from Christchurch to join our team.

We'd put on a show for the kids and I was the connecting link. All through it, even though we had a lot of fun, was the blunt message — Maori could say it to Maori — that we all had to do better at school. I gave a chronology of what I went through at the same age; how I left school without School Certificate and how hard I had to try to achieve the goals I'd set for myself. I talked about the cultural difficulties I went through and about not having sufficient qualifications for a decent job.

And the crunch for the kids was when I told them that when I was touring with the Quartet in the early years, I realised I needed to improve my education. I told them I did this by taking correspondence courses in things I was interested in — history, geography and English. I explained to the young people that as an entertainer you didn't just get up and sing songs. You had to be believable; you had to be articulate; you had to sound intelligent. The feedback from the pupils showed that they had got the message loud and clear — success comes from hard graft and dedication.

To add further relish to our programme of entertainment, plus the challenge of putting it in their hands as far as achievement was concerned, Irirangi Tiakiawa explained martial arts Maori-style with the taiaha and the patu. He was a master with both weapons and would explain the meaning of them, the use of them and how long it took to learn to use the weapons correctly. Young Temuera played his student and they went through a series of moves which left the whole assembly entranced. And you could see it instilled a lot of pride in the Maori kids, boys and girls. You could feel the vibes. Hey, this is *our* culture!

The icing on the cake came when I introduced Peter Kahukiwa. He was a fine-looking young man, but when he told them who he was, ex-president of the 'Filthy Few', there were gasps. To a lot of the young Maori kids, Peter was a cult figure. He'd hammer home the essence of why he was with my team. The message was: 'If we'd had this programme to assist people like me when I was at school, there's a good chance that I wouldn't have gone off the rails.' He was very open in saying to them: 'If you kids want to stuff up your lives, go ahead and do it. But I've been there and done that, and I like the way I'm feeling now, trying to tell you kids that there is a better way.'

Before we went to the schools, we gave out papers so the pupils who wanted to be interviewed could give their names, their parents, their tribal affiliation, where they were living and their career hopes. On average about a third would be filled in before we got to the school but after our presentation, our 'show', they all stood in queues to be interviewed. They weren't worried which particular person they spoke to. The vibes we were getting back was that they were rapt to have the opportunity of talking to somebody about how they felt, about school and about where their lives were at that time.

All this was hard work, and it would not have succeeded without the cooperation of the schools and their staff. We were arriving at

Chatting with pupils at Kawerau College during a Tu Tangata school visit.

Morrison family collection

school at 9am, going right through the day, having lunch with the staff and re-evaluating after school finished at 3pm. Sometimes we wouldn't get out until five and six o'clock.

We all became totally involved in the evaluations. We matched what the young people were telling us with what the teachers were saying about their pupils. Sometimes they were in conflict; sometimes it was of assistance to us because the teachers were able to steady us up in not believing all that we were told. But the exercise proved to be a success. After our interviews, we went back, sat down to correlate our information and agree on what the follow-up should be. We'd either endorse some of the aspirations that the school leavers already had or offer options with programmes that we had.

Some of the trickier ones involved the 'problem child' — which invariably meant we found a problem family. This is where the caring teachers at school were helpful. They could see the behavioural patterns of the child and they knew them better than we did. What they couldn't do, especially the pakeha teachers, was to follow up some of the pupils they felt were badly at risk by visiting their homes. The parents would have told them to go jump in the lake — to put it mildly. This didn't apply to us, because we were extended family. We went to the parents to talk about their children and where they could help. Our people who followed up into the homes did a tremendous job and they are among those unsung heroes of society; giving their time out of love, out of aroha.

We hammered students in third and fourth form to stay at school, those in fifth and sixth form to be looking at career options or tertiary training. People like Peter Kahukiwa were invaluable in telling them there was no shortcut; that the shortcut of leaving school early was a tightrope out into the open world and if they fell off they'd be statistics of the worst kind.

The formula we used meant asking the community services sections of all our departments throughout New Zealand to visit all the schools in the first term, do follow ups in the second term and again, where required, in the third term. In the first term of 1978, we used the Waiariki district as a test area and brought all the community services senior staff from other district offices to Waiariki to see how the recipe worked. Once we were on a roll everyone became very enthusiastic, especially the people from the other districts. My team had to be extended.

On a national basis, I was also getting assistance from other paragons of the intelligentsia in Don Selwyn, Selwyn Muru, Pita Sharples and Alby Williams, the huge, articulate, overweight but lovable manager of the South Auckland office at Wiri.

Our programme set out to put faces on the statistics. Once we established the formula in the Waiariki district, I took my team on the road to assist the other district officers. Support came from Kara Puketapu and head office as we had a programme that supported their aims and objectives. All the vibes were positive and we knew we had a winning formula.

One of the first districts we visited outside Waiariki was Wellington and the newspapers were now interviewing Morrison in a totally different light. From the front page of the *Evening Post:* Howard Morrison claims that the national average of Maori pupils leaving school without any qualifications is as high as 75% . 'The alarm bells are ringing but, instead of pontificating about it, we want to go into the schools and assist them to do something.' It made good copy. There was a photo of my team, our work in the schools was reported on and we made the TV news. It all gave a very high profile to the programme we were calling 'Tu Tangata' (Stand Tall).

However, the Minister of Education, Les Gandar, came out and said my revelations were not only exaggerated, they were dangerous and incorrect. He having answered the gauntlet I'd thrown down, I threw his department's own statistics back at him in a following article. And then all went quiet on the Western Front, and from the Minister's office.

We really rattled some cages. By 1980 the school profiles we'd been doing on pupils were showing their worth. There were more pupils staying at school longer and more response to our trade training programmes. As well as the predictable diesel mechanics, butchery and so on Maori school leavers were branching into other areas.

Another aspect of Tu Tangata was obtaining funding from our general pool to promote marae wananga. Wananga is a place of learning and we started utilising our kaumatua, our elders, our tribal people on various maraes around New Zealand to house kids from other districts for a week during the May and August holidays. Some of them had never been on a marae before or experienced that atmosphere. The main theme was to instil a little self-confidence, a little self-esteem — the Maori way.

The youth wananga programme on maraes was aimed at what might be called 'at-risk' children, potential non-achievers who lacked not so much acumen, but any desire to succeed at school. This exposed another problem, a lot of peer pressure to not succeed. Believe it or not, there was pressure not to be a 'clever Dicky', to stay dumb like us. The pressure on some brave ones not to succeed was tragic.

By the end of 1978, I and my 'Swat Team' had covered every district where we had a Maori Affairs office, from North Cape right down to Invercargill. The programme was up and running. The programme at this stage was being facilitated and sustained only by the community services section of the department. I wanted to get more support from other sections — clerical, housing, Maori Trust — but ran into resistance and apathy. Here we were, trying to consolidate the programme, and there were fierce divisions within the department.

Racism was rearing its ugly head. Kara Puketapu was the first Maori to be appointed Secretary of Maori Affairs. In 1978 and '79, the retiring district officers, all pakehas, were being replaced by Maoris. Neville Baker, later to gain notoriety through the Quality Inns deal, was the first to be appointed. Then came Alby Williams and others were to follow. Up until then, a hangover from the old colonial times, even from my dad's time, it was always expected that district officers would be pakeha. This change rankled with some of the entrenched pakeha staff. The warts started to appear and there were divisions within the department.

I do not make these comments lightly. We were subjected to comments like 'Maori Affairs has no business getting into education programmes exclusively for Maori'; 'Everybody has the same chances to succeed at school'. That many Maori pupils needed extra attention didn't seem to count as a reason for our department to assist.

In 1979, I said to Kara that if he wanted this programme to succeed with me at the helm, I'd have to be looking at a permanent, or fulltime, appointment. A vacancy had come up for Director of Youth Development with Maori Affairs and I had to line up against other candidates. I was interviewed in Wellington and, from out of nowhere, with no public service record at all, I was appointed to a 007 rating! It was probably the greatest leap that anyone ever made in the public service.

I've mentioned that Don Selwyn and Selwyn Muru worked with me closely during this time. Robin Ruakere was another who joined the ranks. He also had an entertainment background as well as a strong administrative side in business. Robin died of a heart attack in November 1991, aged 50. The heart attack was sudden and he died in his car after a round of golf. It was a great shock to all of us because Robin was much loved and had not received the recognition in life he richly deserved.

One of my closest allies was a guy called Bill Kaua, a real livewire, very energetic and very committed. People said we made good bookends because we were a pair of blowhards. Hello New Zealand!

Some of us hadn't come up through the public service so we didn't really comprehend the fear within the ranks or the internal resistance. Our Tu Tangata programme brought variety to the otherwise humdrum existence of the department. A lot of the staff enjoyed it and were very good. The community staff in our Rotorua office had their hearts in the work. For many it was a new experience to get into the schools and mix it with pupils and staff. So, while there was resistance, we were making progress on different fronts to what the department was accustomed to.

I was then starting to pull in some of my contacts in the business world. I went to Hugh Fletcher and asked him for support. Wilson

Whineray, of Carter Holt, Don Rowlands, of Fisher and Paykel, Jack Christie, of Tisco, and similar people were very helpful in setting up subsidised training modules within their industry. The department had never had that type of involvement before.

We were enthusiastic about the moves we were making. Tu Tangata was endorsed by Prime Minister Rob Muldoon and his government; Ben Couch, the Minister of Maori Affairs, was very supportive.

To give the programme a national profile, and allay fears about it being anything other than constructive, I put on my show biz hat again and said: 'The best way to focus on Tu Tangata and the good it can do is to do a tour of the country.' Show biz with a message. The Quartet came back together for the tour. The other boys could see the importance of what we were trying to do and, again, there was that marvellous bond, that loyalty, that still endured after 15 years apart.

At rehearsal in Ngaruawahia for the 1979 show which launched Tu Tangata.

NZ Herald

Wi Wharekura couldn't join us, but it was a superb show. I had Toni Williams in place of Wi and I had Noel Kingi and Gerry Merito, who were both very committed. Our support artists were Toni, on his own, Tina Cross, the Morrison family . . . and intermediate school kids from around the country. Everything came together but not by chance — there was a lot of hard work first. I had to lobby hard both politically and show biz-wise. I called in Dennis Brown to give me some assistance to promote the show. The Maori Queen was in attendance; there were various MPs; Ben Couch was there and made a nationalistic and patriotic appeal to the audience.

The end result was a televised show at Turangawaewae and then a national tour, giving the Tu Tangata philosophy a national face. The tour was a sellout and it really gave our programme, and the department, a profile they'd never had before.

For that tour we also brought in another person to assist in the promotion — Philip Munro, very artistic, bi-lingual, very strong in Maori culture. He was sent ahead to instruct chosen intermediate school pupils from the towns we were visiting, so they could appear on stage with us. We had the stage set up so they were on tiered seating behind the band, in full view of their home-town audience. The highlight of the evening came when, after seeming simply part of the audience with premium seating, they suddenly joined in as part of the show.

These intermediate children were tremendous. None of them embarrassed us by yawning or going to sleep. And there were some real magic moments with those kids and their full-throated singing of songs like *We Are Sailing* in Maori. They contributed so much warmth and 'oomph' to the show that newspaper reports consistently said such things as: 'If this is what Tu Tangata is, then New Zealand must support it. Our children are our future, and those on stage last night with Howard Morrison and his troupe showed how bright that future could be if they're guided in the right lines . . .' We were leaving towns not only with on-stage involvement of children from that community but we were also establishing the reason for promoting and supporting Tu Tangata for all our children.

The message went further than just the stage. The newspapers were reporting the tour before we arrived and carrying reviews of the show after we left; we were getting publicity from other media outlets such as radio interviews. With the telecast of the Turangawaewae show coming out before the tour, Tu Tangata certainly gained a national face. On the way around New Zealand, we involved the community service staff in each area that had a Maori Affairs office. For instance, at Wanganui Bill Kaua had a successful school visitation programme and he promoted it very vigorously with his staff. He involved other resource people of the ilk I've mentioned before — Maori Women's Welfare League, health organisations, a lot of retired 'grey power' people, kuia and kaumatua. After we left each area, it just meant follow-up.

I pulled in everyone I could to give Tu Tangata the highest possible profile. Hika Reid, the 'happy hooker' of that time, Bryan Williams and Ruia Morrison were more than willing to give their time; the heroes and heroines of New Zealand could tell their own story to the kids at school. When the kids went back and talked about this Tu Tangata programme at home, there were some rednecks who would say 'just another Maori thing'. But when they heard the type of people who were prepared to be involved, national heroes and heroines, they started to sit up and take a bit of notice.

All things being equal, in 1979 we would have set the pattern for the next 10 years.

I guess I should mention that I did manage to achieve one or two other tasks in 1979, in between and around my fulltime involvement as National Director of Youth Development and my promotion of Tu Tangata. One such task was to undertake a 'C'mon to New Zealand' promotional tour of the United States for the Tourist and Publicity Department.

It was a busy year.

13

HOW GREAT THOU ART

FOR OUR TU TANGATA programme, 1979 and '80 were very good years. Full of promise for the future, full of good things done. But what happened next was a dissipation of our work as head office started bringing in other programmes. It took all the impetus out of our work because it suddenly removed from us a lot of the people we needed to work on nothing else but visiting the schools and furthering our youth development programme there. This was the launch of the Kohanga Reo programme which again fell under the umbrella of community services people.

In 1980, except for Wanganui, Waiariki and parts of Tai Tokerau, up in the north, personnel were moved as the instruction came from head office: drop everything you're doing; this is what you've got to do now, Kohanga Reo. The Kohanga Reo programme was to address the problem of the language dying. Kaupapa Maori. 'Language nests' for pre-schoolers. Nobody is arguing with the merits of Kohanga Reo. It's very necessary, very worthwhile.

While our Tu Tangata programme was aimed at school visits, looking after those who were salvageable and losing some of those who weren't, the new remedy was get 'em while they're young, before they go to school! Ideal, right? Fine, if we had the resources to do both. But hang on a minute! Later in those two years, 1980 and '81, another

Probably a lot of New Zealanders don't realise just how highly
Howard rated in the East. In all the shows I worked with
Howard overseas, he got a standing ovation. Every one. When
you're up there, there are always people wanting to knock you
down. But I won't hear a word against the man. The knockers
don't know what he's really like and all the things he's done for
others. I remember a time we did a show at a prison near
Christchurch. It was so moving. Most of them were our people,
Maori, and Howard really touched them. He had the prisoners,
hard men, in tears — and we were all crying as we left.

— **Charlie Te Hau**

programme came flying into the community services portfolio. That
was Matua Whangai, a programme to foster counselling to some of our
people in institutions, to help rehabilitate them, to assist them to rejoin
the mainstream when they came out. On sheer merit, you couldn't
argue with either programme.

It was unreasonable, however, to expect that one section of Maori
Affairs in each office, community services, could cope with these two
and Tu Tangata as well. They couldn't.

On the face of it, in terms of promotion and publicity, this Tu
Tangata programme was magnificent. It was working. They're looking
at pre-school; they looking at people at school; people who are leaving
school; and now they're looking at the problems of many young Maori
in borstals. It made persuasive reading when you are taking your
estimates to Government for approval. But like a paint job that needed
an undercoat and a primer, there was nothing underneath.

It has to be acknowledged that Kohanga Reo is presently very successful and growing all the time. However, its success in my opinion is
due to the programme being taken away from the department. It now
enjoys Education portfolio funding and Maori Education Foundation
administration.

Having said that about Kohanga Reo, I believe that Kara Puketapu's 'master plan' was that funding and resource people for the Tu
Tangata school programme would be picked up by the Education
Department, but with input from specially appointed resource people
from Maori Affairs. Similarly, the Justice Department would become
involved in funding and supporting Matua Whangai. All this could
have happened if a task force comprising representatives from the
departments of Maori Affairs, Social Welfare, Justice and Probation,
Health and Education had been set up to work out the how! I did
suggest this and was quoted accordingly in a *Sunday Times* article. The
result was a stern rebuke from Kara Puketapu, who told me very clearly

that I was forbidden to talk policy. End of story!

From my own point of view, it was very clear that all of the programmes were going to suffer. A lot of it was going to depend on our resource people out there who would work for nothing — insufficient funding, insufficient numbers and deteriorating enthusiasm.

I was disheartened. As Director of Youth Development, I couldn't be on the coal face all the time. There was only one of me, and I didn't have enough bodies to keep up the momentum in all the districts. It was assumed in head office that now it was up and running the youth development programme would take care of itself. But it wasn't happening that way. From the schools, the principals and staff, guidance counsellors in particular, in areas where the visits we'd promised weren't being kept up by local staff through other impositions on their time, we were starting to get negative responses — 'fly-by-night programme; here we go again'. Forget all the pre-conceived doubts about the programme, we gave them the justification for criticism without any help from the 'antis'. All show and no go. I found that very hard to take, because a lot of it was falling back on my head.

The programme justified thorough follow-up. We had it consolidated; all it needed was a further push from head office. But an opportunity was lost, through taking on more than we had the resources for! Incidentally, in February of 1992, I made overtures to Doug Kidd, Minister of Maori Affairs, about considering the merits of reinstating the Tu Tangata Youth Development programme. It looks like it's going to be one of those 'don't call me, I'll call you' stories!

What I had taken on back then was an extension of the Tu Tangata programme — 'indigenous bachelor of business studies'. A Tu Tangata Bachelor of Business Studies programme was set up by Dr Ralph Love and Neville Baker at Massey College, where we subsidised young Maori school leavers with UE minimum to Bursary A and Bursary B. We gave them extra sponsorship through the Tu Tangata programme at Massey. My son-in-law, Anaru Grant, was one of the first to go in. Not nepotism — he went on merit!

That was when I really started knocking on doors — AHI, Fletchers, Tasman and had a great deal of success with Westpac Bank. The recipe was this: I went to them and said, during the holidays why don't you take on some of our trainees who live in your area so they can have practical experience which would be complementary to what they are studying at university. In one particular year, Westpac actually had 33 students in branches through the country and they were very happy with the people they had.

A lot of firms were grateful for the opportunity because they were disquietened by the lack of young Maoris applying for the jobs that were there. 'Look, we advertise and we don't get any Maoris.' This is where we were very helpful to these firms, who couldn't put in their

The Howard Morrison Golf Classics raised a good bit of money for various causes — and I wasn't going to miss out on the fun of participating. My expression says this was a good shot . . . who's to prove otherwise?

Troy Restieaux

newspaper advertisements: 'Our staff at the moment reflects 99% pakeha in middle management; we'd like a few brownies if they have the formal qualifications — please apply.'

While I was not happy with the lack of progress in the school visiting programme, specifically its failure to continue the way it had been envisaged, I was still kept busy setting up these subsidised training schemes with big companies around the country.

I'd said publicly when I joined the department in 1979 that I would not be singing professionally per se. I had, by the way, received permission from the State Services Commission to do extracurricular work, in other words entertaining, as long as it didn't interfere with the work I was doing. But, of course, my background and instinct as an entertainer made my work in expounding the Tu Tangata philosophy so much easier. So any performing I was doing was actually to complement the work I was doing in Tu Tangata. And I have to say this, since a lot of people know about it: much of my extracurricular activities were to raise funds for programmes that I had started and believed in, that had no other source of funding.

One of the most satisfying was the celebrity golf matches. I went straight to the top! Our then Governor-General, Sir Denis Blundell, agreed to be patron. And it really was something to have Geoff Howarth flying down guys like Allan Lamb, Ian Botham and Lance Cairns — all sponsored — to play in a golf tournament in a little place like Te Puke. I had real celebrities from different sporting persuasions. In three years we raised enough funds to build what we call a kokiri centre on Whakaue Marae at Maketu. It was formally opened by Sir Denis in 1982. It was there not only for Kohanga Reo but as a place where young people at school could go and do their homework and study. Some of them didn't have that facility at home.

I was involved with a lot of charity work, right up and down New Zealand. In fact, once it was out that I was doing this type of thing to assist the programme in various areas, the demands on my time became overpowering, unsustainable. So I guess that in 1979, '80 and '81 I was working harder than I ever had in show business. I was going to schools and visiting companies during the day, hustling for opportunities and openings for our young people and loving it; I was doing shows at night, too many to mention. The Kohanga Reo Trust at Matamata, say; then up north to do one for someone else. What I did was choose the ones that I felt weren't relying on the show alone to get them off the ground.

In other words, if the community got together with me and my team to go to the school during the day, and I could maximise the visit through the press and a show at night, then it was worthwhile. But I had to get to the stage of saying: look, I'm not going to wherever to do a show just to raise funds for this project, when the community hasn't been doing the base work. Underlying this rationale was that I was getting a bit suspicious about where the funding might go — sometimes unfairly, perhaps, but if I did something I wanted to know the destination of all moneys raised.

By the time 1981 came along, engrossed as I was in my restricted field of endeavours, visible though I was to Maori communities and young Maori people, I was almost a non-event on the national entertainment scene. I hadn't had a hit. Nothing on the radio. I wasn't getting any television. The stigma was still there: Morrison's too hard to handle. Or he's too busy with Maori Affairs. But no one was asking me. I was seeing my contemporaries like Ray Woolf getting shows and a feller called Billy T. James was making a huge impact on all fronts in New Zealand show business.

Ray and Billy's success was the reason I asked State Services for permission to do other work. I was hoping, actually, to get the opportunity to do my own show on television. This would have helped me to promote the Stand Tall concept again, as well as remind people that Howard Morrison, Entertainer, hadn't joined a monastery.

So 1981 wound its way until the royal tour, to take place in September, became imminent and I was asked by Tom Parkinson, Ricky Stratful and Phil Warren to participate. What to do? It wasn't just the public who'd lost touch with Howard Morrison. HM had lost touch a bit, himself, with the current entertainment scene.

I was at a Tu Tangata hui in Auckland and *Whakaaria Mai (How Great Thou Art)* came up as part of our opening prayer and dedication. When it came to the chorus, my hair stood on end. I said 'That's it!'

Tom Parkinson had wanted me to do a comedy skit, one he'd seen me do on television with Billy T. James, *The Mail Must Go Through.* I was highly indignant. How dare you demean my standing by implying that I am just a prop for a comedy skit? Do you realise I was awarded

---

In my first term as an Auckland city councillor, I chaired the committee responsible for organising the Royal Variety Show in the St James' Theatre, part of the royal visit of 1981. I asked Howard if he would be part of the show, with no money involved, and he agreed. Tom Parkinson, the director, and I were a bit concerned when we learned Howard planned to sing *How Great Thou Art*, because it was a hymn and might have been taken wrongly. It turned out to be an inspired choice. Howard was magnificent and it was the first time anywhere that the Queen and the Duke came up and met the performers on stage, in front of the public with the curtain up. We did a rush release of the record and it sold very well. *How Great Thou Art* was the rebirth of Howard's career.   — **Phil Warren**

the Order of the British Empire? Don't you think I might want some say as to what I do in front of Her Majesty and Prince Philip? I was really on my high horse!

Tom, being the nice person he is, said, 'Okay, okay! What do you want to do?'

'I want to do a hymn. Specifically, *How Great Thou Art.*'

There was silence from Tom on the phone.

'Are you there?'

Tom probably thought I had taken leave of my senses, but said okay. He, Phil Warren and Bernie Allen have since admitted they thought I was pushing my luck, but agreed that if anyone could pull it off, it would be HM.

I don't think I would have picked that song if I had been entertaining fulltime at that stage. I would have thought, like a lot of the artists on that show (bless their souls): how can I promote myself and my image in the best possible light as an entertainer? I was so far removed from the show biz circuit that I thought of the occasion first. I thought of the honour, and what I could bring to the show.

Doing *How Great Thou Art* in both Maori and English was something I'd worked out in my therapy ward, in the Urewera country. I went to my mentor, my Uncle Tupara, and asked him for some help in how to put the song together. I told him I wanted to do it in both languages, and he was very complimentary about that. Then I asked him if it would be okay for me to greet the Queen in Maori. He asked me if there was any other Maori content in the show. I said no, because there was to be a full Maori welcome that day at the Domain. Essentially I was the only person who was going to do 'something Maori' or, more precisely bi-cultural. So he said that's okay. You're allowed to greet your Queen.

We worked out what I was going to say. This, you may recall, came in the middle of the song. An expression of our respect, of our appreciation of the opportunity this occasion gave to say how we felt.

At rehearsals the organisers were having a bit of a problem about who goes where. We had a few superstars on the programme and everyone was clamouring for the prime spot. Who's going to close the show?

Tom Parkinson said to me: 'Would you insist on closing the show?' I said no.

'That gets away from a problem,' Tom said. 'John Rowles would like to close the show.'

And John *was* international, you know. I said fair enough — but can I get to say where else I want to be in the show? No problem. There was an opera section, a ballet section and then the rock 'n roll era — Tom Sharplin, Dinah Lee and that effervescent girl who has done very well, Sharon O'Neill — all the dancers on TV at that time; it was a non-stop action medley of rock 'n roll.

'I'll go straight after that,' I said.

'John Rowles follows you,' Tom reminded me.

'That's okay.' I could be gracious.

There is still a naughtiness in me; I still like a challenge. Going into a show like this, I didn't have the feeling of, 'How can I steal the lime-light?' I thought of the occasion and I knew I'd picked the right song. If I'd had any doubts, the MC, my good friend Peter Sinclair, convinced me otherwise. But when it came down to the nitty gritty of going on stage and performing, I have no qualms about saying that it was my intention, and will always be my intention, to go on, perform, walk off and say to anybody who was going on after me: Follow that! That's professional pride, competitiveness.

I picked a song that was absolutely right, as it proved. It was repeated on the Sunday. I suddenly realised that we had a potential hit. Eventually RCA got it out — three months later. The Royal Variety Show was held in September. On Christmas Eve, in the last *Ready to Roll* of the year, *How Great Thou Art* went straight to No 1. When *RTR* came back in late January, it was still on top; in February, the same. You've heard stories, I'm sure, about exaggerated ratings of songs and records. For *My Old Man's An All Black* the figure was 60,000. I've been told recently that it was as high as 78,000. But to have *How Great Thou Art* make such an impact two decades later — well, it wasn't bad for an old feller, eh? And both were recorded live, again amplifying where my strengths are.

The stories from producers about Howard and TV studios were legendary. Unfortunately, they were all true. He hated studios, being without an audience; he was totally undisciplined; he hated backing tracks; he'd change key in the middle of a song, forgetting he didn't have a live band which could change with him. Howard, by instinct, education and experience, is a live performer. Four metal cameras and a group of technicians too busy getting their job done to react to Howard's performance is not the setting for him. For Howard, all performances are a two-way show. If he gives, he expects to get; and if he gets, he gives. So Howard and TV were little short of a disaster area — until the Royal Variety Show in 1981. With a director (Ricky Stratful) who understood the needs of entertainers, the Royal Variety Show was an outstanding success. And Howard, the old trouper with new tricks, came out No 1. That was the turning of the road for Howard as far as television was concerned. Our next show, the 90-minute *Howard Morrison Special* from the Founders Theatre in Hamilton, was equally successful.   — **Tom Parkinson**

The clever commercial thing to have done at that time (which, thinking selfishly, I sometimes regret not doing) would have been to ask for leave of absence from the department. I would have cleaned up on a tour round New Zealand. But I was thinking of what I'd dedicated myself to. When I saw *How Great Thou Art* doing so much for me, it was another opportunity to give Tu Tangata a good boot. And did it ever get a boot!

Until then, the kids at school only knew me from the Bic ads. And, the power of TV being what is is, they did know me, right down to the little guys. But now I became a pop star hero in their eyes because of having an *RTR* hit — and it was a hymn! It brought a different class of song and, in many cases, another perspective to 'churchy' music, to the attention of young kids.

What a full circle I'd taken! I was working with young kids, a great percentage of whom were entirely devoid of the spiritual training and environment that I'd enjoyed at their age. Here they were, able to feel the strength of spirituality through a song that came to them through *Ready to Roll* and hit parades. So here am I all those years later, coming back to the essence of the teachings that were indelibly imprinted on my mind by people like John Tamahori, our pastor at St Faith's, like Wi Huata, Sam Rangiihu, Manu Bennett, Henry Northcroft and all those people.

And I can tell you that when I went back to the schools and I started singing, just with guitar accompaniment, *How Great Thou Art*, the reaction from the kids was extraordinary. I couldn't do the same mihi in the middle part that I'd done for the Queen, of course, so I changed it to a dedication to the kids and their school.

On the side I was now doing extracurricular work on the weekends, in the RSAs and Cosmopolitan clubs. The same thing was happening there; what was different was the faces. I had the cherubic, innocent vulnerability of the kids at school . . . and the smoke-filled haze and ruddy faces of the clubs. But they came together. These were the parents and grandparents of my Tu Tangata age group, and I was not backward in promoting the programme in these venues. It was very well received, too, I must say. That's where I've been lucky. How do you feel about entertaining? HM's answer: It's easy to touch people if you're clever enough, and good enough at what you do. But to be touched in return — ah, that's the reward.

So 1981 was, for me, a resurrection. Another one!

14

NEW DIRECTIONS

HOWARD MORRISON WAS Flavour of the Year in 1982 and my first big project was to set up the first New Zealand Maori Businessmen's Conference. The venue was Trillo's, the guest speakers were Sir James Fletcher and Sir Denis Blundell, and the guest list included other corporate heads and successful and aspiring Maori businessmen. As special guests were successful Hawaiian businessmen. The conference was held in February and was very successful. This was the direction in which I was now moving.

A consequence of my high profile in 1982 was a call, out of the blue, from the Minister of Broadcasting, Dr Shearer, to join the New Zealand Broadcasting Corporation board. This was a big deal. The NZBC still had a virtual monopoly of radio and television, two branches of the media with the potential to wield enormous influence.

Well, my three-year term on the Broadcasting board was interesting in that I learned a lot and gained a lot of insight into how things work at that level. But it was frustrating in that I felt at the finish I had achieved little and scant progress had been made in what I saw as important areas. Scant progress? No progress!

It was ironic, and appropriate, that the end of my term, in mid-1985, coincided with a month-long 'celebration' of New Zealand television's first 25 years. The headline on a Graham Scott interview with me in the NZ *Herald* summed up my view: 'TV's 25 Years of

Standing Still'. I came onto the board at a time when state television and radio were being separated — the old NZBC became TVNZ and Radio New Zealand — and at a time when TVNZ was having to see private TV as not a distant threat but an imminent challenge. It was a time for forward thinking, a time when the opportunities for change and growth were there.

In that Graham Scott article at the end of my term, I pointed out that television whitewashed its failure to give appropriate exposure to Maori music and culture by claiming it was a specialist area outside its field of expertise — nonsensical in my view. Yet in my last year on the board, the New Zealand Symphony Orchestra had been propped up to the tune of $4.5 million. A fine body of musicians, I'm sure, but their appeal is to a small percentage of the population. *Close To Home*, a 'soap' which could well have ended up on the cutting room floor if its merits had been more rigorously examined, was allocated a budget three times that approved at the time for Maori programming.

I didn't see myself as a 'one issue' person on the board. I was concerned about the lack of quality New Zealand programmes generally.

On the three-hour special which launched the silver jubilee of New Zealand television, I sang a song called *Hine Hine*, which probably got fitted in because it was the basis for the Goodnight Kiwi theme. That and the Patea Maori Group was the sole Maori content and reflected pretty accurately the lack of priority which New Zealand's television system had accorded Maori culture and music during those first 25 years.

Why else would the New Zealand Maori Council make a claim to the assets of RNZ and TVNZ in 1992? The claim is the result of long-term frustration.

Similarly, where on that special were the successful pop groups like DD Smash, Hello Sailor, Split Enz, Dance Exponents? Pop music on television in New Zealand had virtually disappeared when Kevan Moore and Tom Parkinson opted out of the system. Compare the treatment accorded to the Symphony Orchestra.

Elitism, closed-door strategies and hierarchical arrogance were ingrained in the television bureaucracy; as were costly duplications of resources and costs in Wellington and Auckland.

I know my frustrations were echoed by the producers and programme makers. The structure of RNZ on one side, TVNZ on the other, with Corporate Services in the middle, made innovation difficult.

Corporate Services were the bureaucrats who controlled the financial and political agendas of RNZ and TVNZ. Broadcasting policy was firmly controlled by the government of the day through the Broadcasting Act, which limited the BCNZ in capital expenditure or borrowing money. Control of the corporation was designated to the chairman, who was also the Chief Executive. This was unusual and

In full facial tattoo for the Howard Morrison Special *in Hamilton's Founders Theatre.* Morrison family collection

Final rehearsals for the 1981 Royal Variety Show. Left: Clowning with director Ricky Stratful. Below: With Ray Columbus and Peter Sinclair.

Morrison family collection

The Maori culture group assembled (with the blessing of Ngati Whatua) to perform at Heritage Park.

Meeting a proud old chieftain from a different race and culture . . . HM in Papua New Guinea.

With Michael Fay, Chris Dickson and the KZ7 team in Fremantle.
Morrison family collection

OVERLEAF: *On stage with family and friends after* This Is Your Life. *Yes, they did catch me by surprise!* TVNZ

With the Maori culture group (a couple of whanau in there!) at the Hawaiian Trade and Cultural Expo 1986.
Morrison family collection

On stage for the Aotea Centre show, September 1990.

Hinemoa and Tutanekai.

Jane Ussher/Listener

With Invercargill friends at a Child Cancer fundraiser.

probably not healthy for a corporation that size. TVNZ executives were desperate for long-term strategy but, in the main, the board was being involved in short-term housekeeping.

Therefore my claims about '25 years of standing still' and 'bankrupt forward thinking' were echoed, I know, by many within the organisation. Not as an emotional outcry but fact. In television particularly, the duplication of positions, facilities and costs obviously affected the amount of funding that was available for local programmes. You would have a person in Wellington with a job description and a person in Auckland with a similar job description.

Most of the on-screen talent in entertainment and drama lived in Auckland, therefore the cost of flying them down to Wellington and lodging them increased production budgets three-fold.

Avalon, built at great cost in Wellington, never reached its full potential because a lot of the effective directors, producers and technical people were domiciled in Auckland and didn't want to move to Wellington. Avalon was and still is the ultimate 'white elephant' of broadcasting; built in the wrong place (it's a packed lunch distance from central Wellington) in the wrong city and for the wrong broadcasting system. Being stuck with it, the administrators had to make it work. And, like all mistakes, it became a black hole for money.

Government policy that Auckland, Wellington, Christchurch and Dunedin should all have major TV facilities with local production meant more duplication of resources and manpower. More than a decade down the track, we have new television headquarters in Auckland, built at a huge cost and with a huge debt-servicing commitment. This would never have come about if the right homework had been done and the right decisions made before Avalon was built.

When I joined the board, I didn't expect to change the world in six months. I didn't go in with preconceived ideas, because I didn't want to be accused of being the brown face that was going to promote brown programmes only. It was my first experience of being on a board at that high-powered (as I thought) level. I expected to spend the first six months looking and learning.

What I didn't expect was that I, and other board members, would have so little power to bring about change. The whole structure was too unwieldy, too cumbersome. The agendas were massive and, by the time you considered reports from all the department heads in television and radio, it was inevitable we were doing a certain amount of rubber-stamping. I couldn't help feeling that the agendas were manipulated to that end.

As well as not regarding myself as a one-issue person, I didn't regard giving Maori culture a higher and more appropriate profile as a one-race issue. Maori music, dance and story is the only culture that is uniquely New Zealand's. It is something to be shared by all New

On stage during the Howard Morrison Special *at Hamilton's Founders Theatre, all the nationalities of New Zealand represented through our children. And yes, that imposing Maori chieftain is HM.* Morrison family collection

Zealanders regardless of colour and ethnic origin. And the most effective means of sharing it is obviously through television and radio.

Radio New Zealand, from my observation, had a far greater commitment to Maori programming at that time than TVNZ, despite the fact that the general philosophy of both services stated: 'The primary need is for programmes which reflect Maori attitudes, culture, events and aspirations to a wide and general audience.' If you accepted TVNZ's square-off that they did not have the staffing skills, production budgets or technical resources, it seemed to me that the answer was to find solutions, not simply put it in the 'too hard' basket.

In my second year on the board, I prepared a paper for the Te Arawa Trust Board in which I outlined the Maori content of Radio New Zealand and TVNZ programming. I pointed out, incidentally, that while Radio New Zealand had an outside committee of 15 Maori and Pacific Island people who met regularly with senior staff, TVNZ had no outside advisory committee, and no fulltime Maori consultant like RNZ's Bill Kerekere. Maori broadcasters attached to *Te Karere* (which did come about during my term) and *Koha* had no influence on decision-making or policy.

My recommendation (fully supported by the Te Arawa Trust Board after they considered my paper) was that submissions be made to the government to establish a Maori Broadcasting Unit in the New Zealand Broadcasting Corporation; that the Maori Broadcasting Unit be totally funded by the NZBC. It's objective: to provide a service that 'enriches the indigenous culture of New Zealand . . . to emphasise its importance to New Zealand in terms of history, tradition, culture and spirituality.' And, I might have added, that enriches the fabric of New Zealand society, and New Zealand's identity, as a whole.

Nearly a decade further on, a Maori Broadcasting Unit has not taken shape. As I said earlier, my three-year term on the board was one I look back on more with a sense of frustration than achievement.

If the comments I made when I finished my term on the board seem harsh, look at the situation now, seven years later. At present we have a surfeit of Australian programmes on New Zealand television, a further indictment of the lack of commitment and forward thinking by programme planners past and present. Think about the last time we had a New Zealand series with any musical content and you would have to go way back to the early '80s and Billy T. James. TVNZ no longer has an entertainment department and the last head of the department, Peter Gratten, is now contracted to an outside production house. How's that for a massive leap backwards?

I support privatisation of one of the TVNZ channels as long as the majority shareholding remains in New Zealand. I also agree with my former boss, Ian Cross, that TV1 should be made a non-commercial station.

In September 1982 I came out of the cold in terms of TV appearances. The *Howard Morrison Special*, recorded live at the Hamilton Founders Theatre, was shown on television. It was a huge production and rated the top programme for that week, ahead of the National News. More than that, it outrated the premiere of the series *Roots*. New Zealand was the first country in the world where the *Roots* premiere had ever been beaten — 'Take that!'

Was I happy? Man, I was over the moon.

During and at the completion of my term with the Broadcasting

On stage at the Founders Theatre for the Howard Morrison Special — *the show that out-rated* Roots.

Morrison family collection

board, I was still with the Department of Maori Affairs, but associated more with special projects. One which came up as a priority in 1985 was extending Maoridom's participation in the tourism industry. There was no voice representing Maoridom. We had, in many ways, the culture being abused through ignorance because the main game players, the tour operators, were pakeha. While their intent was to be conscious of the culture they had no sounding board is the kindest way to put it.

We saw an opportunity for Maoridom to be directly involved. At the direction of Koro Wetere, it was my task to put together the first Maori Tourism Conference. It was called Manaakitanga, meaning 'hospitality'.

I went to the leading players from the Tourist Department, to Neil Plimmer, to Tourist Industry Federation executive officer Tony Stannaford, and then met all the decision makers, the Duncan Hamiltons and Rodney Walshes and so on, to get their support, not only in principle but also to be present at the Manaakitanga conference. The expression of support and goodwill was more than cosmetic. It was very well supported because the industry did feel they needed a sounding board representing Maoridom.

We had no representation where all the decisions were being made, for instance, on the Tourism Council, which is the last step before matters go to the Minister. We had nobody on the board of the Tourist Industry Federation; we had no representation at regional level. We had Maori people who were in the industry, doing their own thing, but they had no voice at influence level.

The conference was held in Rotorua and, unlike a lot of hui sponsored by the department at this time, was user pay. Out of that conference came the appointment of a task force which was chaired by former Bishop of Aotearoa, the Right Reverend Manu Bennett. Appointed to that task force were Neville Baker, Ted Butt, Bert Mackie, and, ex officio, Howard Morrison. Robin Smith and Graham Butterworth were co-opted as researchers. We had six months in which to put together a white paper on how we would see a proposed Maori Tourism Association working. Also required was a dissection from our point of view where we felt tourism was, where we thought it was going, historical background, where Maoridom wasn't, where we would like to see it involved.

The task force met regularly and I suppose the first measure of our success was that we had one of our own task force members, Ted Butt, appointed to the Tourism Council. He was also appointed to the THC Board. Later Dr Ngatata Love, from Massey, was appointed to the board of Air New Zealand. So we succeeded in getting some direct input at high level, pretty quickly, although the task force duties were not completed after six months, and its term was extended.

During this time span, the first half of the 1980s, there were several other projects that I put together which related to entertainment and tourism.

The first one came as Maori Affairs representative to the board of the New Zealand Maori Arts and Crafts Institute. During my tenure there, I put together something which has flourished ever since —

lunchtime Maori concerts at the institute's meeting house, Te Aronui A Rua. The idea was that tourists coming in and out of the institute during the day, independent travellers who might come to Rotorua for the day, weren't catered for because the only Maori concerts were at night in the hotels. Some of the tour operators were apprehensive, fearing lunchtime concerts might take the gloss away from the hangi concerts at the hotels in town. But the board of the institute fully approved the project and it has proved to be a tremendous crowd pleaser as part of the institute's overall attractions. During the summer they now have two matinees, at 11.30am and 1pm.

I also worked with the Department of Labour to put together a training programme which resulted in 11 young Maori people being placed with various sectors of the tourist industry, after a 20-week training course.

In 1983, after consultation with Tom Parkinson, who was then head of South Pacific Television, we decided that we could put together a programme to train young people in the entertaining arts. I suppose it was our modest equivalent of the College of Musical Arts that was featured in that TV series *Fame*. The tutors were Robin Ruakere, who was with the department at that time, and Joanna Paul, who had just finished at Waikato University. Joanna was very strong in drama, acting and dance.

With headquarters at the South Pacific studios, we used their administration arm and Tom Parkinson was also able, during the 20-week course, to bring together a group of people with skills in entertainment to make contributions to the training of these young people. I put in my two cents' worth as overseer and also as a contributor to things like stagecraft and voice production.

The results of that programme are easily enough judged. We all know Joanna Paul became a very successful television personality — we'll take some credit for her. Others who were part of SPATS (Performing Arts Training Scheme) included Temuera Morrison, actor; Margaret Urlich, singer; Jay Laga'aia, actor; Kim Willoughby, singer (with When The Cat's Away); five out of 11 who still have a high profile. Again, it was a successful outcome and I was a popular boy with the Department of Labour, because the two programmes I had initiated with them were both successful.

Buoyed by this, I was approached by a chap called Terry Beckett, who was putting together a dream. That dream was to establish a theme park which would offer a complete taste of New Zealand within 10 minutes of downtown Auckland. Established on a former quarry site in Mt Wellington, it would provide an accurate presentation of the native flora, fauna, agriculture and Maori cultural experience.

Originally Terry joined forces with Mogul Corporation, which had been working on its own cultural world idea. They came together with an Australasian investment company. Terry also brought some American consultants in to help design the park; to make it physically and environmentally pleasing. The people he brought in had been involved with Disneyland, Knott's Berry Farm, Universal Studios and a host of other projects worldwide.

Terry's park was a huge project, the budgeted cost of development was somewhere around $7.5 million. Not a bad price, really, when you consider that the area was 12.5 hectares, an enormous undertaking. In 1983 the Minister for Tourism, Mr Talbot, planted the first tree on the site. This was quickly joined by several hundred others as bulldozers and heavy earth-moving equipment began shaping the landscape. A man-made lake, containing two islands, was created. The irrigation systems were put in place and by the time it was finished there were something like 10,000 trees, bushes and shrubs.

The concept had features such as Nature World, featuring the native plants and native animal life of New Zealand. Agra World showed the importance of agriculture to New Zealand; there were displays of exotic timber trees, horticultural crops, farm animals, shearing, milking.

Where I came in was Culture World, which was to incorporate two spectacular international-standard audio-visuals, one showing New Zealand scenery and the other illustrating New Zealand's development to the present day. Culture World was also to include live displays of Maori arts, crafts, songs and legends and entertainment; with craftspeople, quality souvenirs and things of that nature. Part of my brief was to commission carvings and pou pou to be placed at the entrance into Culture World. For this I commissioned Laurie Nichols, a relation of mine from Rotorua, who did a magnificent job. They are still there to be seen today, at Heritage Park in Mt Wellington.

Then, of course, we needed bodies for the live performing side of Culture World. Along with Terry Beckett, I interviewed a group of young Maori people, male and female, from all parts of the Bay of Plenty. Most of the group were school leavers. The advantage of this was that this was going to be their first job, so we could train them the way we wanted.

The comprehensive training programme covered Maori heritage, culture studies, history, weaponry, weaving and other skills. Also important was background as to their tribal affiliation, so that when tourists came to the park and were guided around by these young Maori people, there would be no ums and ahs when asked: are you a Maori? Yes — then what is a Maori? What is your background, your whakapapa, your heredity?

We conducted two 20-week sessions, working with Derek Packham of the Labour Department, Rotorua, and included practical visits to other tourist-related industries. When they had trained to the point where they could entertain, I led them at several important international conferences in Auckland and Rotorua, to give them some familiarisation with what was meant by the word multi-functional. They not only had to be performers, they had to be guides, purveyors of their history and all the complexities of Maori heritage.

During the training, as word got out, there was opposition from local Maori. Heritage Park was in Auckland; why should this group from Rotorua come up and trample on our territory? Or less polite words to that effect. Tribalism was rearing its ugly head — we were on the boundaries of the Tainui confederation of tribes and Ngati Whatua.

With Irirangi Tiakiawa, who'd been involved in my school visits programme, I went to a paramount chief and high priest of Ngati Mahenga, a sub-tribe of the Tainui, Te Whati Potene Awaitaia. We took him to conduct a special dedication service for the area. There wasn't any complaint about that because he represented pretty strong clout tribally. But Terry Beckett was taken to task and I had to go to Auckland because there were complaints that we were intruding in their area and why couldn't we have trained people from Auckland?

Some of the short answers to this were, one, that the funding came out of the Department of Labour in Rotorua; two, that the venue for the training was provided by my old Waikite football club; three, that Rotorua was the hub, the No 1 tourist destination in the country and the home of the practising culture as it relates to tourism. So part of the training of these young people was made easier by the tourist attractions right on our own doorstep.

However, we found it necessary, and highly desirable, to seek the support of Ngati Whatua. We are related to Ngati Whatua and they are wonderful elders up there; Doc and his men and ladies received us at Orakei marae. We brought our whole delegation up plus the paramount chief of Te Arawa, Hamuera Mitchell, to plead our case in formal etiquette on the marae.

After the explanations and the formal requests to accept our people — who were also their people, in terms of the wide representation we had within our group — our young people put on a performance for the Ngati Whatua. And, in a Maori way, they were absolutely blown away by the standard these young people had reached. They accepted the group, and myself, and our hopes and aspirations, gave us a mandate of support and it was a beautiful way of smoothing the way to our entree into Heritage Park.

For this project, I sought leave without pay from the Department of Maori Affairs. It was a full commitment that I had made, and don't regret. In November of 1984, after the 40 weeks, we had 33 young Maori people placed in employment as contributors to Heritage Park.

The park was opened by Prime Minister David Lange on November 30, 1984.

The training: successful.

The park; not so successful.

There have been many reasons put forward as to why Heritage Park never took off. Some suggested the word 'Heritage' had a museum-like connotation; my feeling was that 'Heritage' obliterated the fun aspect of what the park offered. Another reason was that there wasn't a good marketing plan put together (the marketing person left the park after only about five weeks). So all the promises and the rainbows on the horizon about this theme park, offering a complete taste of New Zealand only 10 minutes from Auckland, the gateway to New Zealand, failed to materialise. It had some very sticky moments and a lot of our young people who were in their first job were laid off.

I think it's a bigger tragedy that Heritage Park never got the public support which I believe it deserved. Maybe the real situation is that Auckland is indeed just a gateway; a place where you arrive and go through, return and go out.

Yet it made a lot of sense to have all this on offer so close to the heart of Auckland and you have to ask yourself, as I still do, why didn't it click? Certainly the domestic market stayed away from Heritage Park as if it carried disease. The local population didn't support it at all. Mind you, the market crash of '87 has worsened the situation. A lot of parks and public attractions have closed or struggled since then.

What about the young people? Why I believe it was a bigger tragedy for the park not to succeed than for them to be laid off is that a lot of time and effort went into the development of these young people, in all the disciplines that we had in the programme. When Heritage Park folded, many of our young people were snapped up in a wide range of work, a lot of it associated directly with tourism.

During that same time span, Richard Hartman, manager of the Sheraton Hotel Auckland, which was due to open in October 1984, approached me to commission samplings of Maori art and murals. A giant mural on display in the Rendezvous Bar of the hotel, depicting a village scene pertaining to hospitality in pre-European times, stems from that approach.

The original concept was to have Maori artwork prominently displayed throughout the hotel. But the interior decorator and his associates spent so much money on items such as marble (from Chile, would you believe, at great cost) that the Maori content was savagely diluted. I was very disappointed at the outcome. What an opportunity to have an international hotel with a uniquely New Zealand flavour! To amplify that point, I don't know of any hotel that has a prominently indigenous New Zealand ambience, in direct contrast to the major hotels of Hawaii and those in the great cities of the East. A visitor could wake up in any hotel in New Zealand, look around and wonder what country he was in.

State of Hawaii

Senate Certificate

SUPPORTING THE NEW ZEALAND TRADE EXPO IN HONOLULU

WHEREAS, in recent years the aboriginal peoples of Hawaii
and New Zeland have reestablished historical bonds of Polynesian
affinity through a number of meaningful exchanges of culture,
education, language, and economic development; and

WHEREAS, the first NEW ZEALAND TRADE EXPO will be held in
Honolulu at the Sheraton Waikiki Hotel between June 29 and
July 1, 1986, representing the Maori culture of Aotearoa and
the Maori Tourism and Business Investment Task Force, and pro-
moting a full display of cultural and economic aspects of
Maoriland and New Zealand; and

WHEREAS, the Maori and Hawaiian business communities will
begin the event with traditional Hawaiian and Maori ceremonies
of welcome; and

WHEREAS, the Maori Tourism and Business Investment Task
Force, chaired by the Rt. Rev. Manuhuia Bennett, Bishop of
Aotearoa, and Howard Morrison, Department of Maori Affairs,
wish to further Maorian marketing opportunities in trade and
tourism by seeking the support of the Hawaiian people; now,
therefore,

BE IT RESOLVED by the Senate of the 13th Legislature of
the State of Hawaii, Regular Session of the 1986, that this
body supports the intent and activities of the NEW ZEALAND
TRADE EXPO to be held in Honolulu.

On a brighter note, Richard Hartman, who was one of my guest speakers at the Maori Businessmen's conference, committed his hotel to assist 'coal face training' of some of our Heritage Park trainees.

In 1985, an executive in the Department of Maori Affairs, Neville Baker, persuaded me to reapply to the department and I was reappointed to work on special projects. Neville had been passed over for the job of Secretary of Maori Affairs; the job going to Dr Tamati Reedy. Now I'm not going to get into a bun fight over the merits of a man I respect as much as Dr Reedy, but I feel that in the history of the Department of Maori Affairs no one person has been more badly treated than Neville Baker. He took early retirement in 1992 when the Quality Inns Affair, prodded and fuelled by Winston Peters, hit the headlines.

Neville, in my opinion, was the most lateral-thinking, most creative and most visionary person it has been my pleasure to work with in the department. And I say that without being embarrassed that he is a very close mate. Back in 1985, he and I became a team. We had already established a very creditable working association. It was he and I who put together the New Zealand Maori Businessmen's Conference in Auckland and our next big project together was working on the Manaakitanga Conference. We spent a lot of time, too, consolidating our

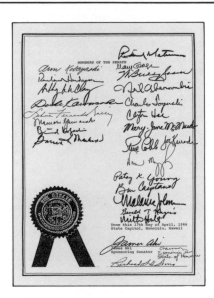

Endorsement for the See, Hear and Taste promotion in Hawaii.

contacts in the business community to encourage subsidised work opportunities for young Maori people.

Early in 1986, Dennis Brown came to talk to the task force with an idea of promoting a See, Hear and Taste promotion in Hawaii, at the Sheraton Waikiki. The idea was that we would hook up with the Hawaiians we had hosted at the Maori Businessmen's Conference. Where better to get a sounding board than in Hawaii, where the heart of Polynesian tourism is actually anchored? We also saw it as an initiative that would show we were pretty serious about what we were doing.

A coup came my way when I received endorsement from the Senate of the Hawaiian State Legislature. It was quite an honour.

We wanted to promote New Zealand by selling off booths where different people and companies could promote their products. There was quite a wide range from the Maori sector; as well as the predictable souvenirs and wool products, there was an effective display of Maori art — paintings and weavings and carvings.

We made contact with duty-free people and they were very keen to promote some of our arts and crafts goods. I also went to people outside Maoridom and got support and participation from Feltex, who not only paid for a booth but were successful in getting a million dollars worth of orders in two days; AFFCO came to the party and did a lot of business with their products; Matawhero Wines, who donated the wine for the launching banquet, secured orders from the Sheraton Hotel chain in Hawaii — 12 or 13 hotels.

But the Maori side was a bit of a disaster. Our contact with the Bishop Museum and the Polynesian centre, though showing a lot of promise, actually fell through. And it was a catastrophe; nothing less than that. The presentation, the promotion, the display was a success, but the spin-offs at the end weren't so good. In trying to get the product back it was pilfered at the different ports and when we returned we faced some very angry Maori artisans who got only part, or none, of their product back. There was reason for severe recriminations and the department was right in the firing line.

I felt for Dennis Brown because while he was trying to run a commercial promotion it did not end up well for him in financial terms. Very badly, in fact.

I took over a cultural group (with family, of course) which I arranged finance for independently. Presentation-wise, I know we did a superb job. But the outcome wasn't good.

Part of the outcome was having a gentleman named Rocky Cribb

The poster advertising the launching banquet for Dennis Brown's 1986 trade and culture promotion.

Presented by ■ JOE BROWN ENTERPRISES (USA) LTD & The DEPARTMENT OF MAORI AFFAIRS.

Featuring
Royal Command Performer

SEE HEAR & TASTE
NEW ZEALAND

HOWARD MORRISON
New Zealand's best known Entertainer and his MAORI Revue.

An Entertainment and Food Spectacular
as part of the

The Pacific's Number One
air new zealand

NEW ZEALAND TRADE & CULTURAL/EXPO 1986

The Pacific's Number One
air new zealand

SHERATON BALLROOM
Monday 30th June Commencing 6pm

ALL INCLUSIVE PRICE $25.00
Includes A Special Buffett Dinner Featuring New Zealand Food Delicacies, Wine Beer & Cheese

*SPECIAL
GUEST APPEARANCE*
by
DANNY KALEIKINI
The Ambassador of Aloha and his Ohana Group

MARLENE SAI

TICKETS
*Tickets Available Sheraton Cabaret Desk,
Telephone 922-4422
Charge by phone 9222411
Pat Kelly Tour Desk
Funway Ticket Outlets*

QUALITY
NEW ZEALAND PRODUCTS
On Display and Available For Sale:

*Arts & Crafts including
Carving, Paintings, Pottery Food Products Sheepskin Products*

Proudly Printed by ACADEMY PRESS LTD.

over there when we met people from the Hawaiian Affairs Department to see how we could further exchanges in trade.

Rocky came to Hawaii on a look-see vacation basis, but everybody was fascinated by his business acumen and forward thinking. So much so that on our return, in an appointment with Koro Wetere, he was not only given expenses to fly back to Hawaii to cement some of these possible deals, he was also given a letter, signed by the Minister, saying that Robert Cribb represented his and our interests. The letter gave Rocky authority to negotiate on the department's behalf '. . . agreements that will enhance the trading opportunities between Maori people and the Hawaiian business community.' (Negotiate but not to finalise!)

Rocky was having some rocky experiences with his own business dealings (unknown to us at the time), and I'm sure he saw the opportunities of being the Minister of Maori Affairs' representative to Hawaii as very attractive. Armed with this authority, the ebullient and very aggressive Mr Cribb eventually made contact with Michael H. Gisondi, who claimed on his letterhead to be a certified financial planner. Gisondi brought in one Max Raepple, who was the contact to some financial authority in Kuwait.

Essentially the deal went as follows: The amount of money sought (of Rocky's own volition) was from $US250,000 to $US300,000 for the purpose of establishing a bank or financial institution in New Zealand 'on behalf of Maori peoples and the nation of New Zealand'. At the closing of the deal, the borrower would pay a 'finders fee' of a maximum of 6% to be shared by the agents — Gisondi and Raepple. The term was 25 years and the interest rate was not to exceed 4% per annum. I guess the collateral was that Rocky's authority was shown as 'representing the Maori peoples and the nation of New Zealand'. That sounds like all of us, doesn't it?

The deal included special conditions. 'These funds are made available to non-Communist aligned, non-oil-exporting countries. The funds are to be used only for development of economic infrastructures of the governments which borrow the moneys.'

This deal was brought back to the Minister — I presume. I lost contact at this stage when it went direct to the Department of Maori Affairs; the secretary at that time was Dr Tamati Reedy. Well, of course, the proverbial hit the fan through the disclosures made by Winston Peters, who had been made aware of the negotiations. It had wide ramifications.

It is now history that the notorious 'Maori loans affair' propelled Winston Peters into the forefront with all the news media. And it badly embarrassed the government, because his insinuation was that Koro was doing all this without the knowledge or permission of the Minister of Finance, the Prime Minister, or Cabinet. In fact, the request for money never got as far as the source of the supposed loan — namely Kuwait. It was cut off at the pass and Koro actually had nothing to report. All that had happened was that Rocky had made contact with Gisondi and Raepple and an agreement had been set out which was dependent on the deal going through for the loan at the Kuwait end.

My personal feelings are that, at 4%, it would have been a very good deal. But, of course, that's history too. Some sections of Maoridom claimed that the political interference was a form of economic genocide; that Maori people were blocked from the opportunity of becoming economically independent. Anyway, nobody from Kuwait sent word to Koro Wetere through his emissary Rocky Cribb saying do you want a government to government dialogue.

From that period, in October of 1986, the Department of Maori Affairs lost its way, and its confidence, in many priorities. There was a witch hunt after these disclosures were made and my mate Neville Baker was made the scapegoat. He had to front up to the State Services Commission; a lengthy inquiry was held which lasted four, five, maybe six months, at the end of which Neville Baker emerged squeaky clean.

The Prime Minister at this time made an unfortunate remark to the effect that the devolution of the department was appropriately imminent; that the department should be disbanded before they did it themselves from within. It probably echoed the sentiments of a lot of rednecks out there who felt Maoridom was incompetent to administer any economic development independently and it was the sort of thing which did nothing for morale in the Department of Maori Affairs.

By now our task force, set up at the first Manaakitanga conference in Rotorua, had completed its findings and put them into booklet form for presentation to the government about where they saw Maori tourism initiatives going into the year 2000. The report was in parts critical of establishments such as the Tourist and Publicity Department and asked for stronger Maori participation in New Zealand's fastest-growing industry, highlighting where Maoridom could participate more prominently, especially with information about this very important aspect of the New Zealand tourist industry, the indigenous history and culture.

It actually took till 1987 for the second Manaakitanga conference, again held in Rotorua, at which the association was formalised and a board, representing Maori tourism interests and operators, was chosen.

Again, HM was conveniently pushed aside. I don't think I was being vain or egotistical in thinking I would be virtually an automatic choice. Through my frequent sojourns in the East, I'd had experience in promoting New Zealand internationally which no other aspiring candidates could match; I'd grown up and spent my New Zealand life in a tourism centre of the country; I'd been a prime mover in the very first moves to organise Maori interests in tourism.

I think I was about the 18th nomination to be on the board. After listening to some of the glowing bio's of the other people who had been nominated, the skills with which they were supposedly endowed, I was actually quite embarrassed that my name went forward at all. My qualifications were humble by comparison. What I am really saying is that for most of those who were nominated, their promo-bio's were laced with delusions of grandeur and more than somewhat out of touch with actuality. So in 1992, seven years after the Maori Tourism Association was launched, it is now called the Aotearoa Maori Tourism Federation. Halleluia! It may be a harsh judgement but, as far as I can tell, so much time has been lost, so many opportunities wasted.

I hope we can make progress from now, because tourism is still the biggest growth industry and it still offers the greatest opportunities for our people to participate at all levels, as operators, managers, administrators, in their own right.

There were shock waves when the new Tourism Board appointed by John Banks in late 1991 did not include a Maori representative. This

Recording our KZ7 song (written by Howard Jnr) before I departed for Perth to give the New Zealand challenge moral support. Morrison family collection

was rectified in February 1992 when the president of the Aotearoa Maori Tourism Federation, John Heremaia Marsh, was added to the board. John Marsh is a very competent administrator and, through him and the Maori Federation, hope springs eternal that Maori aspirations in tourism will make more than just a colourful impact.

As I've said, from 1986 and for the next couple of years, there was a loss of confidence and direction in the Department of Maori Affairs. I still had a contract with them for special projects but there was not much initiative forthcoming and I was getting a bit fidgety.

A bit of light relief to all this drama of the 'Maori loans affair' was when I was appointed a 'cultural ambassador' by Mike Moore and went over to Perth to lend my support to the hype involving the America's Cup challenge of 1986–87.

The Kiwis were the new kids on the block, in yachting terms, and it was only that lack of experience which prevented them from meeting the Australians in the final — that's my layman's opinion. The first day I was there, part of that inexperience showed up in that some things were badly handled — again, in my layman's opinion. That was when they picked the team, well before the playoffs on the water, that was going to be on KZ7. This caused a tremendous dip in morale. I was on the plane with two of the wives who went over and were looking forward to seeing their husbands, only to be greeted by dark and gloomy faces because they'd missed out. It was badly handled. Chris Dickson at that time was an island unto himself.

I gave them a talk — not telling them how to sail a yacht, obviously! — and I was looking around at the faces, because I do know how to read an audience. There were the quizzical, where's-he-going faces; there were the listening to every word I was saying faces; I had an attentive audience. I think I made Michael Fay shuffle in his seat once or twice. What I can still remember, vividly, was looking over in the direction of Chris Dickson. Unlike his father, Chris wasn't outgoing and sociable. He was sitting on his own and I made eye contact with him a couple of times while I was talking; there was absolutely no reflection of interest, disinterest, or anything else from these cold grey eyes. A man seemingly in isolation — by choice!

It was an interesting interlude, though, and we did have some exciting times on the water even if we didn't make it through to sailing off for the America's Cup.

Back home, though the Department of Maori Affairs was going through its period of uncertainty and inaction, there were activities, like the trainee placements from the Bachelor of Business Studies programme, that were still simmering along as well as some of the high-profile projects that I was involved in — and pushed aside from!

As part of my involvement in diplomatic roles in that 1986–87 time span, I was invited to Rarotonga to launch their Aids Awareness programme. I became involved in this through Koro Wetere, who has very strong ties in Rarotonga; they love him over there.

Aids Awareness . . . it was quite frightening, thinking about that trip, because you could see the vulnerability of a small island. On every international flight, on every merchant ship that visited, you'd have no idea of who the carriers might be. And the disease would decimate the population so swiftly if it gained a hold.

The Rarotongans as a people are closer to the New Zealand Maori than any other Island group. I have performed there many times and I feel a real bond of friendship and identity with them.

In 1987, going into '88, I felt my role with Maori Affairs was getting less effective all the time. Koro Wetere wanted me to stay on, and I did; I was put on a contract that allowed them to come to me to promote different programmes and I was otherwise free to do other things for myself.

In 1987, Ron Beardmore of AGC appointed me to the selection board of the Young Achievers competition that was initiated in 1986. Man, the depth of talent that abounds in this country of ours! And what a privilege to have assisted in the final selections. A leading finance company, AGC are to be warmly congratulated on their philosophy: 'An important dividend on investment is the human resource.'

Early in 1988 I took in a show at the Travelodge, promoted by Peter Heremaia, featuring Toni Williams. Peter was taking Toni around the chartered clubs circuit. It wasn't especially lucrative, but it was work.

The bottom had really fallen out of the theatre business. No New Zealand artist, including myself, would have been game to go on the road at that time because the cost of putting on and travelling a show was so outrageously high. Unless you were backed with sponsorship there was a good chance you'd go down the tubes. Since the share market crash times had been tough all round.

The club circuit looked like it could provide a good opportunity to combine some of my national work for the department and tour New Zealand. In touring terms, it was definitely not the high profile of appearing in theatres but we were going to where the audiences were. People were going to chartered clubs rather than to pubs; rather than risk wearing a jug around the ears, they were going to an environment where they knew the company, had their own friendships, their own parties.

I went on the road in about May of 1988, with my own band, and went right through to about November. It was hard work, but I really enjoyed it. One of the upsides was that I was away from the places I was performing at by about 9.30pm, whereas in theatre shows it would be 11.30pm before you'd get home. Another plus was that I was going to audiences I'd never actually lost, the people who used to see me in the '60s and '70s and were now chartered club members. Before I was putting on a show and they were coming to see me, now I was going to their territory.

It never entered my mind that I was lowering my standards. There's no room for snobbishness in this country. There is also an acceptance of whatever is right for the time. I think if they felt I was demeaning myself by going to places like that, they would be demeaning themselves. Sure, I think there were elements among followers of mine who felt it wasn't an atmosphere where they would expect me to perform. But professional entertainers work where the market is at the time.

Towards the end of 1988 I had a couple more trips overseas promoting New Zealand as a tourist destination — my first trip to Indonesia, which was something new and interesting, and to my old stamping grounds in Malaysia and Singapore.

There were more such trips in '89, when I headlined the show the New Zealand Armed Forces put on as a salute to Singapore; they were getting ready to move out. And I went on the chartered clubs circuit again.

When I got back from Indonesia late in 1988 I had a heart-racing problem which hit me out of the blue. It lasted about four hours; what they call atrial fibrillation where the heart goes out of control and the pulse is erratic — scared the hell out of me! I went to the hospital on the quiet and they were about to admit me overnight and give me some tests when it swung back into regular rhythm. I was given some pills to keep the heartbeat regular and sent on my way.

The next day I went back for a checkup and they put the pictures up which appeared to show nothing organically wrong. But I feel to this day that if they'd put me through the stress test it probably would have shown what was eventually picked up in 1991. I say that because the buildup in the tubes didn't happen overnight or in six months. It had been happening over a period of time. I couldn't very well say that the hospital weren't very efficient in not following up every avenue, because the truth is I wanted to believe it was just one of those things. I was still keeping myself fit and Morrison's ego wasn't going to accept anything other than that I was indestructible.

When they did open me up in 1991, they found some scar tissue on the bottom of the heart which indicated a previous attack. And it was either than one, or when I went to France, where I also became really ill.

France, you say? Yes, France! In 1989, in a new learning curve for me, I was front man for a TV documentary, *Inside France with Howard Morrison — Kia Ora, Bonjour*. Kia ora from me, bonjour from them! It was a new discipline and a challenge that I enjoyed. The production house responsible for the documentary was a group called Impact, dissolved as a company not long after this documentary. It is nice to know that the brothers Bradley (the Impact directors) have recently enjoyed success with their 1992 movie *Chunuk Bair*.

The *Kia Ora, Bonjour* producer was George Andrews, well-known in the documentary field, and his skill was valuable to me. He could be a bit of an old tart at times, but then again so could I, so we probably deserved one another. But when it came to the nitty gritty we were a very good team.

Right from my early years at school I've always been a fascinated student of history and geography and in France I was overwhelmed by the feeling of being in the presence of so much history . . . Notre Dame, the Champs Elysee. In Bordeaux, the heart of wine-making country, we saw trenches that were dug where the first vines were planted by the Romans in 50BC.

We went to Marseilles, which has been a strategic port for generations, for centuries, and it made me realise, when I got home, how well off we are and what opportunities we have. We are such an infant nation and yet we're finding it difficult coming to terms with problems like racial issues. You have a look at a place like France, in particular Marseilles, after all those centuries they haven't got it right yet. With our brief history, we've surely got a better chance of facing up to our problems and solving them.

I really enjoyed going into the hinterland and meeting the real stock of France, as it were. They can't stand any comparison with what they feel are 'pretenders', the Parisiens and other big-city people.

We first went to France to capture Bastille Day, and were we lucky! Funding came from the French government because in the year of the bi-centennial celebrations of Bastille Day they wanted to show themselves off as pretty good people, in a light less uncomplimentary than the aftermath of the *Rainbow Warrior* affair.

Through the commitment of George Andrews and his team, we managed to get a prime spot right on the Champs Elysee, on a raised platform, where we could film the Bastille Day parade. The amount of money spent on those celebrations was mind-boggling. The parade of the armed forces alone would have wiped out our national debt and left change to restructure the industrial capacity of this country. But the more the parade progressed, the sadder I got. There seemed such terrible wastage. I'm looking at all this firepower, manpower, pomp and influence — yet basic problems like poverty and starving millions remain unsolved. There's something wrong somewhere, almost like we haven't come far from the gladiatorial days of the Roman Empire. And that fell on its bum!

I saw a lot there that fascinated me, Bordeaux most of all, a special place on earth. It has the absolutely correct soil, it has the absolutely correct climate, the right warmth and period of sunshine, and, at a given time, almost to the day, the grapes are kissed by just the right amount of rain to bring them to fruition at the exact time of harvest. Combine that with the hundreds of years of tilling skills, you've got an unbeatable combination. It's almost as if you had a shaft of light from Heaven and a voice saying: this is going to be the perfect place to grow wine.

While I was in France, unknown to me, events were taking place which were again to have a dramatic effect on the life of Howard Morrison, entertainer. They had begun, of course, even earlier.

When I was on the chartered club circuit late in 1988, I met

During our Kia Ora Bonjour *documentary in France . . . with French rugby winger Jean Baptiste Lafond at his vineyard. Not a bad drop, either!*   TV3

Rosemary McLeod, a journalist on *North and South* magazine. She was in the audience at the Wellington Club. I said I liked her work and she expressed interest in doing a story about me. I said she was welcome — provided she came on the road with us. I wanted her to see me warts and all, the upside and downside, rather than just me telling her the things I wanted her to hear.

She did come on the road and she saw the lot. She saw my compassion; she saw my short-wick temper. She saw my love of singing; she saw our family closeness.

The article appeared in *North and South* of March '89. It was an excellent article, I thought — a potted biography interwoven around the tour; the light and shade, the drunks and rowdies and 'old faithfuls', the battle to be taken seriously. It quoted my mate Neville Baker, then my direct superior in Maori Affairs, as saying that someone like me who could communicate music and culture was 'pivotal in terms of where we're going as a nation. Howard's a pretty unique New Zealander, because he can move comfortably between the cultures. People are looking for the bridge. They don't want confrontation or polarisation.'

I quote that small passage not to massage my ego but to indicate that the article made the point that I felt I still had important social contributions to make.

The *North and South* article activated the interest of Bob Parker of *This Is Your Life*. The advantage for them in keeping it away from my pretty attentive antennae was that I was moving around a lot. I got back from France two days before *This Is Your Life* was sprung on Howard Morrison. A lot of people have asked whether I knew or guessed beforehand. The answer is no, but it certainly played into their hands that I was overseas at the crucial time. And, of course, I'd been ill in France and arrived back dead beat. I wasn't looking forward to rehearsing for a show on the road. I was supposed to be straight back into the club circuit with Peter Heremaia.

The day after I returned I went down to Wellington, to resume the circuit. We were staying in the Burma Lodge, where that night's show was supposed to be held, and some strange things were happening. I had only that day to rehearse the show and the band was not cooking, they weren't quite with it.

I was very impatient with them and getting the pricker with all and sundry. That nobody seemed to know about the show was aggravating me even more. Was I giving Peter Heremaia and the hotel management a hard time! How did they expect to have any people there if nobody knew about it?

As an escape route, there was a meeting set for the Sir Robert Kerridge Trust Board. They'd written to me before I went to France saying they would have it in Wellington, not only to fit in with my schedule but to suit the other trustees. The meeting was set for that day at 6pm and I thought it was a good opportunity to get out of the hotel for a couple of hours. It was one of the few occasions that I would wear a tie.

In *The Dominion* that morning I'd read that *This Is Your Life* was going to be on that night. I'd thought 'lucky blighter!' because it said the guest was so special that they were going to make it an hour-long programme. That afternoon, on my way to the Michael Fowler Centre, I heard on the car radio that they needed more people for the audience for the *This Is Your Life* programme. I chuckled under my breath and thought, 'Nobody's going to turn up for whoever it is!'

I went to the Michael Fowler Hotel by mistake. When I got there at the appointed time, 6pm, no one knew what I was talking about. Somebody realised that I should have been at the Michael Fowler Centre, so I went there and parked around the back. There was a TV van parked there, but it didn't register. My mind was elsewhere. I wanted a distraction from the show I was to do that night; I didn't want to be back in the hotel stewing about it.

I was directed to the place where the meeting was supposed to be and the expected trustees were there — Ray Columbus, Robert Kerridge Jnr, Bill Rowling — and they introduced me to Bob Parker, who was sitting in. My eyebrows went up, internally at least: what the hell's he doing here? Bob Kerridge introduced him as a new member of the trustees. That was fine — but he was wearing makeup!

I'll tell you for nothing that I looked around but couldn't see any cameras. I admit I thought for a moment, 'I'm the subject of *This Is Your Life*.' And I admit to being disappointed that I couldn't see any cameras! They were there of course; hidden behind a partition.

Anyway, Bob lumped it on me. When he gave me the book I sort of backed away from it as if it was red-hot coals. I'm used to creating things. I'm the author of situations. No one pulls these stunts on me!

I have to say that they wouldn't have got away with it if I'd been back in New Zealand. I'm meticulous about details, and in normal circumstances I'd have got to the bottom of the nonsense at the Burma Lodge. Being just back from France, tired and not very well, I let things run.

What happened after that, of course, is now documented history. I must admit that when we went to the studio I felt a bit embarrassed. Thousands of people out there watching this self-indulgent show, Howard Morrison and his family, and I wasn't responding very well. I was definitely put on the back foot and I wasn't used to that. But by the second break, by the time Gerry, Wi and Noel came on, I'd warmed to the task. I'd really relaxed inside and I felt very comfortable with it.

You go out in the world to try to make something of yourself and if sometimes you succeed you spend the rest of your life trying to get recognition and respect. At first I was feeling embarrassed for all the

Thinking about my research into the Howard Morrison *This Is Your Life*, the main memory that returns is the sense of family. Howard is at the centre of an extended family — mother, sisters, children, nieces and nephews, cousins, family and tribal connections — that seem to extend like a web across not just the showbiz world but the whole country.

In researching *TIYL* I remember being told by many in the television business about Howard's tantrums, his huge ego and his demands on people. The impression created for me was of a man of shallowness. In the aftermath of *TIYL* I grew to know the man a lot better. I came to a few opinions of my own.

The picture he drew for me was of a man who has learned about showbiz the hard way. He is very wary of the exploitation that goes on in the entertainment industry.

Howard has earned his stripes standing on the dusty floorboards of every cold hall in every town this country has to offer. He has been the toast of the nation, and he has been yesterday's man, and he has come back. You don't go through a lifetime like that without learning a lot about human nature.   — **Bob Parker**

thoughts I'd had from time to time of not being appreciated. Once I relaxed the night just whizzed through. There was a collection of people there who made for terrific television. Apparently they took hundreds of calls of good wishes.

I didn't stay too long for the after-match function; I was still on Cloud Nine anyway. Worse, I had to get up at seven the next morning to fly to Auckland to record my song for the Commonwealth Games opening . . . an arrangement I wouldn't have made if I'd known *This Is Your Life* was going to be on. Furthermore, I had to fly back to Wellington that afternoon, to do a show at a hotel that really was on the itinerary. Not the Burma Lodge, by the way.

The reaction to the *This Is Your Life* programme right around the country was absolutely unbelievable. When I was at the studio in Auckland next morning recording *Tukua Ahau*, I was fielding calls from Pam Corkery down in Wellington and Phil Warren at 1ZB. They had to put a stop to the calls so I could finish off the recording.

When I walked on stage in Wellington that night the whole audience stood up and applauded . . . not so much because I was coming on to perform but because of the *This Is Your Life* show the night before.

It took me a while to get my faculties together and start singing. The pipes were in bad nick, because I'd sung for about four hours earlier in the day trying to get *Tukua Ahau* down, and it was at the absolute top of my register. But the audience carried me, and I had a lot of mates in. Eddie Low came and I got him up and we got through the show. It was almost as if the last bits of energy had drained out of me, like pulling the plug out of a sink. I went back to bed that night and slept halfway through the next day, I was so exhausted and exhilarated.

It was a tough few days. Paris to New Zealand is no short hop, and that had been followed by flying to Wellington for (as it turned out) *This Is Your Life*; back to Auckland the next morning for recording and back down to Wellington the same day for an evening show. A tough few days — but worth it.

The reaction to *This Is Your Life* was astounding. All my chartered club shows were full anyway but after the programme they were banging on the doors. I'd also had the theatre booked at Nelson to do a show for IHC. The Nelson show was four days away and we had only about 200 bookings. The day after *This Is Your Life* it booked out.

When I saw the response from the public, it kicked me into gear. I said I'm not going to let this go like I did in 1981–82, after *How Great Thou Art*, when through pride and commitment I said I wasn't going to commercialise myself and take some time off from the department to chase the dollar.

While I was still with the department, it was now on a consulting basis rather than eight to five clock-in; it was more picking up on jobs as they came up. Peter Heremaia got Brian Richards to put together a tour of the theatres that could carry on from the 'little tour' I was doing, the chartered clubs.

Well, it was phenomenal.

When the 'little' tour finished I had a show in Brisbane, for the New Zealand Society there, and it was just two weeks before we'd set the itinerary for the major tour of the big cities to start. It would have been a promoter's dream to have known I was to be on *This Is Your Life* and it was going to be such a huge success. We could have started the planning and arrangements back in April. As it was, we had to do it almost 'stop press'.

Brian did a hell of a job. Of the Young Turks — that's the next age group after the Benny Levins — he probably is the most creative theatre man around. Expensive caviare and champagne tastes can get in the way but as long as those are kept in check he does a great job.

A sincere word or three of thanks and appreciation is appropriate here to Peter Heremaia, a leading promoter of shows to the chartered club circuit. He put me in there, which led to the McLeod article in *North and South* and then on to *This Is Your Life*. Thanks, Pete.

While I was over in Brisbane word came that not only was every theatre booked out but Brian Richards was asking if he could put on a second show. We did two shows in Dunedin, one only in Christchurch, two in Wellington at the Michael Fowler, two at the Logan Campbell

Backstage with whanau at the 1989 Christchurch Variety Spectacular.

Morrison family collection

in Auckland (that's 3000 people plus!), two in Hamilton and three in Rotorua. Three in Rotorua! The *Bible* says a prophet is without honour in his own country and my home town has always been the hardest for me to crack, in show business terms. But we did three shows in Rotorua — unreal!

My family has always been there for me when I've needed them. But this tour was the first in which I integrated them into a formal part of the show. It was magic being able to share this 'Howard Morrison is back' tour with the family. Barely a year earlier, no New Zealand artist, myself included, would have been game to tour the theatres. This was the biggest all New Zealand show since the Quartet years. No other local artist had put on two shows, and twice filled, the Logan Campbell.

Things went crazy in 1989. After our last show at the Logan Campbell, the family and I were part of the Variety Club show recorded for television and I'd been booked to do a Christmas Carol show at Mt Smart. Also in '89, back in August, I'd had Neil Roberts of Communicado following me around doing the first of the *Magic Kiwi* shows.

So what I had in the can was *Kia Ora, Bonjour, Magic Kiwis* and the Variety Club show; by Christmas Eve I had the Christmas Carol show I was compering . . .

After the *This Is Your Life* show in September, Barry Shaw wrote in the *Herald* that it was great television; now, what about a Morrison TV movie? By the New Year, he was writing that we were in danger of seeing too much of Morrison.

This is where you have no influence over people cashing in on the fact that you are 'hot'. Commonsense tells you that all this exposure and publicity is lovely, but you'd like to spread it over a year or so. In fact, you have no control over it, everything comes in a rush — and suddenly you're 'over-exposed'!

My *Magic Kiwis* segment wasn't intended to be the first one on the air but, with Morrison in such high profile again, it was promoted to lead off the series. So, following *This Is Your Life*, they put on *Magic Kiwis*, they re-ran the *Don't Let It Get You* movie from the sixties, they put on *Kia Ora, Bonjour*, the Christmas Carol show, the Variety Club show . . . I think there were seven different shows in which I was on television. Talk about overkill — I was getting sick of me myself!

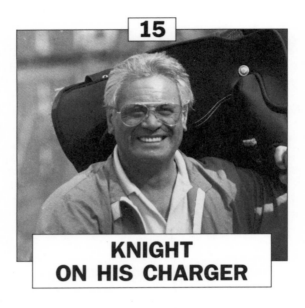

15

KNIGHT
ON HIS CHARGER

COME 1990, AND A good leveller to bring me down to earth again
was being part of the Commonwealth Games opening ceremony.
I spent enough time involved in the preparations to see, for instance,
that many of the boys and girls involved in the cultural segments of the
opening ceremony were unemployed. These young people had been in
rehearsal for weeks to get it right and that was probably the most
positive Social Welfare money ever spent. They were on the dole but
were gaining mana, pride, through participating in a national event.

When I was doing my song in rehearsal, these kids were looking at
me in awe. 'Aw, gooday Howie! Cher!' They got a buzz out of the fact
that I was one of them. And I got a buzz out of *being* one of them.
Because I wasn't headlining, I felt equal to them, part of the show with
them. I never felt any butterflies. We did the dress rehearsal the night
before, and when my name was announced you'd think it was Caesar
come to greet the loyal legions.

When the real thing happened, I was still in the mind frame that
I was part of something we were all proud of. No butterflies, no dry
throat. I just went out and opened up and went for a note at the end
which I wasn't brave enough to do in rehearsals. There was no tentative
sneaking into it. Just whack! That's how carried away I was. A lower
note would have been perfectly acceptable, because I had strings, brass,

plus 600 voices behind me! When you see that you are singing to the mass movement that Logan Brewer had created, depicting waves, and migrations, and Polynesian influence and other aspects of New Zealand's history and lifestyle — I was just carried away with the euphoria of the occasion and gave it everything. It was a proud moment for me; proud to be part of it all.

So 1990 carried on from where 1989 had left off. In February I began to step up some promotional ideas for The Culture, so to speak. I got a very good hearing from Drew Stein of Electricorp Marketing about a project to do television vignettes on Maori myths and legends. This was an idea I'd first begun to push when I was on the Broadcasting board. Now seemed an appropriate time to do something concrete. With all the mileage and the publicity I was getting, again there was that commitment to give something back, something meaningful and long-lasting.

In places like Singapore, Indonesia and Malaysia they actively promote their indigenous culture through simple TV programmes like their equivalent of *Sesame Street*. I thought why not start with short vignettes of Maori myths and legends. I put this idea to Stein and Electricorp Marketing became a sponsor together with New Zealand on Air. The commitment from TV3 was to show the programme on a regular basis between 2pm and 5pm and sometimes as fillers during the weekends and even during adult viewing hours.

It became a major project and brought to the surface a lot of latent talent in the form of graphic artists, producers and directors. We used high profile people to tell the stories and launched it in September 1990. Yet another magic September!

We completed 60 vignettes which are still being shown. There was also a compilation made available to schools as a teaching aid. It was a nice, subtle way of taking it into the homes with no intimidating factor of the culture being pushed down people's throats. TV3 have put the whole compilation out for public sale and the sales have been very good, proving that after two years a demand for the tapes has been established.

If I was asked to name any one contribution to television I'd like to be remembered for, top of the list would be creating *Maori Myths and Legends*, combining with a good friend and a man I admire a lot, Tom Parkinson of Isambard Productions, with Don Selwyn there to keep us honest.

The preparatory work on *Maori Myths and Legends* got under way in February, the month I went over to Bangkok again to put on a show for the New Zealand Society there for Waitangi Day commemorations.

In April of 1990, after Billy T had gone through his heart transplant operation, he made a comeback at the Aotea Centre and I supported him on that show. It's funny, looking back; I had that tickle up in 1988, the irregular heart-beat problem. And when Billy went down in 1989 with a heart attack, it really scared the hell out of me. I was wondering how far away I was from the same situation. When I quizzed him, some of the symptoms he described were alarmingly similar to what I went through at that time. When he did the comeback show in 1990, there was almost a reluctance of people to come to the show; almost ghoulish. There was this hidden worry.

Billy did virtually the whole show; to my mind he did too much. He wanted to show the audience and New Zealand that he was alive and kicking — the show was called *Alive and Gigging*. He didn't have to work as hard as he did and I mentioned that to him on stage during the show. It was a magic night, though. We had a wonderful post-match reception where everybody was so thrilled to have Billy back on deck.

Meantime I was rehearsing songs for a show I was planning at the Aotea Centre with the Neophonic Orchestra. I started putting things together in May, because I have to live with songs for a while before I feel I can produce the delivery to do them justice.

I was wearing five or six different hats — working on *Howard Morrison Live at the Aotea Centre*, keeping an overseer's eye on *Maori Myths and Legends*, a doco on the Cook Islands for TV3. And, at the same time, I was looking at realising an ambition I'd long held, to do a ride round New Zealand on horseback. I was inspired in 1988 by Susan Devoy walking the length of New Zealand. I thought there must be an easier way; I'll do it by horse!

I initially went to Murray Deaker, who was then the executive director of FADE, an organisation set up to combat drug abuse. I was also looking at Child Cancer as a possible recipient of any proceeds from my ride when it came to my notice that Sharon Hoggard was putting together a trek with a guy called Moa Larkin, promoting Life Education. They were already some way down the track, so I decided to go with them.

So there was a lot on my plate as May turned to June. And there was one other event in and around all this. The 1990 Queen's Birthday Honours List included the name of Sir Howard Morrison, KBE.

Murmurings of a knighthood began to reach my ears in the latter part of 1989. I've since found out that there had been a number of overtures prior to that from different sectors of the public to have me knighted. Mike Moore told me something interesting. He said that his government felt neat, giving it to me, but added a rider that it was funny about how 'dirty' opinions of a public figure could also be. What

A lot of people thought, 'How does this soft, nightclub entertainer think he's going to ride the length of New Zealand? He won't make the first 50 kilometres!' But I didn't go in cold; I got plenty of practice on my trusty steed!

NZ Herald

he was intimating was that my name had come up on previous occasions but, for one reason or another, had been passed over. I frankly thought that it could have been before my time anyway. I was embarrassed when people came up to me asking how I'd feel if my name went forward for a knighthood. What do you say to something like that? But I got used to it after a while and I'd just say . . . well, it would be bloody marvellous.

— I don't know how much ego was attached to that, there'd have to be plenty. But, at the same time, my goal was always to succeed; to honour my father, to honour my family.

Through these initial murmurings I didn't really think a knighthood for HM was a possibility. But some more approaches were made in January, and the Maori Trustee, Neville Baker, asked me for an updated biography, apparently to support submissions from other people and organisations. Actually he wasn't giving much away, and neither was Koro Wetere. What had a lot to do with it, I think, was *This Is Your Life*. I know that programme once more accelerated me into the public domain; made me very high profile again. Well, it makes sense doesn't it? *This Is Your Life* showed in September 1989 and almost two weeks later these approaches were being made about a knighthood — the ripple effect.

After these subsequent approaches I forgot about it and carried on with 1990, which was already shaping as an exciting year. When the preparations for the Commonwealth Games were coming together, I got to thinking that it would have been mind-boggling to have a couple of billion people throughout the world watching the opening and closing ceremonies of the Commonwealth Games, with a Knight doing a part of the opening and a Dame in the closing ceremony!

In early April 1990 I received a letter from the Governor-General's office. When I saw 'Government House', I instinctively knew. Sure enough, the letter from the Governor-General said I had been recommended for the honour of Knight Bachelor. When I actually saw it in print I couldn't believe it. When your highest hopes are realised, when you actually read it . . . I went all prickly, my palms were wet, I grabbed Kuia and gave her a hug. Then I sat down, stunned. For the next week or so I wasn't communicating well with anybody. I stayed away from people, went for rides in the Urewera country, let it sink in. I felt humbled by the whole thing.

The next communique you receive is the day before the announcement of the honours — 'Congratulations'. Up until then anything could happen because the first letter asks if you'll accept the honour. I think the envelope was still hot when I sent my reply back — I felt like hand-delivering it!

From the first letter from the Governor-General to the announcement, I told only Kuia. I kept it a secret from the rest of the family.

This photo mightn't win art awards but it could have had historic significance. It's the shot of my horse I took while I was having chest pains in 'the outback'.

With Mum and all four sisters on stage in Christchurch, 1989. Morrison family collection

Always a special delight . . . performing with my mother.
Morrison family collection

Uncle Tupara in 1990.
Morrison family collection

Daughter Donna shows her skills with the pois.

OPPOSITE: *Oldest son Howard Jnr . . . winner of 'Best Male Leader' at the Polynesian Festival, Ngaruawahia 1992.*

My younger son Richard, also skilled in haka and Maori martial arts.

Daughter Donna and her husband Anaru Grant. A love of Maori culture brought them together.

Back to show biz, fully recovered, October 1991.

Hot Shot Studios

As I travelled around the country with him on the 'Ride For Life Education', it became apparent that Howard has a clear picture of his own worth, to himself and to those who want to exploit him.

It is fair to say that much of the exploitation is unwitting; people asking for more at the end of a hard day that they haven't thought about — 'Get up and sing us a song, Howie'; a fan demanding that Howard come and meet his friends, or a pakeha not understanding the protocols of Maoridom . . . 'The local organisers thought it'd be great if the local Maoris welcomed you down at the marae . . .' (Howard's mana demands time-consuming ceremonial.)

Thus Howard sometimes says 'enough' and the rest of us can get a little wound up by this. We want him to do it our way, of course! However, with a little increased awareness of the pressures of his lifestyle and his tremendous work experience, we can begin to appreciate the wisdom he has accumulated from all those years on the road. It can be frustrating for those working around him, but Howard is usually right.

He is a man of considerably more depth than probably even his strongest fans realise. He is personally and politically aware. Look at his work with young people, especially young Maori. He never missed a chance to encourage the young tangata whenua to get on with life, to get involved and take advantage of opportunities that are there for them. It's as if, as he has grown more aware of his own rights, more assertive in his own career, he has also been keen that others, too, break out of the mind constraints they place on themselves.

I began to wonder whether 'Ol' Brown Eyes' might have one more major career move still to come — politics. Nah, too many small halls to play and he's done that. Governor-General at least!
— **Bob Parker**

To be honest I didn't know how to handle it, I was a bit nonplussed. So I decided Kuia and I would go to Hawaii, get right out of it while the announcement was made. But I got the dates wrong, went a week too early and got back before the announcement anyway!

Just the same, the trip did me good. I was expecting the announcement to be made while I was overseas, so I told my American friends in Hawaii on the quiet that, though I hadn't heard anything else since, it looked like I was getting the knighthood. My American friends were overwhelmed. You'd have thought they were standing beside the Queen's direct representative. 'Say, I've never met a real Sir before!'

It put me in a better frame of mind. I got back home and thought, 'You selfish bugger; this is a time for sharing and thinking about how other people feel.' When the Honours List came out there was a front-page picture in the *Herald* of me and my grandson having a bath in our mineral pool. That's when I made the statement that I didn't know whether I could be serious about what a knight is supposed to be, or how they are supposed to look, except that I didn't feel like a knight.

Sir Charles Bennett looked and acted like a knight. Sir Apirana Ngata looked and acted like a knight. Sir Hepi Te Heu Heu, chief of the Tuwharetoa, looked the part. Graham Latimer was more my speed — gumboots and a swannee. Dame Kiri Te Kanawa was a natural, because she was a diva, bringing international recognition to her

This rather cheeky cartoon by a gentleman named Ellison summed up the differing attributes of the three new knights — his version, anyway!

country. But Richard Hadlee and I were a departure from tradition. In Maori terms I was only a bit of a pup to be knighted, not a tribal leader; and for a sportsman like Richard, who was still playing first-class cricket . . . I definitely felt we broke the mould.

The announcement of the knighthood in June meant I was Sir Howard Morrison when I undertook my Ride For Life. I'm sure it helped to lift the stature of the fund-raising trek.

The Aotea Centre concert came first and on the day of the show we did the launch of the Ride For Life with a ride up Queen Street. I had a cowboy hat on and the gear which I would usually wear riding. I had to come back to more accepted equestrian garb, skull cap and so on, later. Billy T, All Black Zinzan Brooke and other well-known personalities lent their presence and support to the launch.

The Aotea Centre show that night was the realisation of some dreams of mine. I'd worked with the family before, but I'd never done a show with a full symphony of strings behind the sort of front line I'd normally use; three saxophones, three trombones, three trumpets and a strong rhythm section. In all we had 60 musicians plus six backing vocalists. I worked with Carl Doy as my musical director to put the whole thing together.

I brought the family in and had up my sleeve a few surprises. Buck Shelford really enjoyed himself that night. He led 'Kamate kamate' as a surprise during *My Old Man's An All Black*. I changed the words around: 'My mate Buck's an All Black, he wears the silver fern, his mates just didn't want him so they gave Zinzan a turn (who does some modelling on the side!)'

Billy T's entrance caused an electrifying response from the audience. That was his payback to me, for my supporting him on his show earlier in the year.

The day after the Aotea Centre show I recorded an interview for the TV series *When The Haka Became The Boogie*. Then I was on the plane for Invercargill to start the Ride For Life.

There was a lot of apprehension about me undertaking that ride. How could Howard Morrison, entertainer and cabaret performer, ride a horse the length of New Zealand? Did he know what was involved? What wasn't generally realised, of course, was that I had ridden horses from an early age and I'd stepped up my riding during the course of the year to increase my 'saddle fitness'.

As if 1990 wasn't busy enough, it was also the year of Telethon for the elderly. I was appointed one of the trustees to distribute the funds and producer Andy Shaw gave me the honour of doing the theme song *The Living Years*. I was very comfortable with the words of *Living Years*, about how we should appreciate our elders while they're around, and some of the lyrics had special significance for me as they pertained to me and my dad.

'I wasn't there that morning when my father passed away . . .

'I didn't get to tell him all the things I had to say.'

Very poignant.

That Old September Song again — Telethon, the launch of the Ride For Life, the televised Aotea Centre shows . . . all in September.

By the time I got to Invercargill, I was completely whacked — but I was really ready for the ride. I had only one discipline to attend to, one project to concentrate on. We'd got a huge sponsorship response to start the ride when we launched in Auckland and when we got to Invercargill to start the ride proper there was another huge donation from Trust Bank. We were a quarter-million in front before I put a leg over the horse.

The ride started in lousy weather, but because of the sheer novelty

My 'million dollar' Ride For Life mate Nero (right) meets double Olympic gold medal winner Charisma at Tirau.   Waikato Times

of it there was no discomfort or pain. From Invercargill through to Balclutha was the wettest part of our ride but it didn't dampen our spirits or the enthusiasm of the crowds who turned out in their hundreds. In Balclutha they were led by the District Mayor, Keith Fyall, and the Clutha MP, now Speaker of the House, Robin Gray. What a character he is!

I can't detail the highlights of the Ride For Life — I'd need half the book to recount them all. So, having mentioned the first stages of the journey, I'll leap up to the middle of the North Island and then to the top.

We had a huge parade going into the Waikato town of Cambridge and that section of the ride remains vivid for two reasons. One, we called in at Patrick and Justine Hogan's Cambridge Stud, where the champion thoroughbred stallion Sir Tristram stands. And on the way in to Cambridge, from Tirau, we were joined by the great horse Charisma, of Mark Todd and Olympic fame. What a beautiful walk that horse had! He carried himself like a ballet dancer. I was on Nero, who must have felt a sense of occasion. His ears were pricked and he was ambling at such a majestic gait that it was almost like horse to horse; I'm as big a star as you are!

Now we leap to the Far North. The daybreak church service we had at Cape Reinga was very spiritual. There we were, right at the tip, the leaping-off place for the spirits of our ancestors. Spine-tingling stuff. Wind-swept, we sang our hearts out. That day we completed our longest ride, in one day, of the whole trek, some 72km.

In Whangarei we met the mayor, Stan Semenoff, and his wife — a former vocalist with our Showtime Spectaculars of the 1960s, Kim Kreuger.

You couldn't have orchestrated a better way of meeting the people, the whole cross-section of New Zealanders, from kindergarten, through to the retired and the elderly. The kids at the schools were the ones who really kept the momentum up and they were the programme's target.

The radio stations, Bob Parker in particular, did an outstanding job of promoting the ride. 'Howard will be at such-and-such a school at such-and-such a time. . .' It was on the air all the way and the kids were outside all the schools, chanting Howard! Clap-clap-clap. Howard! Clap-clap-clap. Great stuff, absolutely amazing. I felt absolutely

Early in the ride, at Timaru — a fistful of dollars. Timaru Herald

fulfilled. Just let me finish this ride and I could fall off my horse into my grave and die happy. That's how I felt. Almost prophetic, as it turned out!

The ride encapsulated all those elements but the kids were the driving force. Towns turned out, the streets were lined. The warmth of the reaction again proved to me that New Zealand is a very caring country. New Zealanders are very patriotic, and they'll link arms to support something they see as worthy of support. I found the country was alive and well, and full of hope. And the people found our programme, Life Education, was one they could relate to as saying something positive about the future.

Motorists along the way were great. When they saw our entourage they waved out and tooted their horns; it was practically an automatic gesture to wave back. Of course the Ride For Life nurtured my ego. My head didn't swell so much that I nearly fell off the horse, but of course I felt good about it and good about myself. I thought about those years of influence, about my dad, my brother, Canon Wi Huata, my mum and Kuia; I thought what a great thing to have happened to me, in my lifetime.

But it *was* the Ride For Life. The message was never lost. It wasn't an odyssey to promote Howard Morrison. Pardon my saying so but I was already famous; my knighthood had already been announced. As Paul Holmes said in his interview at Christchurch, this is the kind of thing people take up to get knighted!

I had two horses. One belonged to Moa Larkin, the day-to-day trek road boss; a big horse, 17 hands high, named Phoenix. The other was Nero, owned by a university student named Amy who generously lent him to me. They were quite different characters. Phoenix was a do-the-business horse, no tricks up his sleeve — except when other horses went past him when we were having a gallop down Moeraki Beach, just out of Oamaru. The bugger bolted with me, so I used the old Ruatahuna training and headed him straight into the cliff face. He stopped and I almost carried on!

Nero had a real personality. Like his rider and now owner, a hell of an actor. But I could ride along a line of kids and know he wouldn't tramp on them. They'd 'high five' with their hands and I could lean right over to touch their hands without having to do any reining to keep on a straight line. Nero had a very fast amble, a beautiful pace. I've clocked him at 15km/h and he could sit at 10km/h for an hour. Both horses were very strong.

Some people have trouble riding a horse that is pacing but I was brought up with 'amblers' in Ruatahuna. They were a favourite type of horse. And a pace is only a fast amble. I can sit an amble all day, whereas the equestrian one where they trot and you lift your bum with every stride and down again — I can't do that.

All through the Ride For Life the kids kept the momentum going.

Cambridge Independent

I believe I had a more comfortable ride than the others although I got mushrooms on the old bum after the first week. I'd been wearing those bicycle pants under my jodhpurs, plus a sheepskin on the saddle. I didn't care if people said I was a cissy; it was my bum and I wanted to be comfortable. But the bicycle pants caused humidity — ideal for growing mushrooms! I had an uncomfortable two or three days but I hardened to the task. My upper body and thighs became very strong. During the first eight days I got very stiff and sore around the neck and top of the shoulders. It was almost as if the weight of the helmet and

It was nothing for Howard to do five media interviews before he got on the horse. That was the interest the Ride For Life created. Howard had incredible charisma. It was fascinating to see him interacting with people from all sectors of New Zealand's population; children at the schools, elderly folk in retirement villages, 'middle New Zealanders' in the street, mayors and dignitaries. He had this incredible respect from all parts of our society; he captivated them. — **Sharon Hoggard**

the gait of the horse combined to put pressure up there. But that wore off. And I chopped off about 10lb during the trip.

We had an itinerary which could not have been finished unless we took some short cuts. In other words, we had to float the horses at times between towns to meet the timetable. I have no qualms about admitting that. I know there were some cynics who said it's a sham, he's not riding all the way. What was the point in riding through thirty miles of deserted plains waving to the sheep? The job was to take the message to the kids. The regional organisers were doing a great job, all voluntary. They wanted us to come to places important to them, and if that meant taking a few shortcuts that was no problem to me.

That's another of the great things about this country. While you've got a voluntary base driving a project, you might not have the professionalism and the polish. But you can excuse that because they'll generate more enthusiasm and support than an organised, paid-for, synchronised team of professionals. You'd call Bob Parker a professional, which he is. But he only did it for digs and transport costs, because of his commitment to Life Education.

The run-up to the elections was on during the ride, and it was amazing the number of politicians who were falling over themselves to hop on a horse and come riding with Howard. Going into Rotorua I had Max Bradford, Peter Tapsell and Paul East; in Christchurch Ruth Richardson joined the cavalcade (no side-saddle for Ruthie) and in East Coast Bays it was Don McKinnon, whose horse and helmet both looked too small for him!

The Ride For Life was so successful that we could go back to the areas we never touched and do it again, and it would meet the same reception. I want to do just that some time. Well, we proved that. Nine months after the event we did the East Coast and met the same sort of reception.

An outstanding thing for me was to meet, among that cross-section of New Zealanders, many who had supported me over 30-plus years in entertainment. Face to face, shake their hands and talk to them. So the ride meant more than Life Education for me. It was another way for me to reach out and say thank you; you helped to put me there and I'm grateful for the chance to promote a worthwhile cause that we're all supporting.

The Ride For Life was a great success, not only in the way it was received by people throughout the country but in practical terms, in the money it raised for a very worthy cause: Life Education.

Midway through the tour, of course, I had to take a break for my investiture, that stirring and dramatic ceremony with which I began this book.

In November, when I'd completed the ride, I launched into a three-week concert tour and the people turned out again — this time

> Howard was not only generous with his time, his personality, his speeches, his singing, his charisma, but during the whole 42-day trek he charged not one cent. No fee. I remember him saying that New Zealand had been good to him and this was an opportunity to give something back.　　　　　　　　**— Sharon Hoggard**

for the entertainer. A moving experience of the concert tour was having the honour to present, on stage, a cheque for over $100,000 to the class-mates and families of the Aramoana victims. I was only the messenger on behalf of the people of Auckland, who had responded generously to the tragedy.

Thank you Auckland and a big thank you to my fellow trustees. Come December, when the tour finished, I said to myself: Self, it's getting harder to scrub the act up and get the body together because it feels shot to bits. I will not work for six months in 1991.

Before I went on the ride, after many approaches from publishing houses, I had accepted a proposition to collaborate with John Costello on an autobiography. So I thought okay, for the first six months of '91 I have a reason to tell anyone who wants me to do something to go jump in the lake. By then, too, Labour was out and National was in. The Department of Maori Affairs was in for some radical change, led by Winston Peters. Part of the change meant there were going to be some cuts. The head of Iwi Transition, Wira Gardiner, indicated to me that my contract with Maori Affairs for 1991 would be under review. I could anticipate that until such time as the restructuring was completed, I would be on hold as it were.

On hold? Well, in fact I got notice from Gardiner in January of 1991 that my contract would not be renewed. Neville Baker's letter of November 1990 had been more promising . . .

> . . . Thinking back to the time when you joined the Depart-ment of Maori Affairs in 1978, it was clear that your appointment was a result of the very high profile that you enjoyed at that time. The task that you were given, to identify the destination of school leavers and maximise the opportunities for young Maoris' further education, training and employment, was a very good idea. However, it soon became obvious that the bureaucracy of Maori Affairs steadily resisted your appointment and your full value as a high-profile leader/entertainer was not taken advantage of.
>
> In retrospect it seemed to me that many of the top managers in Maori Affairs saw you as someone to compete with, or as a threat, rather than a person to get behind and utilise the obvious talents and contacts that you had at that time . . .
>
> Your many activities both nationally and internationally with

the Department of Maori Affairs would normally have brought major advantages to that organisation and to Maori people. But this potential was never quite realised, because the leadership failed to recognise the value of an entrepreneurial appointment . . .

It seems also that the Iwi Transition Agency has under-estimated your ability to be a major contributor towards the development of opportunities for other Maori people and also as a commentator on the real state of race relations in New Zealand . . .

. . . your most recent venture [Ride For Life] illustrated that New Zealanders see you as representing what New Zealand is all about and what it should be in the future . . . [It] demonstrates the practical way in which you have contributed to New Zealand and highlighted the need for everyone to recognise that the health and livelihood of our children is in fact our future heritage . . .

I am keen to ensure that as we are now moving into a new era we do not make the mistakes of the past. I believe we need to plan for the way ahead, so your contribution is better managed and supported . . .

16

KNIGHT IN DANGER

THE END OF 1990 saw Kuia and I take our annual sojourn in Hawaii before undertaking another discipline: putting words and pictures together for a book. In Hawaii, Bill Tavares is our host. This friendship goes back to when the American forces used New Zealand as a base in 1943. Bill and his buddies Peter Wong and Phillip Kam met up with our extended family in Mitchellville (Ohinemutu, Rotorua) while on R&R with the 65th Combat Engineer Battalion. Visits of families to families since the war have now passed through three generations and will continue, I'm sure, ad infinitum.

Back home after the New Year festivities, I decided that I wanted to give up smoking. I returned to the Urewera country, where I worked out and wrote a few notes for the book. I was up in Maungapohatu, the stronghold of Rua the Prophet, with my son Howard Jnr; living in a little bach there courtesy of the Tuhoe people. We were up at 3000 feet there and after fishing with Howie one day we were walking back up these steep hills and I felt a bit of shortness in the breath. 'Thank goodness I'd given up those wicked fags,' I said.

The next day I went for a ride and hunt up this beautiful valley, full of history, where Rua the Prophet established his own kingdom; with his own bank, his own police force, his own flag. The imperialists couldn't stand for that — and they went in and arrested him on a trumped-up sly grogging charge. The atmosphere in the valley is time-

After the hustle and excitement and razzmatazz of late 1990, I headed up to my Ruatahuna therapy ward to relax — and think about an autobiography. I look pretty relaxed in this photo from an earlier visit . . . but things didn't go to plan.

Bruce Jarvis

less. You can feel the history; you can almost feel the spirits of Rua and his followers.

It was quite early in the morning. The horse I was on was no Bonecrusher, but these mountain horses could be relied on to walk all day and into the next week. After an hour or so I decided to tie the horse up and do a stalk, although I wasn't very serious about hunting; if a silly deer poked his head out, I'd bowl him over for the meat.

I'd walked only about 100 yards from where I'd tethered the horse when I felt this peculiar tightening right in the middle of my chest. There were no sharp shafts of pain, it just made me feel very uncomfortable. I know my body so well that I instinctively felt this was not only something different; it was something I should be worried about. I paused and, for no reason at all, took the camera I was carrying around my neck and photographed the horse. Funny the things you do! I didn't think I was going to snuff it, not if I had any say in the matter, and I knew I'd be easy enough to find; Howie knew which area I was going to hunt. But in case anything happened, I thought, let me record this event.

I lay down after that, put my feet up on a log and let the blood go down. I got up after half an hour and continued the walk. Then it happened again. So I said to myself: Self, I think we had better go back to horse and trundle back to the hut. Which I did, but I really took my time. In fact, for the first hour, going downhill, I chose to walk the horse. The pain and the effect of this spasm, or whatever, had left me by now. But I thought it would be better for me to be walking rather than riding the horse in case I involuntarily tipped off.

Even though the pain had gone away I really took my time. It was about 11 in the morning when I started back. Just on dark, many hours later, both walking and riding, I eventually got on to the road which would take me back to the village and our bach. About half a mile away from the hut, which is beautifully placed on a rise overlooking the valley, I saw the lights of a vehicle approaching. It was my son Howie who, knowing I'd been out all day, was getting a bit worried and was coming to look for me. I didn't say anything to him. We had a meal — he'd cooked a great stew — and then I said: 'We've had our time communing with nature; I think we'd better head back to the concrete jungle tomorrow, refreshed and on top of the world.' I kept the conversation light-hearted.

When we got back to Rotorua I didn't say anything to Kuia, either. Silly me. But the next morning, which was a Sunday, I saw our doctor, Dr Sill, and told him — sort of. I told him I'd had these pains and, just for my own peace of mind, could he give me a note for the Cardiology Unit in Green Lane to check me out. He said I'd had a hard 18 months, I should have a thorough check-up and he put together a bit of a case history and a general resume of the state of Howard Morrison to take up to Auckland. And off I went to the 'smoke'.

At 7am the next day I had to do a breakfast show. Air New Zealand and the Pan Pacific Hotel had brought out some tour operators and representatives of a radio station to promote the country. It was a great initiative and I was asked to talk about myself and our country live on air to Los Angeles.

Before I left my hotel to go to the Pan Pacific I had an involuntary sweating condition and I was pretty tied up constipation-wise. Anyway, I put on a brave face, did the radio show and had some breakfast. Then I trotted off to Green Lane and showed the receptionist my note from the doctor. What made me feel more comfortable was that the receptionist was Bonnie Allen, wife of my ex-musical director, friend and confidante Bernie Allen.

Bonnie sent me up to the Cardiology Unit, where I was received and thoroughly quizzed by a young doctor. I went through some tests:

blood pressure great, pulse rate great, cholesterol level normal, X-rays clear. While I was waiting for the final test, which was going to be the stress test, they told me that Billy T, unknown to the public, had been in there for about a week. So I went along to see Billy.

'Hello, doy! How are you, doy?'

'Oh, I'd not be feeling the best, doy,' says Billy. 'And what are you doing here, doy?'

He thought I'd come up to see him, and how did I find out? I told him I'd be the check-up-have-a, using our old slang, and so far I'd be the Okay one. He said you look after yourself and I said never mind telling me look after myself, you'd be the looker-after of yourself!

I said to him that I had one more test to do and I'd come back to see him before I left the hospital. The stress test was a treadmill job and I started off at a nice easy pace. Then they inclined the treadmill and increased the pace and after about three minutes I felt the tightening in my chest. I guess the attack of biliousness and indigestion I had in the morning was another signal of things not being too good in the heart department.

So it only took about three minutes and everything on the screen was going haywire. They told me to sit down while they looked at the charts, talking in lay terms. The young doctor brought the cardiologist, Dr Harvey White, and he said: 'We would like to do an angiogram and see what your heart is doing.'

I still hadn't told anybody; I was up there on my Pat Malone. So there I was, half past four, and they took me up, gave me a local, pumped this dye up through my veins and that showed how the arteries were functioning. They didn't talk much because they were concentrating on what was coming up on the screen. Actually, I was yapping my head off but they wouldn't answer me! Fancy, free entertainment and they'd not be the reactors!

I was taken back to the ward and I had a room next to Billy's. I poked my head around the corner: 'Hello again, doy!'

'Hello, doy! Still here?'

'Yeah, you'd better shift over, mate. I don't think I'm going anywhere!'

We had a bit of a chuckle, a bit of light relief, because inside I was pretty worried. And it didn't take long to get the news. When Harvey White had looked at the pictures he came to me and said: 'I'll give it to you straight — you're in the big league! You have two arteries completely clogged with plaque and bits and pieces in the third one. You're a heart attack waiting to happen and the immediate thing that has to happen is a triple bypass operation.'

Well! I reckon I took that pretty calmly, especially when he said I was in the big league. No ingrown toenail problem for Morrison — this was the big time!

I called home, told Kuia the bad news. Said I was OK, that I was quite resigned to the fact that I was a sick boy. Yes, it was a life-saving operation and I put my faith in the fact that these people were experts and knew what they were doing. It was almost a relief, in a way, because I'd known for some time that there was something not right inside. Particularly in 1989, when I was in France and after I came back, I'd get drawn and a bad colour too easily. My eyes weren't bright and they reckon the eyes reflect what's inside.

Dr Sill said I was one of the most perplexing patients for an MD to have. My blood pressure always tested OK, my cholesterol level was always OK, my pulse rate, apart from that one time when my heart raced, was always all right and my X-rays showed clear. It wasn't till they did the stress test and pumped the 'ink' into my veins that they found the clogging of the arteries. People like me, he said, could go through life and suddenly die of a massive heart attack. It was perplexing.

So I'd be the lucky one, especially when you consider that my real warning hit me when I was a lot of miles, and many hours, into the bush on my own. My inner feelings tell me that fate was on my side. Something drew me back to the place of my childhood and that something may have saved my life. Yes, oh yes, I'd be the believer!

The first things they look at when trying to diagnose the reason for a heart condition are genetic factors, blood pressure, cholesterol, whether you are a smoker. In my case the first three were all clear. Being a smoker obviously was a definite factor.

One aspect which cannot be defined medically is the role that stress plays. While cardiologists recognise it is indeed a contributing factor, they can't put it under a microscope and identify how much stress individuals are suffering or its effect on the heart. I think it is a major contributing factor. People generally who overburden themselves with work develop a variety of harmful stress reactions and the entertainment business imposes particularly high demands. Over the years, just reading through my bio to this point, the life and times of Morrison as an entertainer from 1960 onwards definitely put me in the high risk bracket as far as stress was concerned.

While I've always seen the need to balance the hyperactivity with time for relaxation, my only real escape was into the Ureweras and I obviously didn't do it often enough. Anyway, when you get years of comments like 'Morrison is a ball of energy; the fittest and most well-adjusted fella in show biz,' I have to admit you get delusions about your strength and power. The key is to have the ability to keep a balance between confidence and conceit; to maintain humility and honest self-assessment.

Meanwhile, back on my back in Green Lane, the die was cast. Howard Morrison was in there and by the next day, February 19, the bush telegraph from the hospital had spread the word that I was laid

Sir Richard Hadlee lends his support to the Ride For Life. The two of us were knighted in 1990, heart patients in 1991.

up with a heart condition. The six o'clock news on TV confirmed that I was in Grecn Lane and said it was understood I was suffering a heart condition which necessitated a triple bypass operation.

When this was confirmed, an unfortunate situation arose when one Deirdre Kent, of the anti-smoking group ASH, was very quick on the bandwagon to claim that people like myself and Billy T. James were in hospital with heart conditions that related directly to smoking.

She made a big issue out of it and, when taken to task about it on the 20th, was unrepentant about the comments she had made. When she was later criticised about the bad timing of her comments, in view of the fact that I was about to go under the knife and that it had brought a lot of distress to my family, she tried to square off by saying it was her understanding that I'd already been in there 10 days and was therefore still going through tests. This, of course, was a convenient way out but not true. But when I was recovering back at my home we had a live hookup with the *Holmes Show*. She apologised and I expressed the hope that it might indeed do some good to promote the work that ASH was doing in the community.

My 'sweeping the decks' in Green Lane to get everything tidied up included a bedside update on my last will and testament. The family arrived in force and all stayed at my sister Linda's place in Auckland. I had my four sisters, my mum, my wife and my children around to comfort me.

The operation was a success. The surgeon in charge was Ken Graham, who turned up in full running gear for his morning visits to patients. Perhaps this was a ploy to get his patients up on their feet quicker, because he certainly is a no-muck-around man. I was out of hospital on the seventh day and back home in Rotorua, armed with all the information for the recuperation plan.

What a tremendous experience that operation was. We all know that the health professionals in the hospitals are underpaid and over-worked. But when you see it first hand, the matter-of-fact acceptance, commitment and dedication that they have towards their work, it's mind-boggling. It made me realise how fortunate I was.

I love entertaining, I love seeing smiling faces, I love making people happy. I love it and it's contagious. Hospitals present a different set of circumstances. These people are dedicated to making people better and there are many sad moments when they lose their patients. Yet the dedication is so profoundly evident that you become very aware of how much you have to be grateful for, how much you should enjoy the life you've been given and look after the life that you've got.

I made rapid progress, riding my 12-speed bike and doing other exercises after four weeks. I wasn't extending myself, I was just doing what I felt my body could handle. It certainly soon sent out the signals when enough was enough and it needed to rest. And wasn't I pleased

With some of the Get Well messages I received while recuperating from my heart operation.

NZ Herald

that at the end of 1990, after doing that tour which followed the Ride For Life, I'd said to myself that my body was shot to bits; I would take six months off, not do any work, and concentrate on the book and getting my body right. OK, my body was more shot to bits than I'd realised and 'getting it right' was a more major undertaking than I'd anticipated, but I hadn't made any commitments so I wasn't in a situation where I had to cancel a whole screed of engagements.

It was appropriate that in Green Lane I wasn't given any special treatment; I was given the same care and attention as any of the other patients. And why not? All my professional life I'd been a public person. Why shouldn't I be in a public hospital?

While I was there I was overwhelmed by the cards, letters, telegrams, faxes . . . all manner of written communication. The Get Wells from all over New Zealand numbered hundreds, from people in all walks of life, many from people I didn't know.

Overwhelmed is probably an understatement. I used to look at them and shake my head. I not only felt grateful but I honestly felt very special. It made me go into myself spiritually and give thanks that I'd been given another chance. The down-to-earth expressions of concern and support from hundreds and hundreds of New Zealanders reminded me that I'd been around a while, that I'd made a lot of people happy and that they were out praying for me and wishing me well . . . which, I have to say, beats a standing ovation any day.

I actually find it difficult to express now damn fortunate I was. I don't usually have much problem painting pictures with words, but this experience, even a year and more after the event, is still very difficult.

What a dramatic and unexpected start to 1991!

At least my recuperation period allowed me time to sit back and put some thoughts together for this book. And it put me in the right frame of mind to look back over my life in a positive way.

In looking back, from my childhood right through to the present time — man, I realise that I really have lived! The passages of my lifetime have been rocky, smooth, high and low. But no saying would be more appropriate than that Frank Sinatra phrase:

'Regrets, I've had a few

'But then again, too few to mention . . .'

Okay! Enough of Maori tears, fears and thank you God! Foremost in my mind when I had that period at home to think how the book should go was that it should be as honest as I could possibly make it. And I wanted it to be basically an entertaining book, with as much fun as possible but warts and all.

So here is a resumé of the women in my life . . .

•   •   •

But seriously, many of the people who have influenced me in a forthright way have been women. I emerged from my teenage years with the influence of my mother; Kuia is a stalwart who has always been there for me; when I started singing, Mrs Whatarau was a strong influence. I have four sisters, whom I love and respect; a lot of my close friends have been women. Their personalities are wide and varied.

Perhaps my respect for women is not only attributable to my Maori side because there are indications that the Irish side of me may have passed down the same values of respect for womanhood. Though feminists might disagree, there is a very strong Irish tradition of near-reverence for maternity which is reflected in the status accorded to womanhood. Be that as it may, on my Maori side the womb of woman is sacred for obvious reasons. That's where all mankind comes from and, for once, that chauvinist 'mankind' is appropriate because without women there would be no mankind. The earth is sacred in Maori mythology, being called Papatuanuku (Earth Mother).

One of the main reasons my Te Arawa protocol forbids women to speak on the marae in formal ceremonies is a hangover from our traditional past. In pre-European times these formal occasions sometimes developed into physical altercations because the marae was not only a sounding board for praise but also a platform for airing grievances. This could lead to bloodshed as a speaker could be challenged to one-on-one combat. Obviously a woman speaker would be put at a considerable disadvantage if insulted during these proceedings.

Going a little further, if a woman speaker had been pregnant then the insult would be two-fold, and have a domino effect of insulting the family and the tribe. Despite the fact that insults being hurled across courtyards in my area are now few and far between, don't hold your breath waiting for Te Arawa to change their ways.

Getting back to the 'other women', that I'm not going to talk about, I spoke to Kuia about this aspect. She didn't raise her eyebrows, merely saying, 'I think that's private. Things like that have always stayed within our four walls.' She's a realist. When John Costello asked her how she'd reacted over the years to the 'other women' that, in his words, seemed part and parcel of a high profile in show business. Kuia's very quick reply was 'We're still here!'

Kuia has a wicked sense of humour, too. I wouldn't want to give the impression that she is a passive or submissive woman and that 'what he does is OK'.

I started Kuia running about 10 years ago and she has been running ever since, including completing the Fletcher Marathon in May 1992. She's played top-grade squash and she's off a 10 handicap in golf. So she keeps herself fit.

By the second week in May 1991, I was fit enough to caddy for Kuia at the Maori golf tournament in Taupo and Sharon Hoggard, of Life Education, got in touch with me as to whether I'd be OK to support the presentation of a Life Education mobile classroom donated by the Williams Family Trust for use in the Tairawhiti area — Gisborne and the East Coast. I thought it a wonderful opportunity to get Nero out of the paddock and throw a saddle over him and not only

Not the most glamorous photo of Kuia — but why would it be? She has just completed a marathon, aged 50-plus! Proud of her — then, as so often.

ride around and say hi to the kids and promote Life Education but also to go to an area we'd missed in 1990.

We arrived in Gisborne in June for the presentation, a formal fund-raising dinner at the Sandown Park Hotel. After the dinner, which was very successful, I went back to the room definitely feeling off-colour. I had an uncomfortable clammy feeling and the discomfort grew. By two in the morning I was in a lot of distress with pain in the lower side just below the ribcage.

Kuia got the hotel people to ring a doctor, who came around and diagnosed that I probably had gallstones. So there I was, in an ambulance at three in the morning and admitted to Gisborne Hospital. We didn't want any guesswork about this one so I got Sharon Hoggard to ensure that the appropriate press statement was issued. I didn't want anyone confused that it was a heart condition; it was totally unrelated. I was under the spotlight again: Howard Morrison admitted to Gisborne Hospital. But gallstones . . . not very glamorous! It meant, of course, that we had to cancel our Ride For Life up the Coast, which was very disappointing all round. (I completed the ride in November 1991.)

Three days later I had the operation and I was very well looked after. My recuperation for the first 24 hours was quite rapid but then, for some strange reason, I found it a painful experience over the next 24 hours. In terms of discomfort and sheer pain, it was worse than recovering from the triple bypass. That was a bit of a shock, but again there was the heart-warming response in cards and messages; I remember some beautiful posters from the schools I'd visited the day before I went into hospital.

I was in Gisborne Hospital for three or four days and got myself pretty upset because my irregular heartbeat came back again. Even though they gave me what I call electric pad shock to try to bring it back, it persisted and really made me like a bear with a splinter in its paw. I'd been thinking, of course, that the triple bypass would have cured the irregular heartbeat. But no sir! It had not.

I have to say that I was very down as I could see myself being vulnerable to more heart trouble for the foreseeable future. I went to Green Lane to see my cardiologist, Harvey White, and they were about to give me another electric pad shock when, lo and behold, the heart beat went back to normal.

I suppose a lot of it was anxiety. We're talking about having another operation four months after the triple bypass so my confidence was very low. I must have aged 30 years in front of my own eyes; very despondent and not the happy one!

Time had to be set aside for recuperation . . . I was used to it by now! I slowly came back to being mobile; a return of confidence and positive thinking made me realise that time heals all and don't be impatient. Harvey White and Dr Sill were in contact all the time, keeping my spirits up, and the family was always there to humour me as much as possible and give me comfort.

I returned to some form of active duty, in terms of putting more words together for the book, and my duties with the Telethon Board of Trustees who were selected in 1990 to distribute the funds to various organisations who service the needs of the elderly. By the time I came back on the scene most of the decisions had been made and what a sterling job the board did! There were thousands and thousands of applications.

Frankly, I was quite pleased that I'd had an enforced hiatus from that responsibility. The three meetings I did attend were enough for me to realise that one could get paranoid about the right and fair perspective on all these written applications. Thankfully the Telethon executive staff, especially Bridget Farrelly, did all the donkey work, giving us very thorough overviews and recommendations.

After the last meeting of the Telethon board, on August 7, I had business in Auckland so I flew from Wellington that night. I was leaving the terminal to pick up a rental car when a taxi driver came running over to me and asked whether I knew if it was true that Billy T. James had died earlier that day.

I couldn't answer him; it was like a thunderbolt. Just a sort of gasp came out. I didn't say much to him at all, that I can remember. I got in the rental car and, within five minutes, the news came over the radio confirming that Billy had died.

17

FAREWELL BILLY T.

I PULLED THE CAR over to the side of the road and had a big sob. And just cried out why, oh why, oh why? By the time I got back to the hotel, TV3 and people from the *Holmes Show* had phoned asking if I could give a comment. I wouldn't. I couldn't. Simple as that.

In the meantime Billy's body had been taken back to the house that night. The next day I learned what the arrangements were — to keep Billy at the house, have a memorial service in the cathedral in Auckland and then to take his body to Taupiri Mountain for burial. That was apparently his last wish, asked of his wife Lyn.

I phoned Lyn that night and tried to comfort her as best I could. I was worried about the Maori side. Local Maori people felt that Billy should have been lying in state on the marae in Auckland and the Tainui people felt that Billy had to lie at Turangawaewae if he was to be buried on Taupiri Mountain.

The next day Paul Holmes interviewed me. I hadn't had a very good night and when I saw the playback it looked like I hadn't slept for a week. I looked aged — maybe I should have applied for a Telethon grant!

In that interview, I made the statement that, in Maori terms, it was impossible for Bill to go to Taupiri Mountain until he had lain in state on a marae chosen by his people. The day before I remember saying to Elaine Hegan, Billy's agent, that I had the feeling his body might be more or less hijacked. We all know the aftermath. While the debate raged on talkback

Two brown caballeros in the Queen St parade which launched the Ride For Life, September 25, 1990.

radio and other media, with everybody giving forth opinions, the rights and the wrongs of it, Billy was taken back to Turangawaewae. He was buried without Lyn being there but his daughter Cherie was with him at the marae and at his burial.

My comment about the situation is simply that Billy, unfairly, asked of Lyn something that she was strong enough to try to make happen. Billy wanted to lie at home; he wanted a service in the cathedral; he wanted to be driven straight to Taupiri Mountain for the burial.

Why would Billy have asked for that? Simply, he didn't know the protocol. When you die it's out of your hands. Billy was illiterate in terms of tradition, kawa, etiquette.

It ended up a real shemozzle. What could still have happened, to have kept everybody happy, was that the memorial service could have been held with his body present at the cathedral — and then his body could have lain in state at Turangawaewae before the burial on Taupiri Mountain. But there was so much anger, so much stubbornness and definitely a lack of communication.

A group of us, including Tom Parkinson, some of Bill's colleagues from Isambard, Don Selwyn, Selwyn Muru, Robin Ruakere, Charlie Te Hau, Craig Te Hau and Dennis Brown, all seemed to conveniently arrive at Turangawaewae at the same time. So we all went on together to pay our respects to Billy. In my speech I said to Bill (which is the way we go; we talk to the person as if he is still alive, because his spirit is still alive) that he had unfairly put Lyn in a position where she was trying to meet his wishes, out of his own ignorance.

But there was also the compassion, in the tears that we all shed for Bill, that our poor mate was so far estranged from his own culture that he didn't bother to find out, in the event of his death, what the right procedures would have been and how they could have married up with his own wishes.

I still blame Bill, because he faced his own mortality in 1989 when he had the quadruple bypass and later when he had the heart transplant. And then, when I was in hospital for my triple bypass in February, he was on the decline from that time. Yet the silly bugger still didn't take care of business. I'm talking about business-business, too, in terms of how his assets were to be dealt with. He went to the grave leaving behind a whole lot of financial problems that his family didn't deserve, let alone leaving a country in turmoil about the rights and wrongs about what the procedure should have been after he died.

I admire Lyn for being so stalwart and so strong in what she saw as her duty to fulfil her husband's last wishes. I definitely became one of the 'baddies' in her eyes. When I phoned her the night Billy died, she asked me as a special favour if I would be one of the people who paid my respects at the cathedral. When I came back to the memorial service at the cathedral, there were a lot of people who were not only looking

Even backstage, Billy found it hard to keep a straight face. NZ Herald

at me sideways because I was one of 'them' (Maoris), but it actually brought to the surface some bigoted views from those who knew no better.

The night before the memorial service, Tom Parkinson phoned me — I know it was very difficult for him to tell me this — and he said: 'I hope you understand, Howard, that I am merely the messenger, but it is Lyn's wish that you don't participate in any acknowledgement to Billy at the cathedral.' I wasn't devastated. I accepted that. But I was still there.

After the church service I drove back to Rotorua with my son Richard and his girlfriend Rawinia and we stopped at Taupiri Mountain. We had the mountain to ourselves. I made my karakia, my prayer, to the mana of the mountain; to its sacredness and to its earth that embraced the bodies that rested in peace there. And it is a sacred mountain; kings and queens, high priests, common people, all whanau. I went up to our mate's grave and said to him, 'Well, buddy, I don't know whether or not you wrote the script for this one but it certainly was a humdinger. You'd be the stuffer upper! Rest in peace dear friend. Go to your mother, go to your relations, go to your ancestors. Rest in peace.' And I felt good. I didn't feel uncomfortable.

I wrote to Lyn and told her that, irrespective of what had happened, tradition had been observed and I didn't feel one of the 'bad guys'. It's a great comfort to me that when Richard met Lyn by chance some time later she told him she had received my letter and carried it around with her in her purse; that one day we must get together and talk. That day will come soon, before the anniversary of Billy's death, because my desire is to be one of the many who will be by her side when we remember the passing of this great man Billy T.

A legacy that Bill should leave to this country is the realisation that there are many people, of the same age group and younger, who are ignorant of the most sacred of Maori traditions, the tangihanga. Bill's passing highlights the need for greater understanding of the indigenous culture — which does not belong, and I've said this many times, to Maori people alone — for the benefit of all who may, in the future, be affected by a similar situation.

The tangihanga is not just a sad occasion. It is also an occasion which allows the extended family, the extended tribes, to gather and pay tribute on the marae the person belongs to; tribute to his heredity and the environment the person has been part of during his living years with the bottom line the mana of the person who is being paid homage.

Part of the privilege of acknowledging one's Maori side is to know your traditional roots. Billy did not but he did express a strong desire to learn more.

In a span of less than a decade, Billy T. James became such a celebrated entertainer. Always the raconteur, the quick wit, a man who made millions laugh; even though he died before his time, he left us memories which, with the help of his films, TV shows, cartoons and poetic narrative will always be there for us to remember and, for generations to come, to enjoy.

Yes indeed, William James Te Wehi Taikato. He touched everybody's hearts.

Let's not forget, of course, that Billy's fine-honed talent didn't happen from the time he started out with *Radio With Pictures* and reached tremendous popularity. It was the result of many years of paying his dues. He toured with the Maori Volcanics and with show bands in many countries overseas which required an artist being involved in more than one discipline, in becoming multi-talented. Billy was a vocalist, an impressionist, a musician and, obviously, a comedian.

On stage with Billy T. when he joined my show at the Aotea Centre.

John Dolan Photography

By the time New Zealand saw him, the man was versatility personified. He was ready for his own audience.

It's hard to imagine a guy as funny as Billy being as shy in private as he was. But turn on the lights, turn on a microphone, give him a character, give him the audience — and he was something else.

Selfishly, I regret not having the opportunity to have worked more with Billy, particularly on television. We did a little skit, the two 'brownies', on his comeback show after his heart transplant. Apart from a few lead-in lines, most of it was ad-libs bouncing one off the other. We worked really well, and easily, together, and I'd have loved the chance for us to have done more together. Back in 1986, Billy T and I were proud recipients of 'Entertainer of the Decade' for two respective time spans — me for 1965 to '74, Bill for 1975 to '84.

I don't want to sound ungracious (which means I'm about to!) but I really think I should have at least deadheated with Billy for his winning decade. But that's to give me a bit more credit for what happened in my career during those 10 years, 1975 to '84, rather than detracting from Billy.

We all have regrets about Billy's passing. I guess I express the sentiments of the thousands upon thousands of New Zealanders who remember him with so much affection when I say, 'Thanks for the memories, Billy T. James. Rest in peace.'

FAMILY PORTRAITS

THROUGH THIS STORY, my dad and mum and wife Kuia have obviously featured prominently. Now is a good time to look at the rest of my family, who are also such an important part of my life.

My brother to brother relationship with Laurie in early years came to a temporary halt when the family moved to Ruatahuna. There were four years difference in age between Laurie and myself and he stayed back to attend Rotorua Boys' High School. Laurie spent those years, from 14 to 18, with our Aunty Tiddle and his cousins who lived in the Koutu area, by the lake. This probably had a lot to do with Laurie being a very independent individual. While he was estranged from his family in day-to-day life, he had his extended family, including our favourite auntie, to look after him. But he assumed a very manly role from an early age.

About the time the family came back from Ruatahuna to Rotorua, and I was at Te Aute College, Laurie was on his way to Ruatahuna to teach at Huiarau School. So we missed out on those early years. I was in Ruatahuna while he was in Rotorua; I was at Te Aute College while he was in Ruatahuna. Then I went to the freezing works, and really I never caught up to my brother until he had passed his 21st birthday and was well on the way to a career with the Ministry of Works.

At that time Laurie was better known for his vocal abilities around Rotorua than I was. When I got back he was being called the Dean

Brother Laurie.

Martin of Rotorua, Maori Rotorua anyway. As things progressed after Dad died, Laurie assumed the head of the house mantle, a role he slipped into very easily. During this period we started singing together with makeshift vocal groups. Laurie was baritone and lead singer, I was the tenor. But all through this early part of our singing, it was extracurricular as far as Laurie was concerned, just something he enjoyed doing. The only exception was when he sought leave from the Ministry of Works to come to Australia with us in 1957.

Laurie and I were poles apart in character and nature. He was very serious about detail, and doing things right, and at times it would be fair to say that he 'over-cooked' his attitude as head of the family. Laurie married quite young. He married a girl from the King Country, Hana Stafford, and they raised a family of eight children.

Laurie made rapid progress with the Ministry of Works and was very well respected. On the sporting side he wasn't so much a player as an organiser, and his administrative skills saw him as chairman of the Bay of Plenty Maori Tennis Association. He was also, for a time, chairman of the Waikite Rugby Club and was instrumental in the early stages of fundraising which enabled us to move from our clapped-out old clubrooms on top of Koutu hill to the new clubhouse, further down the road, which he never saw. Laurie was also keen on squash.

Although he chose not to stay with the Quartet when we went fully professional, it didn't stop Laurie being involved with his singing. In fact, he formed a group of his own. We had some hilarious times comparing notes. He didn't listen to me much but I remember one time I suggested to him that he should get his group done up in Indian turbans and call it 'Laurie Morrison and the Turbans'. I made the suggestion very much tongue in cheek — but he took it seriously and followed it through! So we had photos of Laurie and his group the Delkings (thankfully, he didn't use the name I'd tossed in) with these ridiculous looking turbans; no association with ethnic origins or anything else. I was too embarrassed to tell him that they looked stupid, and I was only joking anyway! Again thankfully, it didn't last long.

Laurie instigated the hangi and concerts at the THC in Rotorua. In those early days they were quite a novelty and took a while to get on their feet. But all through the early stages of developing custom for those hangi concerts, Laurie did a very good job. He could be a very provocative character and, if things went wrong, he'd let everybody know from management down. While he was there, he was in charge. Sadly, a little later, management for their own reasons replaced him. The hangi concerts were suddenly going well and there were moves by other Maori group leaders to move in. That's the only word for it. And move in they did. But I can record that, in the promotion of culture, my mother was always in the forefront and my brother Laurie was the pioneer of the now very popular hangi concerts.

On Queen's Birthday of 1974 Laurie was killed in a road accident on his way to Whakatane. He was only 42 years of age; still a young man, with a young family. It was a tragic loss, and affected us all deeply. Mum was devastated. She'd lost Dad at 45, Laurie at 42, and the brother I never had, Charles, at 18 months.

Hana has been very strong in overcoming her loss and did a great job. Laurie's children, all eight of them, have done very well. The best known is Temuera, who has achieved many milestones in acting and entertaining. The others also have individual strengths, in culture and in academia. Laurie would be proud of his children.

My sisters are, from the eldest, Judith Merenia, Rene Kahu, Adelaide (Atareta) Carol and Linda Moewaka. I missed a lot of their childhood when I went to Te Aute College and later to the freezing works and I didn't come back home until they were teenagers. They were brought up with a lot of love.

On the family's return from Ruatahuna, Mum took up the concerts again and played an integral role in the cultural performances that were a feature at our meeting house, Tamatekapua. She got the girls involved and by their teenage years they had all become very proficient. In later years it served them all well because it not only allowed them the opportunity of touring New Zealand with cultural revues but, on many occasions, they were picked to promote New Zealand overseas. And, of course, they did a lot of work with me in places like Hawaii and Bangkok.

Our family has been blessed that our culture has been an integral and important part of our upbringing. It has allowed us to attain many horizons.

Judy married very young. I would say — with not the least bias — that under the tutelage of someone like Dame Mary Leo, Judy would have been a soprano the equal of any this country has produced. Judy is very businesslike and very efficient. She had great secretarial skills, being attached to schools in that role, and was postmistress at Maketu, on the Coast. A take-care-of-business home executive par excellence, Judy's life revolves round her immediate family, her husband Terry, her children (Carol Ann, Lynn, Susan and Terry Boy Jnr) and now her grandchildren.

Where Rene came by her nickname Bunce, heaven knows. Bunce is the professional caterer cum Maori Alison Holst, the kaitiaki of the family. She likes looking after people, organising hospitality for them. Bunce can be relied on to whip up something at home at a moment's notice or to organise feeding people on a larger scale. She's also strong in administration skills and has a fantastic voice. Rene married Ricky Mitchell, son of the great chief Hamuera Mitchell, and their children are two boys, Ricky Jnr and Justin.

Kuia and I have spent and still spend a lot of quality social and recreational time with Ricky and Bunce, going back to the mid-sixties. With my good mate Roger Solomon and his wife Mirth we used to terrorise the water ski lanes of the Blue Lake in Rotorua, bash our way into and through squash tournaments, run the hills back of the Whaka forest and later enjoy the conviviality of dining and dancing as our reward for being so industriously recreational. These days we plod around the golf course, have a kai before dark and lie on the couch.

Adelaide (Atareta) is nicknamed Din. Why Din? Because as a little girl, when she was hungry she'd call out for her dinner — her din-dins! Now Din is the professional cultural person, married to Trevor Horowaewae. They came together through their mutual interest in culture; together they have achieved outstanding success as performers, as leaders of groups both nationally and internationally. They've toured with Inia Te Wiata on the Continent and their son Inia is named after that late, great man. They also have a daughter, Kahurangi. Din and Trevor's cultural work is their passion and they have passed on their knowledge to many others, notably the Ngati Rangiwewehi cultural group (a sub-tribe of Te Arawa).

Adelaide was adjudged the outstanding female leader, against 26 other team leaders, at the 1992 Waitangi Day Polynesian Festival at Ngaruawahia. So 1992 has been a wonderful year of achievement for

Back, my wife Kuia and sister Linda; middle, Mum and Judy; front, Rene and Adelaide. This photo was taken in 1975, when the family toured with me for the first time.

Morrison family collection

> All I have for Howard is accolades. What he has achieved has
> been through professionalism, hard work and that wonderful
> voice of his. With all he's done, all the high circles he has mixed
> in all the honours he has received, he has never changed in the
> heart of him. He has never put himself above anyone. Back home
> we joke and reminisce like we always did.   — **John Morrison**

our family, culturally. It has been well earned because there has been
a lot of hard work and heartache balanced by the success they've
enjoyed. At the time Mum's mokopuna numbered about 18, Adelaide
and Trevor worked in together, Adelaide taking the mantle from Mum,
to develop the tremendous cultural talent in the next generation of the
Morrison family.

So that's Din. She also has an outstanding voice and was called on
to sing the opening song, *Po Kare Kare Ana*, at the cricket World Cup
at Eden Park.

Then comes the baby of the family, Linda Moewaka. Linda was
born while we were at Ruatahuna. She's a real pakeha, fair skin and
freckles. And what a character, always has been. Too young to have
detailed memories of Dad, Linda grew closer to myself and Laurie.

Linda is also strong in culture, but more the producer. She's tried
her hand at many things and is a high achiever in work connected with
the stage. Modelling shows, culture, drama — anything associated with
the performing world is her forte. You could put her out in front to
welcome anyone from Governors-General to visiting Maori groups on
the marae. She is a facilitator and, in Maoridom, is a most under-
utilised person considering the talents she has. I've always believed her
day will come. Linda is more a mate than a sister; I can share with her
things entrepreneurial and promotional. Linda has a son, Aaron, and
mokopuna Charlotte-Anne.

My sisters Judy, Bunce, Din and Linda, together with Mum, have
been a formidable combination — and a huge part of my life. Thousands
of people throughout the country who have supported me over many
years have also taken my family to their hearts but I have also profited
in cementing friendships made through them or the family.

The first time I introduced my family to the New Zealand public
was when the Quartet came back together in 1975 for the reunion concert in the Christchurch Town Hall. Every opportunity I've had since
then to bring the family together, led by the four sisters and Mum, I've
taken. They helped me with the Quartet when we re-formed in 1979
for a tour to promote Tu Tangata. They've always been there for me
and they've supported me in my musical endeavours both on and off
stage. In November-December 1989, following the *This Is Your Life*

programme, I was again flavour of the month. On the road we went again, the family and I, and huge crowds turned out. For the first time since the sixties, a New Zealand show was able to do two shows a night. They've appeared with me on TV, on stage, internationally, throughout the East; they've always been there.

No tours I have been on, in this country or outside, give me as much personal joy and satisfaction as touring with the family. It has meant more to me than even the Quartet years. Everything else has been like an act. But touring and performing with the family combines everything. The voices, the culture, the wairua — the inner spirit, of the family.

I don't know if any other person has been blessed with the same opportunities I've had. Usually, for most entertainers, it would be show business first and everything else, including family, second. For the first part of my show business career it was that way. But for it to turn around from the mid-seventies to where I am now is more than anyone could have asked for. It would have been enough for me to have achieved success on behalf of the family. But for me to share, and have shared, that success with the family, has been such a tremendous God-given privilege.

So to my children. Our first born, Donna Mariana, has grown and developed into a young woman any father and mother would be proud of. In the early years of the Quartet, when Donna was a baby, she travelled quite a lot with us, including some of my stints overseas. The school years were difficult for her at times because of who her father was. It was something I never anticipated or appreciated; in fact, Donna never complained about the hard times she got, especially from intermediate to high school. It made Donna a bit of a loner except that she was very close to her cousins Carol, Taini and Lynn.

I think those early years made Donna more fiercely independent as a person. She was never a cause for worry, always doing well at school, and her interest in culture grew over the years so that, hand in hand with her career as a school teacher, she has done very well. She married Anaru Grant and they have two beautiful children: Anaru Jnr and Hiwaroa (named after Kuia's father). Donna and Anaru's cultural interests have taken them to most parts of the world. Their first overseas trip, which was a cultural experience as well as being a paid honeymoon, took them to the States with the New Zealand National Brass Band.

Donna remains a school teacher. She is very forthright, very articulate and she doesn't stand any nonsense. Donna's main asset, I guess, is her personality. She's not into moralising, or gossiping about how other people should live their lives. Her love of family, her husband, her brothers and her father and mother are her priorities. I'm very proud of her.

Homecoming from overseas trips were always 'dining out time'. Round the table from left: Howard Jnr, Richard, Donna, me and Kuia. Arawa Studios

The difficulty for me in talking about my children is that they are so close to me that I can't be objective. My feelings are deep. But as they are perceived by others, they are very popular, they make friends easily and they give a lot of themselves.

Everybody wants to have a namesake but I actually wanted to call Howard Hiwaroa, after Kuia's father. It was Kuia's decision that he should be named Howard. Well, the poor fellow, he's had to bear a name which, I think, has made life difficult for him. But he's got a great heart; he's very charitable and loving.

Howard recently made the headlines when he wasn't chosen for the cultural group going to Expo in Spain after winning a 'best male leader' Polynesian festival title. I don't want to dwell on that, because he is my son, but I know that he is a leading light as an exponent of Maori culture. In tutorial work he has given his heart to assisting others, and he has also profited from his culture by having the opportunity, like Donna, of entertaining in many parts of the world.

The question again has to be asked: what price culture? It has never been taken as seriously as it should be in terms of getting the right rewards for what our culture means, or should mean, in representing our country overseas. The paradox is that while the culture has been very good to all of my family, in Howard's case it hasn't been a rewarding experience in terms of finding a career for himself. A dream of mine is for people of Howard's experience and level of accomplish-

With first grandson Darren.   Morrison family collection

ment to be part of a Maori theatre which would be given parallel
acceptance and support to, say, the New Zealand Symphony Orchestra.
And I'm just talking about the culture now; not because I believe my
boy Howard should be given a privileged entree into being subsidised
because he is such a great exponent. I'm talking about the hundreds of
people out there who have made culture a foremost priority in their
lives — because they believe it is something intrinsically valuable,
something priceless, which should at all costs be preserved.

Because of his name, I guess, Howard has always found it difficult
to push himself as hard as he should. He has always been reluctant to
make a bold stand for himself. And yet, in what he helped to create for
his Ngati Rangiwewehi club, Howard's endeavours won him Best Male
Leader for the Polynesian Festival at Ngaruawahia in 1992. Howard
not only led them but also composed the music for the poi and action
songs, working in tandem with his Auntie Din, Uncle Trev and Maori
linguist and tribal folklore specialist Uenuku Fairhall.

I'd have to say that at age 29 he has more creative talent than I had
at the same age. His voice is in the same range as mine; he definitely
has the looks and the aura about him. At the moment, following the
festival, he represents quite a celebrity sex symbol if I correctly inter-
preted the reaction of the fair sex, especially after seeing his delivery

and physique portrayed in living colour on television.

Richard Te Tau (Te Tau meaning the dawning, the year, the happening) is named after Canon Wi Huata, Te Tau.

One thing my children have in common is they're all very sensitive. They don't like conflict, they don't like drama and they are givers. They don't badmouth people; they like being liked and they like sharing things. Richard is of that personality and had, from an early age, training in the hospitality trade. He's a natural communicator, a great diplomat, and at present he's a freelance sound recorder in television. Richard is a very striking boy and all eyes turn on him when he enters a room. He's well liked by guys and pretty heavily pursued by the female gender. As a person he is gracious and kind to a fault; he'd give you a dollar if he had only one left. Very strong in culture and a great haka man, Richard has tremendous physique. I started Howard and Richard off in martial arts at an early stage, when I came back from my sojourns in the East. Richard carried on with it. He loves the outdoors, especially diving. He's a fast-lane liver, our Richard, and everybody loves him.

Well, those are my children. We are all very close and, as a family, we like to keep ourselves private. We don't share our problems with anybody outside our immediate family.

As I mentioned elsewhere, you look at your life for achievements and what you might leave behind. I know that my greatest achievements are reflected in the way my children are, and the way their children are, and are going to be.

The children, particularly the boys, adore their mother. And their mother Kuia . . . they're a credit to her. She is fiercely protective of them, right or wrong. Donna I guess is Daddy's girl. As a unit, as a family, we have a lot to be thankful for.

19

HAERE RA
— FOR NOW

THE YEAR 1991 brought life-threatening illness and a major operation; months later a less life-threatening but equally painful and
enervating illness, another operation. It brought the tragic and traumatic
deaths of admired and loved friends and fellow entertainers; it brought
other more personal losses.

One of those losses was my removal from the Te Maori Lodges
board as one of their representatives to Quality Inns. Unfortunately I'm
not at liberty to write about Quality Inns/financial deals/Winston
Peters/the pros and cons. The whole situation is at a very delicate stage
as I write this (May 1992) and I wouldn't want to prejudice ongoing discussions and negotiations. If it seems that I'm backing off, be that as it
may. But I'm not able to discuss the affair in full and I'm not going to
give you just part of the story.

So that was 1991, turning into '92. A year, you might say, to forget.
But to forget would be foolish. Tragic loss comes to all of us at some
time in our lives; so does illness. We grieve, we cope, we can gain
strength. We suffer and, hopefully, we learn.

I am talking of things that have affected me. However, I am also
very mindful of the fears and concerns of a lot of my fellow New
Zealanders. Government policies in 1991 brought hardships that have
been difficult to live with and in many cases they will have long-term

Funnily enough, though my dad and Howard's were great fishing and drinking mates, and my older brother Neil was a hunting mate of Howard's older brother Laurie, I never saw much of Howard through school years though we did meet briefly when at college. Then I went nursing and met Howard through the famous Tama dances at the marae, where Tai Paul's orchestra used to play. Howard was singing at the Sound Shell with a group of six and I didn't take a shine to him at all. But he was a very persistent guy and we started going together. We were married when I was only 19. We were young, but it wasn't considered so young in those days. These days they can plan things more, and wait so they can do this and that first. Maybe they plan too much! But I do regret not finishing my registered nurse exams.

I suppose the show business world puts special strains on a marriage. The absences, the fame, the competition. People — friends and acquaintances — got very possessive about Howard and seemed to expect so much of him. The women who throw themselves at 'pop stars' . . . I know it's all out there in show business, it always has been. But to me, if Howard was misbehaving that was his problem and not my fault. That makes me sound submissive, and I'm not a submissive person. But Howard always knew where his home and family were.

I guess Howard thought I was strong enough to cope with the show business pressures, and I suppose I was. It was Howard who got me into the sporting thing; I played squash every night and tennis every weekend. As a show-business wife you get independent and sport made sure I didn't get lonely or 'stressed out'. I never knew what stress was.

To me, my role as Howard's wife and the mother of our children has been ordinary. I've never gone ga-ga over meeting this famous person or that famous person. I see myself as an ordinary person and I don't think there's anyone I can't get on with.

I know Howard can show an arrogant face to people who don't know him. He can ruffle feathers. A lot of people, top people, don't like his way of saying how it is. But he's really a charitable, loving, giving person. A big softy really. And his responsibility extends beyond this family; to his mum, sisters and on out from there. He's not a vindictive person. When he's been stabbed in the back, as I would call it, he'll say: 'Their turn will come.' When it does, he'll feel sorry for them and try to help.

Howard often wished he had some older person to bounce things off, for advice, and maybe pointers for which direction to take. He has really had to do it all on his own, and he has amazed me at times with what he has achieved. Yet he suffers from a lack of confidence at times. And I'll say; 'You know you can do it. You've already done it!'   — **Kuia Morrison**

ramifications. These policies are intended to turn the economy around; but at what cost? While we have industry leaders looking at an overall improvement on the profit line (and good luck to them) thousands of superannuitants, unemployed or single-income households are looking for ways to survive.

How much strength or incentive is there in middle-ground New Zealand to carry the burden of stabilising the situation? The country is sick, unemployment is at an unacceptable level, violence is rife and armed robbery has become a growth industry. This situation has been building up for a long time and I believe it is a direct result of at least 15 years of flights of fancy and mis-management by politicians we believed in and voted for.

Many politicians do not have the background, the qualifications or the skill to comprehend or facilitate the complexities of their portfolios. Many depend on the advice they get from their departmental bureaucrats — and you know what I think of them! Ruth Richardson's 'mother of all budgets' backfired enough for government to seek out more overseas borrowing in May of this year. How about that for backtracking? There is a lot of anger out there and it may take 10 years or more to turn the human cost around.

Could the mayhem that exploded on the streets of Los Angeles happen here? There are still plenty alive who remember the Queen Street riot of the early 1930s when we had massive unemployment similar to that we're seeing today. One spark could ignite the combustible anger of many of the 200,000 unemployed. Add in the hoodlum element of our society . . . and whammo!

Barely a week before the shocking events in Los Angeles, I was in Seville for the dedication of the New Zealand pavilion at Expo 92 and had long talks with the Bishop of Aotearoa, the Right Reverend Whaka-huia Vercoe, about some positive measures which we could promote among our people. I guess what we came up with was a 'wish list'.

One idea was strengthening the resources of the Maori Wardens and the Maori Women's Welfare League, not only in funding but also in bringing a younger core group into the ranks. Why? Because they could deal with people on the streets of their own age. Another was greater utilisation of marae. This would provide a base for second-chance education, bi-cultural activities for young New Zealanders, a closer relationship with our Polynesian cousins, identifying those brown faces with leadership qualities, working more closely with our schools and tertiary institutions, utilising the services of well-known New Zealanders as role models and encouraging our kaumatua and kuia to participate.

The above suggestions are from a Maori perspective. But, in general, we talked about how we could come to grips with the low morale that exists in our country, battered by the severe recession . . .

With the Senators Showband, my backing group of many years, many tours, many countries. From left: Howard Jnr, Charlie Te Hau, HM, Kim Le Bagge, Rick Waitoko, Rick Heperi, Ray Marama. Morrison family collection

let's call it what it is — a depression!

The Bishop was enthusiastic about the possibility of the church taking a leading role. Could we have a series of massed ecumenical prayer meetings throughout the country, giving thanks for the good things we do have and praying for help with the problems that are before us? That wouldn't be too bad a place to start, would it! By the time this book is published, we may have got beyond the talking stage. We'd better be!

My philosophical discussions with the Bishop (which I enjoyed) were actually inspired by the immense scale of the Expo in Seville — and the extravagance and fervour that every country promoted. It prompted us to think that if a large part of this presentation was to attract people to our country, we'd better do something to clean up our act back home.

Our New Zealand pavilion was a show stopper. Of course, many of the others were mind-boggling in terms of scope and presentation, but ours was unique. While the others gave nothing away from an entrance point of view, ours, with the Young Nick's Head facade, almost spoke and challenged your anticipatory sensors. The anticipation was more than satisfied after entering. I stood among hundreds of

> I was going up to the cemetery for Noel Kingi's funeral and
> Howard called out the window: 'Hey doy! Don't take two cars —
> come up with me.' So we went up in Howard's flash four-wheel-
> drive with all the trimmings. There were two Maori guys
> standing by the road and one of them said: 'Must be big money in
> those Bic shavers!' And the other one said: 'Yeah, and must be
> disposable too!'   — **Gerry Merito**

people of different nationalities who oooh'd and aah'd and broke out in
spontaneous applause throughout the presentations.

Logan Brewer and his team created a pavilion that the media
people unofficially nominated to the magnificent category. The skill
and technology were of a standard that I, as a pretty basic Kiwi, would
have expected from nations with the big bickies. But no, it was little old
New Zealand right up there in 21st century mode, yet the messages
came across clearly as to who and what we are. It was all there, our
tradition, our spirituality, our pride. But if there was one glaring oversight, it was the absence of art (traditional and contemporary) that
portrayed the indigenous culture.

The Waka Maori cultural group performed five 15-minute shows
on a stage just forward of the Young Nick's Head facade. Our pavilion
had a prime position on the main thoroughfare and at every performance by the cultural group traffic came to an immediate halt. The
reception for the group created excitement and anticipation.

Then the throngs moved into the first theatre. Tremendous! The
birth of a nation, a gift from the sea . . . a brilliant audio-visual presentation. Don Selwyn's cultured, booming voice, followed by the
Spanish translation, took us through the early creation of our nation
(flora, fauna, geology) and the settlement from Kupe's first voyages
through to the arrival of the first Europeans — a stunning introduction.

Second theatre: Dame Kiri Te Kanawa in full flight while visual
vignettes show the blending of the cultures, coming together through
survival at sea. Great stuff, too!

On into theatre three, a fast-moving audio-visual showing New
Zealand and the people as we are today; New Zealand's physical
features, way of life, scenic beauties, sporting achievements — all these
interwoven into a tapestry sure to grab the admiring attention of
visitors to the pavilion.

All through these presentations was a very strong Maori theme.
Our art, our waka tauas, our early history and traditional carving
dating back 500 years. On exiting from theatre three, there was an
opportunity to sample our gifts of nourishment: kiwifruit, New Zealand
lamb, our cheeses, our wines, our beer. All the things we are proud of

Backstage at Expo '92 on the night Kiri Te Kanawa thrilled a capacity house at the Seville Opera Theatre. From left, Aroha Cassidy, Dame Kiri, Donna Grant, Kuia, HM. In front, Sharon Ringiau, Kahurangi Maxwell, Ricki Mitchell.

as the stuff champions are made of!

Upstairs was a huge and exquisite display of ceramics, sponsored by Expo 92, the Queen Elizabeth II Arts Council and the National Museum. But there was no physical static display of Maori art, which would have been complementary in my view to the ceramic display.

Remember that the theme of the whole pavilion was New Zealand, Aotearoa, Gift From The Sea. So where are the tangaroas, the

HM and the PM in full flight at a reception on New Zealand Day at Expo '92.

Morrison family collection

marakihaus, the koruru, the proud waka stern and bow figureheads. Where, too, were the works of our more contemporary artisans like Selwyn Muru, Cliff Whiting, Para Matchitt and others? Where were they and what happened?

My understanding is that two organisations were approached. The Maori Development Corporation at first gave warm support and then backed out. The general manager of Iwi Transition was also approached for support in 1991, during the temporary reign of Winston Peters as Minister of Maori Affairs. Nothing happened. Ian Fraser fronted up to the new Minister of Maori Affairs, Doug Kidd, in November 1991. Still nothing! But subsequent to that, it is now my understanding that Te Puni Kokiri (the new Maori Ministry) and its general manager, Wira Gardiner, reopened negotiations. It was so important for Maori taonga to be at Seville, that I hope these negotiations bore fruit. (This is the state of the play as of May, soon after my return from Seville.)

The Expo 92 organisation more than came to the party in the sponsorship of the 35-plus Maori performers. Combined costs of wages, travel and accommodation was in the vicinity of $400,000. This cost covered performances five times a day, seven days a week, for six months.

On Good Friday, three days before the opening of Expo, our South Pacific neighbours' pavilion was burned down by stray sparks from a worker's welding torch. Ian Fraser, our leader, rallied his troops. On Easter Sunday morning the 80 or so people from the South Pacific pavilion, representing Fiji, Kiribati, Vanuatu and Papua New Guinea, came to the dedication of the New Zealand pavilion by Bishop Vercoe. After the dedication we all went to the burnt-out site of our neighbour islands' pavilion. Bishop Vercoe said to us all that on Good Friday Jesus was crucified and he rose again on the third day. His challenge was that the South Pacific pavilion could also rise again.

•   •   •

As 1992 draws to a close, I'm looking forward to the launch of this book in tandem with a nationwide concert tour, when I'll be joined again by my mates from the Howard Morrison Quartet. Sadly, Noel Kingi will not be there, but his replacement, Hori Bennett (brought up with Noel) also has a magnificent bass voice.

As I've fast-forwarded through the proofing stage of the Life and Times of HM, I've realised that God indeed dealt me a pretty good hand (even though it may be said I've been the joker in the royal flush) — I hope He's been happy with the way I've played it.

Distant memories of my dad and a dinghy and days on Lake Rotorua, when the sun, it seems, was always sparkling off the water . . .

A little schoolboy trying to find his way between two cultures, hiding his shoes and socks in the rata tree on the way to school at Ruatahuna . . .

The uncertain adolescent, academic under-achiever . . .

The young man with few qualifications except fitness — and a voice people said would take him a long way one day . . .

The amateur entertainer gradually making strides towards a professional career — and the Quartet who carried him to that goal . . .

The solo performer finding fresh fields to conquer, attaining heights — and losing direction as lifelong disciplines are discarded . . .

The survivor, bouncing back into high public profile just when the spotlight had moved away . . .

The man with the need to give something back to his people, and to his country, in return for the success and good fortune God has bestowed on him . . .

I wonder what's next . . .